NAPOLEON'S MARSHALS

NAPOLEON'S MARSHALS

R.P. DUNN-PATTISON

EMPIRICUS BOOKS
London, England

Empiricus Books
76 Great Titchfield Street,
London W1P 7AF

First published in Great Britain 1909 by Methuen & Co.
Empiricus Books edition reprinted 2001

www.januspublishing.co.uk

Copyright © 1909 by R.P. Dunn-Pattison
The author has asserted his moral rights

**British Library Cataloguing-in-Publication Data.
A catalogue record for this book
is available from the British Library.**

ISBN 1 902835 10 7

Phototypset in 10.2pt Baskerville
By Chris Cowlin

Cover Design Chris Cowlin

Printed and bound in Great Britain

CONTENTS

Introduction ... vii

Synopsis of the marshals ... xiii

1. Louis Alexandre Berthier, Marshal, Prince of Wagram, Sovereign Prince of Neuchâtel and Valangin ... 1

2. Joachim Murat, Marshal, King of Naples ... 20

3. André Masséna, Marshal, Duke of Rivoli, Prince of Essling ... 41

4. Jean Baptiste Jules Bernadotte, Marshal, Prince of Ponte Corvo, King of Sweden ... 60

5. Jean De Dieu Nicolas Soult, Marshal, Duke of Dalmatia ... 78

6. Jean Lannes, Marshal, Duke of Montebello ... 98

7. Michel Ney, Marshal, Duke of Elchingen, Prince of Moskowa ... 118

8. Louis Nicolas Davout, Marshal, Duke of Auerstädt, Prince of Eckmühl ... 135

9. Jacques Étienne Joseph Alexandre Macdonald, Marshal, Duke of Tarentum ... 153

10. Auguste Frédéric Louis Viesse De Marmont, Marshal, Duke of Ragusa ... 167

11. Louis Gabriel Suchet, Marshal, Duke of Albufera ... 182

v

12.	Laurent Gouvion St. Cyr, Marshal	192
13.	Bon Adrien Jeannot De Moncey, Marshal, Duke of Conegliano	203
14.	Jean Baptiste Jourdan, Marshal	208
15.	Charles Pierre François Augereau, Marshal, Duke of Castiglione	215
16.	Guillaume Marie Anne Brune, Marshal	223
17.	Adolphe Édouard Casimir Joseph Mortier, Marshal, Duke of Treviso	232
18.	Jean Baptiste Bessières, Marshal, Duke of Istria	239
19.	Claude Victor Perrin, Marshal, Duke of Belluno	247
20.	Emmanuel De Grouchy, Marshal	254
21.	François Christophe Kellermann, Marshal, Duke of Valmy	263
22.	François Joseph Lefèbvre, Marshal, Duke of Dantzig	268
23.	Nicolas Charles Oudinot, Marshal, Duke of Reggio	277
24.	Dominique Catherine De Pérignon, Marshal	286
25.	Jean Mathieu Philibert Serurier, Marshal	290
26.	Prince Joseph Poniatowski Marshal	294

INTRODUCTION

IT is a melancholy but instructive fact to remember that, in the opinion of him whom nature had adorned with the greatest intellect that the world has yet seen, selfishness and self-interest lie at the root of all human action. 'For,' as Napoleon said, 'in ambition is to be found the chief motive force of humanity, and a man puts forth his best powers in proportion to his hopes of advancement.' It was on this cynical hypothesis therefore, with a complete disregard of those higher aspirations of self-sacrifice and self-control which raise man above the mere brute, that the Corsican adventurer waded through seas of blood to the throne of France, and then attempted, by the destruction of a million human beings, to bind on his brow the imperial crown of Western Europe. In spite of loud-sounding phrases and constitutional sleight-of-hand, none knew better than Napoleon that by the sword alone he had won his empire and by the sword alone he could keep it. Keen student of history, it was not in vain that again and again he had read and re-read the works of Caesar, and pondered on the achievements of Charlemagne and the career of Cromwell. The problem he had to solve was, how to conceal from his lieutenants that his dynasty rested purely on their swords, to bind their honours so closely to his own fortune that they should ever be loyal; so to distribute his favours that his servants should never become so great as to threaten his own position. It was with this object in view that at the time he seized for himself the imperial crown he re-established the old role of Marshal of France, frankly confessing to Roederer that his reason for showering rewards on his lieutenants was to assure to himself his own dignity, since they could not object to it when they found themselves the recipients of such lofty titles. But, with the cunning of the serpent, while he gave with one hand he took away with the other. He fixed the number of Marshals at sixteen on the active list and added four others for those too old for active service. Hence he had it in his power to reward twenty hungry aspirants, while he robbed the individuals of their glory, since each Marshal shared his dignity with nineteen others.

Plainly also he told them that, lofty though their rank might appear to others, to him they were still mere servants, created by him and dependent for their position on him alone. 'Recollect,' he said, 'that you are soldiers only when with the army. The title of Marshal is merely a civil distinction which gives you the honourable rank at my court which is your due, but it carries with it no authority. On the battlefield you are generals, at court you are nobles, belonging to the State by the civil position I created for you when I bestowed your titles on you.' It was on May 19, 1804, that the *Gazette* appeared with the first creation of Marshals. There were fourteen on the active list and four honorary Marshals in the Senate. Two bâtons were withheld as a reward for future service. The original fourteen were Berthier, Murat, Moncey, Jourdan, Masséna, Augereau, Bernadotte, Soult, Brune, Lannes, Mortier, Ney, Davout and Bessières ; while on the retired list were Kellermann, Lefèbvre, Pérignon, and Serurier. The list caused much surprise and dissatisfaction. On the one hand there were those like Masséna who received their congratulations with a grunt and 'Yes, one of fourteen.' On the other hand were those like Macdonald, Marmont, Victor, and many another, who thought they ought to have been included. An examination of the names soon explains how the choice was made. Except Jourdan, who was too great a soldier to be passed over, all those who could not forget their Republican principles were excluded. Masséna received his baton as the greatest soldier of France. Berthier, Murat, and Lannes had won theirs by their talents, as much as by then personal devotion. Soult, Ney, Davout, and Mortier were Napoleon's choice from among the coming men, who in the camps of the Army of the Ocean were fast justifying their selection. Bessières was included because he would never win it at any later date, but his doglike devotion made him a priceless subordinate. Augereau and Bernadotte received their batons to keep them quiet. The names of Moncey, Brune, Kellermann, Pérignon, and Serurier were intimately connected with glorious feats of the republican armies, and so, though only fortunate mediocrities, they were included in the first creation, while Lefèbvre, the republican of republicans, now under the glamour of Napoleon's power, was placed on the list as a stalking-horse of the extreme members of his party. At the time of the first creation, of the great soldiers of the Republic, Moreau was branded as a traitor; Hoche, Marceau, Kléber, Desaix, and Pichegru were dead; Carnot, the organiser of victory, was a voluntary exile; while staunch blades like Leclerc, Richepanse, Lecourbe, Macdonald, Victor, St. Cyr, and Suchet were all more or less in disgrace. By the end of the Empire, death and the necessity of rewarding merit added to the list of Marshals until in all twenty-six batons were granted by the Emperor.

In 1808 Victor was restored to favour and received his baton. After Wagram, Macdonald, Oudinot, and Marmont received the prize, while the Spanish War brought it to Suchet, and the Russian campaign to St. Cyr. In 1813 the Polish prince, Poniatowski, was sent his truncheon on the field of Leipzig, while last of all, in 1815, Grouchy was promoted to one of the vacancies caused by the refusal of many of the Marshals to cast off their allegiance to the Bourbons.

It was a popular saying in the Napoleonic army that every private soldier carried in his knapsack a Marshal's baton, and the early history of many of these Marshals bears out this saying. But while the Revolution carried away all the barriers and opened the highest ranks to talent, be it never so humble in its origin, the history of the Marshals proves that heaven-born soldiers are scarce, and that the art of war, save in the case of one out of a million, can only be acquired by years of patient work in a subordinate position. Of the generals of the revolutionary armies only four, Moreau, Mortier, Suchet, and Brune, had no previous military training, and of these four, Moreau and Suchet alone had claim to greatness. The rough unlettered generals of the early years of the war soon proved that they could never rise above the science of the drill-sergeant. Once discipline and organisation were restored there was no room for a general like the gallant Macard, who, when about to charge, used to call out, 'Look here, I am going to dress like a beast,' and thereon divest himself of everything save his leather breeches and boots, and then, like some great hairy baboon, with strange oaths and yells lead his horsemen against the enemy. A higher type was required than this Macard, who could not understand that because an officer could sketch mountains he could not necessarily measure a man for a pair of boots.

Of the twenty-six Marshals, nine had held commissions ranging from lieutenant-general to lieutenant in the old royal army, one was a Polish Prince, an ex-Austrian officer, while one had passed the artillery college but had refused to accept a commission; eleven had commenced life as privates in the old service, and of these, nine had risen to the rank of sergeant; and four had had no previous military training. It must also be remembered that the standard of the non-commissioned rank in the royal army just before the Revolution was extremely high. The reforms of St. Germain and the popularity of the American War had enticed into the ranks a high class of recruits, with the result that the authorities were able to impose tests, and no private could rise to the rank of corporal, or from corporal to sergeant, without passing an examination. Further, since the officers of the ancient régime left the entire organisation, discipline, and control in the hands of the non-commissioned officers, and seldom, if ever, visited their companies either in barracks or on the parade ground, the non-commissioned officers, in everything save actual title, were really extremely well-trained officers. It was this class which really saved France when the old officers emigrated and the incapable politicians in Paris did their best to ruin the army. Hence it was that, without prejudice to the service, a sergeant might one day be found quietly obeying the orders of his company officer, and the next day with the rank of lieutenant-colonel commanding his battalion.

The art of war can only be truly learned in the field, and the officers of the French army had such an experience as had never fallen to the lot of any other nation since the days of the Thirty Years' War. With continuous fighting winter and summer, on every frontier, military knowledge was easily gained by those who had the ability to acquire it, and the young generals of brigade, with but three years' service in commissioned rank, had gone through experiences which seldom fall to the lot of officers with thirty years' service. The cycle of war seemed unending. From the day on which, in 1792, France hurled her declaration of war on Austria, till the surrender of Paris, in 1814, with the exception of the year of peace gained at Amiens, war was continuous. It began with a light-hearted invasion of France by Austria and Prussia in September, 1792, which ended in the cannonade of Valmy, when Dumouriez and Kellermann, with the remnant of the old royal army, showed such a bold front that the

Allies, who had never expected to fight, lost heart and ran home. The Austro-Prussian invasion sealed the King's death-warrant, and France, in the hands of republican enthusiasts, went forth with a rabble of old soldiers and volunteers to preach the doctrine of the Equality of Man and the Brotherhood of Nations. But the sovereigns of Europe determined to fight for their crowns, and the licence of the French soldiers and the selfishness of these prophets of the new doctrine of Equality soon disgusted the people of the Rhine valley; so the revolutionary mob armies were driven into France, and for two years she was busy on every frontier striving to drive the enemy from her soil. It was during these years that the new French army arose. The volunteers were brigaded with the old regular battalions, the ranks were kept full by calling out all fit to bear arms, and the incompetent and unfortunate were weeded out by the guillotine. By 1795 France had freed her own soil and had forged a weapon whereby she could retaliate on the Powers who had attempted to annex her territory in the hour of her degradation. The Rhine now became her eastern frontier. But Austria, whose Archduke was Emperor of the Holy Roman Empire, would not give up the provinces seized from her; so from 1795 to 1797, on the headwaters of the Danube and in Italy, the representative of the Feudal Ages fought the new democracy. It was the appearance of the great military talent of Bonaparte which decided the day. On the Danube the Austrians had found that under the excellent leading of the Archduke Charles they were fit to defeat the best French troops under capable generals like Jourdan and Moreau. But the military genius of Bonaparte overbore all resistance, and when peace came, practically all Italy had been added to the dominion of France. Unfortunately for the peace of Europe, the rulers of France had tasted blood. They found in the captured provinces a means of making war without feeling the effects, for the rich pillage of Italy paid the war expenses. But, grateful as the Directors were to Bonaparte for thus opening to them a means of enriching themselves at the expense of Europe, they rightly saw in him a menace to their own power, and gladly allowed him to depart on the mission to Egypt. From Egypt Bonaparte returned, seized the reins of government, and saved France from the imbecility of her rulers, and, by the battle of Marengo, assured to her all she had lost in his absence. Unfortunately for France the restless ambition of her new ruler was not satisfied with re-establishing the Empire of the West and reviving the glories of Charlemagne, but hankered after a vast overseas dominion, to include America and India. Hence it was that he found in Great Britain an implacable enemy ever stirring up against him European coalitions. To cover his failure to wrest the dominion of the sea from its mistress, Napoleon turned his wrath on Austria, and soon she lay cowed at his feet after the catastrophe at Ulm and the battle of Austerlitz. Austria's fall was due to the lethargy and hesitation of the courts of Berlin and St. Petersburg. But once Austria was disposed of, Prussia and Russia met their punishment for having given her secret or open aid. The storm fell first on Prussia. At one fell swoop on the field of Jena, the famed military monarchy of the great Frederick fell in pieces like a potter's vessel. From Prussia the invincible French legions penetrated into Poland, and after Eylau and Friedland the forces of Prussia and Russia could no longer face the enemy in the field. The Czar, dazzled by Napoleon's greatness, threw over his ally Prussia and at Tilsit made friends with the great conqueror. In June, 1807, it seemed as if Europe lay at Napoleon's feet, but already in Portugal the seeds of his ruin had been sown. The Portuguese monarch, the ally of Great Britain, fled at the mere approach of a single Marshal of the Emperor. The apparent lethargy of the inhabitants of the Iberian Peninsula and the unpopularity of the Spanish Bourbons tempted Napoleon to establish his brother on the throne of Spain. It was a fatal error, for though the Spanish people might despise their King, they were intensely proud of their nationality. For the first time in his experience the Corsican had to meet the forces of a nation and not of a government. The chance defeat of a French army at Baylen was the signal for a general rising throughout the Peninsula, and not only throughout the Peninsula, but for the commencement of a national movement against the French in Austria and Germany. England gladly seized the opportunity of injuring her enemy and sent aid to the people of Spain. Austria tried another fall with her conqueror, but was defeated at Wagram. Wagram ought to have taught the Emperor that his troops were no longer invincible as of old, but, blind to this lesson, he still attempted to lord it over Europe and his lesson, treated with contumely his only friend, the Czar. Consequently, in 1812, while still engaged in attempting to conquer Spain, he found himself forced to fight Russia. The result was appalling; out of half a million troops who entered Russia, a bare seventy thousand returned. Prussia and Austria at once made a bid to recover their independence. Napoleon, blinded by rage, refused to listen to reason, and in October, 1813, was defeated by the Allies at Leipzig. Even then he might have saved his throne, but he still refused to listen to the Allies, who in 1814 invaded France, and, after a campaign in which the Emperor showed an almost superhuman ability, at last by sheer weight of numbers they captured Paris. Thereon the French troops refused to fight any longer for the Emperor. Such is a brief outline of what is called the Revolutionary and Napoleonic Wars, the finest school the world has yet seen for an apprenticeship in the trade of arms.

SYNOPSIS OF THE MARSHALS

Name	Born	Marshal	Titles	Died	Age
Berthier, Louis Alexandre	Nov. 20, 1753	May 19, 1804	Prince of Neuchâtel and Valangin, Mar. 15, 1806; Prince of Wagram, Dec. 31, 1809	Accident, June 1, 1815	62
Murat, Joachim	Mar. 25, 1767	"	Prince, Feb. 1, 1805; Grand Duke of Berg, Mar. 15, 1806; King of Naples, Aug. 1, 1808	Shot at Pizzo, Oct. 13, 1815	48
Moncey, Bon Adrien Jeannot de	July 31, 1754	"	Duke of Conegliano, July 2, 1808	Natural cause, April 20, 1842	88
Jourdan, Jean Baptiste	April 29, 1762	"	Count, Mar. 1, 1808	Natural cause, Nov, 1833	71
Masséna, André	May 6, 1756	"	Duke of Rivoli, April 24, 1808; Prince of Essling, Jan. 31, 1810	Natural cause, April 4, 1817	61
Augereau, Charles Pierre François	Oct. 21, 1757	"	Duke of Castiglione, April 26, 1808	Natural cause, June 12, 1816	59
Bernadotte, Jean Baptiste Jules	Jan. 26, 1763	"	Prince of Ponte Corvo, June 5, 1806; Crown Prince of Sweden, Aug. 21, 1810; King, Feb. 18, 1818	Natural cause, Mar. 8, 1844	81

Name	Born	Created Marshal	Titles	Death	Age
Soult, Jean de Dieu Nicolas	Mar. 29, 1769	May 19, 1804	Duke of Dalmatia, June 29, 1808	Natural cause, Nov. 26, 1851	82
Brune, Guillaume Marie Anne	May 13, 1763	"	Count, Mar. 1, 1808	Murdered at Avignon, Aug. 2, 1815	52
Lannes, Jean	April 11, 1769	"	Duke of Montebello, June 15, 1808	Died of wounds at Vienna, May 31, 1809	40
Mortier, Adolphe Édouard Casimir Joseph	Feb. 13, 1768	"	Duke of Treviso, July 2, 1808	Killed by infernal machine at Paris, July 28, 1835	67
Ney, Michel	Jan. 10, 1769	"	Duke of Elchingen, May 5, 1808; Prince of Moskowa, Mar. 25, 1813	Shot at Paris, Dec. 7, 1815	46
Davout, Louis Nicolas	May 10, 1770	"	Duke of Auerstädt, July 2, 1808; Prince of Eckmühl, Nov. 28, 1809	Natural cause, June 1, 1823	53
Bessières, Jean Baptiste	Aug. 6, 1768	"	Duke of Istria, May 28, 1809	Killed at Lützen, May 1, 1813	45
Kellermann, François Christophe	May 28, 1735	"	Count, Mar. 1, 1808; Duke of Valmy, May 2, 1808	Natural cause, Sept. 13, 1820	85
Lefèbvre, François Joseph	Oct. 15, 1755	"	Count, Mar. 1, 1808; Duke of Dantzig, Sept. 10, 1808	Natural cause, Sept. 14, 1820	65
Pérignon, Dominique Catherine de	May 31, 1754	"	Count, Sept. 6, 1811	Natural cause, Dec. 25, 1818	64

Serurier, Jean Mathieu Philibert	Dec. 8, 1742	May 19, 1804	Count, Mar. 1, 1808	Natural cause, Dec. 21, 1819	77
Victor, Victor Claude Perrin	Dec. 7, 1764	July 13, 1807	Duke of Belluno, Sept. 10, 1808	Natural cause, Mar. 1, 1841	77
Macdonald, Jacques Étienne Joseph Alexandre	Nov. 17, 1765	July 12, 1809	Duke of Tarentum, Dec. 9, 1809	Natural cause, Sept. 7, 1840	75
Oudinot, Nicolas Charles	April 25, 1767	"	Count, July 2, 1808; Duke of Reggio, April 14, 1810	Natural cause, Sept. 13, 1847	80
Marmont, Auguste Frédéric Louis Viesse de	July 20, 1774	"	Duke of Ragusa, June 28, 1808	Natural cause, July 23, 1852	78
Suchet, Louis Gabriel	Mar. 2, 1770	July 8, 1811	Count, June 24, 1808; Duke of Albufera, Jan. 3, 1813	Natural cause, Jan. 3, 1826	56
Gouvion St. Cyr, Laurent	April 13, 1764	Aug. 27, 1812	Count, May 3, 1808	Natural cause, Mar. 17, 1830	66
Poniatowski, Joseph, Prince	May 7, 1762	Oct. 17, 1813	——	Drowned in Elster, Oct. 19, 1813	51
Grouchy, Emmanuel de	Oct. 23, 1766	April 17, 1815	Count, Jan. 28, 1809	Natural cause, May 29, 1847	81

MARSHAL NEY COVERING THE RETREAT, 1812
From the painting by Yvon at Versailles

ALEXANDRE BERTHIER, PRINCE OF WAGRAM
From an engraving after the painting by Pahou Fils

JOACHIM MURAT, AFTERWARDS KING OF NAPLES
From the painting by Gérard at Versailles

ANDRÉ MASSÉNA, PRINCE OF ESSLING

JEAN BAPTISTE BERNADOTTE, KING OF SWEDEN
From an engraving after the painting by Hilaire Le Drú

JEAN DE DIEU SOULT, DUKE OF DALMATIA
From a lithograph by Delpech after the painting by Rouillard

JEAN LANNES, DUKE OF MONTEBELLO
From an engraving by Amédée Maulet

MICHEL NEY, PRINCE OF MOSKOWA
From an engraving after the painting by F. Gérard

LOUIS NICOLAS DAVOUT, PRINCE OF ECKMÜHL
From an engraving after the painting by Gautherot

JACQUES ÉTIENNE MACDONALD, DUKE OF TARENTUM
From a lithograph by Delpech

AUGUSTE DE MARMONT, DUKE OF RAGUSA
From an engraving after the painting by Muneret

LOUIS GABRIEL SUCHET, DUKE OF ALBUFERA
From an engraving by Pollet

GOUVION ST. CYR
From an engraving after the painting by J. Guerin

JEAN BAPTISTE JOURDAN
After a drawing by Ambroise Tardieu

CHARLES PIERRE AUGEREAU, DUKE OF CASTIGLIONE
From an engraving by Ruotte

BRUNE
After the drawing by F. J. Harriet

ADOLPHE ÉDOUARD MORTIER, DUKE OF TREVISO
From an engraving after the painting by Larivière

EMMANUEL DE GROUCHY
From an engraving after the painting by Rouillard

FRANÇOIS CHRISTOPHE KELLERMANN, DUKE OF VALMY
From an engraving after the painting by Ansiaux

NICOLAS CHARLES OUDINOT, DUKE OF REGGIO
From an engraving after the painting by Robert Le Fevre

1

LOUIS ALEXANDRE BERTHIER, MARSHAL, PRINCE OF WAGRAM, SOVEREIGN PRINCE OF NEUCHÂTEL AND VALANGIN

TO be content ever to play an inferior part, to see all honour and renown fall to the share of another, yet loyally to efface self and work for the glory of a friend, denotes a sterling character and an inflexibility of purpose with which few can claim to be endowed. Nobody doubts that, if it had not been for Napoleon, Berthier, good business man as he was, could never have risen to the fame he attained; still it is often forgotten that without this admirable servant it is more than doubtful if the great Emperor could have achieved all his most splendid success. Berthier, controlled by a master mind, was an instrument beyond price. Versed in the management of an army almost from his cradle, he had the gift of drafting orders so clear, so lucid, that no one could possibly mistake their meaning. His memory was prodigious, and his physical endurance such that he appeared never to require rest. But above all he alone seemed to be able to divine the thoughts of his great master before they were spoken, and this wonderful intuition taught him how, from a few disjointed utterances, to unravel Napoleon's most daring conceptions and work out the details in ordered perfection. Napoleon called his faithful Achates a gosling whom he had transformed into an eagle, but history proclaims that long before the name of Bonaparte was known beyond the gate of the military academy at Brienne, Berthier had established a record as a staff officer of the highest promise; while, before the young Corsican first met him in Italy, the future major-general of the Grand Army had evolved that perfect system of organisation which enabled the conqueror of Italy to control every movement and vibration in the army to be informed of events as soon as they happened, and to be absolutely sure of the despatch and performance of his orders.

Alexandre Berthier had seen twenty-three years' service in the old royal army before the Revolution broke out in 1789. Born on November 20, 1753, at the age of thirteen he received his commission in the engineers owing to his father's services in preparing a map of royal hunting forests. But the boy soon forsook his father's old regiment, for he knew well that the highest commands in the army seldom if ever fell to the scientific corps. When in 1780 the French Government decided to send out an expeditionary corps to assist the revolted colonies in their struggle with Great Britain, Berthier, after serving in the infantry and cavalry, was employed as a staff captain with the army of Normandy. Eager to see active service, he at once applied to be attached to the expedition, and offered, if there was no room for an extra captain, to resign his rank and serve as sub-lieutenant. Thanks to powerful family influence and to his record of service his desire was gratified, and in January, 1781, he found himself with the French troops in America employed on the staff of General Count de Rochambeau. Returning from America in 1783 with a well-earned reputation for bravery and ability, Captain Berthier was one of the officers sent to Prussia under the Marquis de Custine to study the military organisation of the great Frederick. Continuously employed on the staff, he had the advantage of serving as brigade major at the great camp of instruction held at Saint Omer in 1788, and in that year received as a reward for his services the cross of Saint Louis. The year 1789 saw him gazetted lieutenant-colonel, and chief of the staff to Baron de Besenval, commanding the troops round Paris.

When, after the capture of the Bastille, Lafayette undertook the work of organising the National Guard, he at once bethought him of his old comrade of American days, and appointed Berthier assistant quartermaster-general. Berthier found the post well suited to him; inspired by the liberal ideas which he had gained in America, he threw himself heart and soul into the work. Soon his talent as an organiser became widely recognised; many prominent officers applied to have him attached to their command, and, after holding several staff appointments, he was entrusted in 1791 with the organisation and instruction of the thirty battalions of volunteers cantonned between the Somme and Meuse. When war broke out in 1792 he was despatched as major-general and chief of the staff to his old friend Rochambeau, and when the Count resigned his command Berthier was specially retained by Rochambeau's successor, Luckner. But the Revolution, while giving him his chance, nearly brought about his fall. His intimate connection with the nobles of the old royal army, his courage in protecting the King's aunts, and his family connections caused him to become 'suspect.' It was in vain that the leaders at the front complained of the absolute disorder in their forces, of the necessity of more trained staff officers and of their desire for the services of the brilliant soldier who had gained his experience in war time in America and in peace time in Prussia. In vain Custine wrote to the Minister of War, 'In the name of the Republic send Berthier to me to help me in my difficulties,' in vain the Commissioners with the army reported that 'Berthier has gained the esteem and confidence of all good patriots.' Vain also was the valour and ability he showed in the campaign against the Royalists in La Vendée. Bouchotte, the incapable, the friend of the brutish, block-headed Hébert, the insulter of the Queen, the destroyer of the army, decreed that his loyalty to the Republic was not sincere, and by a stroke of the pen dismissed him; thus during the whole of the year 1793 the French army was deprived of the service of an officer who, owing to his powers of organisation, was worth fifty thousand of the butcher generals.

In 1795, with the fall of the Jacobins, Berthier was restored to his rank and sent as chief of the staff to Kellermann, commanding the Army of the Alps, and before the end of the year the staff work of Kellermann's army became the pattern for all the armies of the Republic. When in March, 1796, Bonaparte was appointed commander of the Army of Italy, he at once requisitioned Berthier as the chief of the staff, and from that day till April, 1814, Berthier seldom if ever left the future Emperor's side, serving him with a patience and cheerfulness which neither illwill nor neglect seemed to disturb. Though over forty-two years of age and sixteen years older than his new chief, the chief of the staff was still in the prime of his manhood. Short, thick-set and athletic, his frame proclaimed his immense physical strength, while his strong alert face under a mass of thick curly hair foretold at a glance his mental capacity.

A keen sportsman, in peace he spent all his leisure in the chase. Hard exercise and feats of physical endurance were his delight. Fatigue he never knew, and on one occasion he was said to have spent thirteen days and nights in the saddle. To strangers and officials he was silent and stern, but his aloofness of manner hid a warm heart and a natural sincerity, and many a poor officer or returned émigré received secret help from his purse. Though naturally of a strong character, his affection and respect for his great commander became the dominating note in his career; in fact, it might almost be said that, in later years, his personality became merged to such an extent in that of Napoleon that he was unable to see the actions of the Emperor in their proper perspective. From their first meeting Bonaparte correctly guessed the impression he had made on his new staff officer, and aimed at increasing his influence over him. Meanwhile he was delighted with him, he wrote to the Directory, 'Berthier has talents, activity, courage, character-all in his favour.' Berthier on his side was well satisfied; as he said to a friend who asked him how he could serve a man with such a temper, 'Remember that one day it will be a fine thing to be second to Bonaparte.' So the two worked admirably together.

Bonaparte kept in his own hands the movement of troops, the direction of skirmishes and battles, commissariat, discipline, and all communications from the Government. Berthier had a free hand in the organisation and maintenance of the general staff, the headquarter staff, and the transmission of orders, subject to inspection by Bonaparte; he also had to throw into written form all verbal orders, and he alone was responsible for their promulgation and execution. It was his ability to work out in detail and to reduce into clear, lucid orders the slightest hint of his commander which, as Napoleon said later, 'was the great merit of Berthier, and was of inestimable importance to me. No other could possibly have replaced him.' Thanks to Berthier's admirable system, Bonaparte was kept in touch with every part of his command. One of the first principles laid down in the staff regulations was, 'That it was vital to the good of the service that the correspondence of the army should be exceedingly swift and regular, that nothing should be neglected which might contribute to this end.' To ensure regularity of communication, divisional commanders and officers detached in command of small columns were ordered to report at least twice a day to headquarters. With each division, in addition to the divisional staff, there were officers detached from the headquarters staff. All important despatches had to be sent in duplicate; in times of great danger commanding officers had to send as many as eight different orderly officers each with a copy of despatches.

But it was not only as an organiser and transmitter of orders that Berthier proved his usefulness to his chief. At Lodi he showed his personal courage and bravery among the band of heroes who forced the bridge, and Bonaparte paid him a fine tribute when he wrote in his despatches, 'If I were bound to mention all the soldiers who distinguished themselves on that wonderful day, I should be obliged to mention all the carabiniers and grenadiers of the advance guard, and nearly all the officers of the staff; but I must not forget the courageous Berthier, who on that day played the part of gunner, trooper, and grenadier.' At Rivoli, in addition to his staff duties, Berthier commanded the centre of the army, and fought with a stubbornness beyond all praise. By the end of the campaign of 1796 he had proved that he was as great a chief of the staff as Bonaparte was a great commander. Doubtless it is true that before the commencement of a campaign an army possesses in itself the causes of its future victory or defeat, and the Army of Italy, with its masses of enthusiastic veterans and the directing genius of Bonaparte, was bound to defeat the Austrians with their listless men and incompetent old generals; but, without the zeal, activity, and devotion which Berthier transfused through the whole of the general staff, success could not have been so sudden or so complete.

After Leoben the conqueror of Italy employed his trusty friend on numerous diplomatic missions in connection with the annexation of Corfu and the government of the Cisalpine republic. Meanwhile he was in close communication with him in regard to the proposed descent on England and the possible expedition to the East. To Berthier, if to any one, Bonaparte entrusted his secret designs, for he knew that he could do so in safety. Accordingly, in 1798, finding an invasion of England impossible at the moment, he persuaded the Directory to send Berthier to Italy as commander-in-chief, his object being to place him in a position to gather funds for the Egyptian expedition. From Italy Berthier sent his former commander the most minute description of everything of importance, but he found the task difficult and uncongenial, and prayed him 'to recall me promptly. I much prefer being your aide-de-camp to being commander-in-chief here.' Still he carried out his orders and marched on Rome, to place the eight million francs' worth of diamonds wrung from the Pope to the credit of the army. From Rome he returned with coffers well filled for the Egyptian expedition, but leaving behind him an army half-mutinous for want of pay; his blind devotion to Bonaparte hid this incongruity from his eyes.

As in Italy in 1795 so in Egypt, Berthier was Bonaparte's right-hand man, methodical, indefatigable, and trustworthy. But even his iron frame could scarcely withstand the strain of three years' continuous active service, the incessant office work day and night, and the trials of an unaccustomed climate. After the battle of the Pyramids he fell sick, and before the Syrian expedition, applied to return to France. Unkind friends hinted that he longed for his mistress, Madame Visconti, but Bonaparte, knowing that it was not this but sheer overstrain which had caused his breakdown in health, gave him the desired leave and made all arrangements for his journey home. However, at the moment of departure Berthier's love for his chief overcame his longing for rest, and, in spite of ill-health, he withdrew his resignation and set out with the army for Syria. As ever, he found plenty of work, for even in the face of the ill-success of the expedition, Bonaparte determined to administer Egypt as if the French occupation was to be for ever permanent; and Berthier, in addition to his ordinary work, was ordered to edit a carefully executed map from the complete survey which was being made of the country.

It was to Berthier that Bonaparte first divulged his intention of leaving Egypt and returning to France, and his determination to upset the Directory. Liberal by nature, but essentially a man of method and a disciplinarian, the chief of the staff was quite in accord with his commander's ideas on the regeneration of France, and loyally supported him during the *coup d'état* of the 18th Brumaire. Thereafter the First Consul appointed his friend Minister of War, a position that gave full scope to his talents. All the administrative services had at once to be reorganised, the frontier fortresses garrisoned and placed in a state of defence, and the army covering the frontiers supplied with food, pay, equipment, and reinforcements, while the formation of the secret Army of Reserve was a task which alone would have occupied all the attention of an ordinary man; in fact, the safety of France hung on this army. Consequently, since, by the constitution, the First Consul was unable himself to take command in the field, in April, 1800, he transferred Berthier from the War Office to the head of this most important force. It is not generally known that the idea of the passage of the Alps by the St. Bernard Pass actually originated with Berthier, and had first been projected by him as early as 1795. So it was at the execution of what was really his own idea that for two months Berthier slaved. At times even his stout heart quailed, as when he wrote to the First Consul, 'It is my duty to complain of the position of this army on which you have justly spent so much interest, and which is paralysed because it can only rely on its bayonets, on account of the lack of ammunition and means to transport the artillery.' Incessant work and toil were at last rewarded; but when the Army of the Reserve debouched on the Austrian lines of communication, the First Consul appeared in person, and, though nominally in command, Berthier once again resumed his position of chief of the staff. Without a murmur he allowed Bonaparte to reap all the glory of Marengo, for he knew that without the First Consul, however excellent his own dispositions were, they would have been lacking in the driving power which alone teaches men how to seize on victory. After Marengo, Berthier was despatched as Ambassador Extraordinary to Madrid, 'to exhort Spain by every possible means to declare war on Portugal, the ally of England.' The result of this mission was eminently successful; a special treaty was drawn up and Spain sold Louisiana to France. By October the ambassador was once again back in Paris at his old post of Minister of War - a post which he held continuously during peace and war till August, 1807. The position was no light one, for even during the short years of peace it involved the supervision of the expedition to San Domingo, the defence of Italy, the reorganisation of the army, and the re-armament of the artillery, in addition to the ordinary routine of official work. Moreover, the foundations of the Consulate being based on the army, it was essential that the army should be efficient and content, and consequently the French soldier of that day was not, as in other countries, neglected in peace time. The officers in command of the troops were constantly reminded by the War Minister that 'the French soldier is a citizen placed under military law' - not an outcast or serf, whose well-being and comfort concern no one.

On the establishment of the Empire Berthier, like many another, received the reward for his faithfulness to Napoleon. Honours were showered upon him. The first to receive the Marshal's baton, he was in succession created senator by right as a dignitary of the Empire, grand officer of the palace and grand huntsman to the crown, while at the coronation he carried the imperial globe. But though the Emperor thus honoured and treated him as his most trustworthy confidant, the cares of state to some extent withdrew Napoleon from close intimacy with his old companion. At the same time the Marshal was insensibly separated from his former comrades-in-arms by his high rank and employment, which, while it tended to make him more the servant than the friend of the Emperor, also caused him to be regarded as a superior to be obeyed by those who were formerly his equals. At all times a strict disciplinarian, and one who never passed over a breach of orders, the Marshal, as voicing the commands of the Emperor, gradually began to assume a stern attitude to all subordinates, and spared neither princes or marshals, when he considered that the good of the service required that they should be reprimanded and shown their duty. So strong was the sense of subordination in the army and the desire to stand well with Napoleon, that even the fiery Murat paid attention to orders and reprimands signed by Berthier in the name of the Emperor.

Meanwhile the work of the War Minister increased day by day. The organisation and supervision of the Army of the Ocean added considerably to his work, which was much interfered with by visits of inspection in company with the Emperor, or far-distant expeditions to the frontiers and to Italy for the coronation at Milan.

On August 3rd, 1805, the Emperor created the Marshal major-general and chief of the staff to the Army of the Ocean, and himself assumed command of the Army and held a grand review of one hundred thousand men. Everybody thought that the moment for the invasion of England had arrived. Berthier, and perhaps Talleyrand, alone knew that Austria, not England, was the immediate quarry, and all through August the major-general was busy working out the routes for the concentration of the various corps in the valley of the Danube; whilst at the same time as War Minister he was responsible for the supervision of all the troops left in France and in garrison in Italy, Belgium, Holland, and Hanover. Consequently he had to divide his staff into two sections, one of which he took with him into the field, the other remaining in Paris under an assistant who was capable of managing the ordinary routine, but who had to forward all difficult problems to the War Minister in the field. Even during the drive to the frontier there was no abatement of the strain; during the journey the Emperor would give orders which had to be expanded and written out in the short stoppages for food and rest. By day the major-general travelled in the Emperor's carriage; at night he always slept under the same roof with him, to be ready at any moment, in full uniform, to receive his commands and expand and dictate them to his clerks. Everyone knew when the major-general was worried, for he had a habit of biting his nails when making a decision or trying to solve a problem, but otherwise he never showed any sign of feeling, and whether tired or troubled by the Emperor's occasional outbursts of temper, he went on with his work with the methodical precision of an automaton. To belong to the general staff when Berthier was major-general was no bed of roses, no place for gilded youth, for with Napoleon commanding and Berthier directing, if there was often fighting there was plenty of writing ; if there was galloping on horseback by day, to make up for it by night there were hours of steady copying of orders and no chance of laying down the pen until all business was finished. Thanks to this excellent staff work, Napoleon's ambitious plans were faithfully accomplished, the Austrians were completely taken in by the demonstration in the Black Forest, the French columns stepped astride of their communications on the Danube, and Mack was forced to surrender at Ulm. But Ulm was only the commencement of the campaign, and even after Austerlitz Napoleon pursued the enemy with grim resolution. This was one of the secrets of his success, for, as Berthier wrote to Soult, 'The Emperor's opinion is that in war nothing is really achieved as long as there remains something to achieve; a victory is not complete as long as greater success can still be gained.'

After the treaty of Pressburg, on December 27, 1805, Napoleon quitted the army and returned to Paris, leaving the major-general in command of the Grand Army with orders to evacuate the conquered territory when the terms of the treaty had been carried out by the Austrians; but the Emperor retained the real control, and every day a courier had to be despatched to Paris with a detailed account of every event, and every day a courier arrived from Paris bearing fresh orders and instructions. For Napoleon refused to allow the slightest deviation from his orders:

'Keep strictly to the orders I give you,' he wrote; 'execute punctually your instructions. I alone know what I want done.' Meanwhile the major-general was still War Minister and had to supervise all the more important business of the War Office; while he also found time to edit an official history of the campaign of 1805, and to superintend the execution of a map of most of the Austrian possessions. The work was immense, but Berthier never flagged, and the Emperor showed his appreciation of his zeal when on March 30th, 1806, he conferred on him the principality of Neuchâtel with the title of Prince and Duke, to hold in full possession and suzerainty for himself, his heirs and successors, with one stipulation, that he should marry. He added that the Prince's passion for Madame Visconti had lasted too long, that it was not becoming to a dignitary of the Empire, and that he was now fifty years old and ought to think of providing an heir to his honours. The Prince Marshal never had time to visit personally his principality, but he sent one of his intimate friends, General Dutaillis, to provide for the welfare of his new subjects, and to the best of his ability he saw that they were well governed, while a battalion of picked troops from Neuchâtel was added to the Imperial Guard. But, orders or no orders, the Prince could never break himself free from the trammels of his mistress, and Napoleon gave him but little leisure in which to find a congenial partner, so that it was not till after Tilsit, in the brief pause before the Peninsular War, that Berthier at last took a wife. His chosen Princess was Elizabeth, the daughter of William, Duke of Bavaria, brother of the King. She was married with all due solemnity in March, 1808, and though the exigencies of war gave her but little opportunity of seeing much of her husband, affection existed between them, as also between Berthier and his father-in-law, the Duke of Bavaria. All cause of difficulty was smoothed over by the fact that in time the Princess herself conceived an affection for Madame Visconti.

By September, 1806, the Grand Army had evacuated Austria, and the Prince Marshal was hoping to return to Paris when suddenly he was informed by the Emperor of the probability of a campaign against Prussia. On the 23rd definite orders arrived indicating the points of assembly; by the next day detailed letters of instructions for every corps had been worked out and despatched by the headquarters staff. Napoleon himself arrived at Wurzburg on October 2nd, and found his army concentrated, but deficient of supplies. At first his anger burst out against the chief of the staff, but a moment's reflection proved to him that there was not sufficient transport in Germany to mass both men and supplies in the time he had given, and he entirely exonerated Berthier, who by hard work contrived in three days to collect sufficient supplies to allow of the opening of the thirty days' campaign which commenced with Jena and ended by carrying the French troops across the Vistula. The fresh campaign in the spring of 1807 was attended by an additional difficulty, there existed no maps of the district, and the topographical department of the staff was worked off its legs in supplying this deficiency. Meanwhile, during the halt after Pultusk, the major-general was busy re-clothing and re-equipping the army and hurrying up reinforcements; while in addition to the work of the War Office he had to supervise the French forces in Italy and Naples. After Tilsit, as after Pressburg, Napoleon hurried back to France and left the Prince of Neuchâtel to arrange for the withdrawal of the Grand Army, and it was not till July 27th that Berthier at last returned to Paris.

The Prince came back more than ever dazzled by the genius of the

Emperor; not even Eylau had taught him that there were limits to his idol's powers. But with more than eight hundred thousand men on a war footing, with divisions and army corps scattered from the Atlantic to the Niemen, from Lübeck to Brindisi, it was impossible for one man to be at once chief of the staff and Minister of War. Accordingly, on August 9th the Emperor made General Clarke Minister of War, and, to show that this was no slight on his old friend, on the same day he created the Prince of Neuchâtel Vice-constable of France. For the next three months Berthier was able to enjoy his honours at his home at Grosbois, or in his honorary capacity at Fontainebleau, but in November the Emperor carried him off with him to Italy on a tour of inspection. During the whole of this holiday in Italy the Prince was busy elaborating the details of the coming campaign in Spain, and it was the Spanish trouble which cut short his honeymoon, for on April 2nd he had to start with the Emperor for Bayonne. From the outset the Prince warned the Emperor that the question of supplies lay at the root of all difficulties in Spain; but Napoleon clung to his idea that war should support war, and Berthier knew that it was hopeless to attempt to remove a fixed idea from his head, and, still believing in his omnipotence, he thought all would be well. Meanwhile, as the summer went on, it was not only Spain that occupied the Prince's attention for the conquest of Denmark had to be arranged, and the passes in Silesia and Bohemia carefully mapped, in view of hostilities with Prussia or Austria. Early in August Berthier was at Saint Cloud making arrangements to reinforce Davout in Silesia, owing to the growing hostility of Austria, when, on the 16th, arrived the news that Joseph had had to evacuate all the country west of the Ebro. But Napoleon and Berthier could not go to his help until after the imperial meeting at Erfurt in September. However, on reaching Spain, the magic of the Emperor's personality soon restored the vigour and prestige of the French arms. Still the Prince Marshal could not hide from himself that all was not as it used to be; Napoleon's temper was more uncertain, and the Marshals, smarting under reprimands, were not pulling together. When the Emperor returned to France, after having missed 'the opportunity of giving the English a good lesson,' he left Berthier behind for a fortnight 'to be sure that King Joseph had a proper understanding of everything.' But trouble was bound to come, for the Emperor himself was breaking his own canon of the importance of 'the unity of command' by nominally leaving Joseph in control of all the troops in Spain, but at the same time making the Marshals responsible to himself through the major-general.

In 1809 Napoleon made another grave mistake. He had calculated that Austria could make no forward movement before April 15th, and accordingly he sent Berthier early in March to take temporary command of the Grand Army, with instructions to order Davout to concentrate at Ratisbon and Masséna at Augsburg. His idea was that there would be ample time later to order a concentration on either wing or on the centre. But the Austrians were ready quite a fortnight before he had calculated. The major-general kept him well informed of every movement of the enemy, and pointed put the dangerous isolation of Davout. Still the Emperor did not believe the Austrian preparations were so forward; and a despatch from Paris, written on April 10th, which arrived at headquarters at Donauworth on the 11th, ordered the major-general to retain Davout at Ratisbon and move his own headquarters there, 'and that in spite of anything that may happen.' Unfortunately, a semaphore despatch sent a few hours later, when Napoleon had really grasped the situation, went astray and never reached Berthier. The Prince of Neuchâtel understood as clearly as any one the dangerous position of Davout; the Duke of Eckmuhl himself thought that the major-general was trying to spoil his career by laying him open to certain defeat; depression spread through all the French corps. But after years of blind devotion to his great chief Berthier could not steel himself to break distinct orders, emphasised as they were .by the expression 'in spite of whatever may happen,' and a great catastrophe was only just averted by the arrival of Napoleon, who at once ordered Davout to withdraw and Masséna to advance. Berthier himself was visited by the full fury of the Emperor's anger. But the cloud soon passed, for Berthier was as indispensable as ever, and more so when, after the failure at Aspern-Essling, immense efforts had to be made to hurry up troops from every available source. At the end of the campaign the Emperor justly rewarded his lieutenant by creating him Prince of Wagram.

Once again Napoleon left Berthier to arrange for the withdrawal of the army, and it was not till December 1st that the Prince of Wagram regained Paris and took up the threads of the Peninsular campaign. His stay there was short, for by the end of February he was back again in Vienna, this time not as major-general of a victorious army, but as Ambassador Extraordinary to claim the hand of the Archduchess Marie Louise for his master, the Emperor Napoleon, and to escort her to her new home. For the next two years the Prince remained at home at Grosbois or on duty at Fontainebleau, but in spite of great domestic happiness he was much worried by the terrible Spanish war. No one saw more clearly that every effort ought to be made to crush the English, but he was powerless to persuade the Emperor, and he had to endure to the full and all the difficulties arising from breaking the 'unity of command'. No one understood better what hopeless difficulties would arise when Napoleon ordered him to write, 'The King will command the army ... The Guard does not form part of the army.' To add to these troubles, it became more and more evident that Germany was riddled with secret societies and that war with Russia was inevitable. So it was with a sigh of relief that in January, 1812, he received the order to turn his attention from Spain and resume his functions as major-general of the Grand Army. Not that he desired further active service; like many another of the Emperor's soldiers, he mistrusted the distant expedition to Russia, and feared for the honour and safety of France. Already in his sixtieth year, there was little he could gain personally from war. As he said to Napoleon, 'What is the good of having given me an income of sixty thousand pounds a year in order to inflict on me the tortures of Tantalus? I shall die here with all this work. The simplest private is happier than I.'

The Emperor, knowing the attitude of many of his Marshals, and himself feeling the strain of this immense enterprise, was unusually irritable. Consequently relations at headquarters were often strained, and the Marshals were angry at the severe reprimands to which they were subjected. The controlling leaders being out of gear the machine did not run smoothly: there was nothing but friction and tension. The Marshals were inclined to attribute their disgrace to the ill-will of Berthier and not to the temper of Napoleon. Particularly was this the case with Davout, who since 1809 had suspected that Berthier desired to ruin his reputation. Accordingly the Prince of Eckmühl set down the succession of reprimands which were hurled at his head to the machinations of the major-general, and not, as was the case, to Napoleon's jealousy of him, because people had prophesied he would become King of Poland. This misunderstanding was most unfortunate, for it prevented Berthier from effecting a reconciliation between Davout and the Emperor. Hence Napoleon was driven more and more to trust to the advice of the rash, unstable King of Naples. The major-general's lot through the campaign was most miserable. Working day and night to supervise the organisation of the huge force of six hundred thousand men; mistrusted by his former comrades; blamed for every mishap by the Emperor, whatever the fault might be, he had to put up with the bitterest insults, and while working as no other man could work, to endure such taunts as, 'Not only are you no good, but you are in the way.' Everything that went wrong 'was the fault of the general staff, which is so organised that it foresees nothing,' whether it was the shortcoming of the contractors or the burning of their own magazines by the Russians. But what most moved Napoleon's angel against the chief of the staff was that Berthier, with 'the parade states' before him, emphasising the enormous wastage of the army, constantly harped on the danger of pressing on to Moscow. So strained became the relations between them, that for the last part of the advance they no longer met at meals. But during the hours of the retreat the old friendship was resumed. Berthier bore no malice, and showed his bravery by himself opposing the enemy with musket and bayonet; and on one occasion, with Bessiéres, Murat, and Rapp, he saved the Emperor from a sotnia of Cossacks.

When Napoleon quitted the army at Vilna he left the major-general behind to help the King of Naples to withdraw the remnant of the Grand Army. Marching on foot through the deep snow, with fingers and nose frostbitten, the sturdy old veteran of sixty endured the fatigue as well as the hardiest young men in their prime; and in addition to the physical fatigue of marching, had to carry out all the administrative work, and bear the moral responsibility for what remained of the army; for the King of Naples, thinking of nothing but how to save his own crown, when difficulties increased, followed the example of Napoleon and deserted his post. Thereon the major-general took on himself to nominate Prince Eugène as Murat's successor. But in the end his health gave way, and the Emperor himself wrote to Prince Eugène telling him to send the old warrior home. Berthier reached Paris on February 9th, much broken down in health ; but his wonderful physique soon enabled him to regain his strength, and by the end of March he was once again hard at work helping the Emperor to extemporise an army. With his complete knowledge of this force, no one was more astonished than Berthier at the successes of Lutzen and Bautzen, and no one more insistent in his advice to the Emperor to accept the terms of the Allies during the armistice; but he advised in vain. Then followed the terrible catastrophe of Leipzig, due undoubtedly to Berthier's dread of acting without the express orders of the Emperor. The engineer officer charged with preparing the line of retreat reported that the one bridge across the Elster was not sufficient. The major-general, knowing that the Emperor desired to hide any signs of retreat from the Allies, replied that he must await the Emperor's orders, so, when, after three days' fighting, the retreat could no longer be postponed, a catastrophe was inevitable. Yet, in spite of everything, the Emperor refused to acknowledge himself beaten, and by the commencement of 1814 was once again ready to take the field, though by now the Allies had invaded France. Loyal as ever, Berthier worked his hardest; but he once again incurred the Emperor's anger by entreating him to accept the terms offered him at Chatillon. Still, when the end came and Napoleon abdicated, Berthier remained at his side, and it was only when the Emperor had released his Marshals from their allegiance that on April 11th he sent in his adhesion to the new government. When all save Macdonald had deserted the fallen Emperor, Berthier stayed on at Fontainebleau, directing the withdrawal of the remnants of the army, and making arrangements for the guard which was to accompany Napoleon to Elba. But though he remained with him until the day before he started for Elba, Berthier refused to share his exile, and at the time Napoleon was magnanimous enough to see that, owing to his age and the care of his children, he could not expect such a sacrifice.

So far, the Prince had done all that honour and affection could demand of him. But, unfortunately for his fame, instead of withdrawing into private life, he listened to the prayers of his wife, who keenly felt the loss of her title of 'Serene Princess'. It was at her desire that he continued to frequent the Bourbon court and actually accepted the captaincy of one of the new companies of royal guards. This and the fact that, as senior of the Marshals, Berthier had led his fellow Marshals to meet the King at Compiegne, caused the Prince of Wagram to be regarded as a traitor by Napoleon and the Imperialists. Moreover, the Prince Marshal now saw in Napoleon the disturber of the peace of Europe, so when the Emperor suddenly returned from Elba he withdrew from France, and retired to Bamberg, in his father-in-law's dominions.

It is commonly supposed that Berthier committed suicide, but the medical evidence shows that his fall was probably the result of giddiness arising from dyspepsia. It was on June 1st that the accident happened. He was watching a division of Russian troops passing through the town, and was much distressed by the sight, and was heard to murmur, 'My poor country!' Ever interested in soldiers, he got on a chair on the balcony before the nursery windows to get a better view of the troops, and while doing so lost his balance and fell to the ground.

For the moment the tragic death of the Marshal was the talk of Europe, but only for the moment, for the fate of the world was hanging on the issues of the great battle which was imminent in Belgium. If the Prince of Wagram had been there, it is more than conceivable that the scales would have fallen other than they did; for it was the indifferent staff work of Soult and the bad drafting of orders which lost the French the campaign. Of this, Napoleon was so firmly convinced that he never could efface it from his memory; again and again he was heard saying, 'If Berthier had been here I should never have met this misfortune.' The Emperor, in spite of the fact that in 1814 he had told Macdonald that Berthier could never return, was convinced that he would, and had told Rapp that he was certain he would come back to him. It was this failure to return which so embittered the fallen Emperor against the Prince of Wagram, and led to those cruel strictures on his character to which he gave vent at St. Helena. Moreover, Napoleon, so great in many things, was so jealous of his own glory that he could be mean beyond words. Even in the early years when he heard people praising Berthier's work in 1796, he told his secretary, Bourrienne, 'As for Berthier, since you have been with me, you see what he is - he is a blockhead.' At St. Helena, forgetting his old opinions, 'Berthier has his talents, activity, courage, character - all in his favour.' Forgetting that he himself had taught Berthier to be imperious, he derided his rather pompous manner, saying, 'Nothing is so imperious as weakness which feels itself supported by strength. Look at women.' Berthier, with his admirably lucid mind, great physique, methodical powers and ambition, would have made his name in any profession. He undoubtedly chose to be second to Napoleon; he served him with a fidelity that Napoleon himself could not understand, and he won his great commander's love and esteem in spite of the selfishness of the Corsican's nature. 'I really cannot understand,' said Napoleon to Talleyrand, 'how a relation that has the appearance of friendship has established itself between Berthier and me. I do not indulge in useless sentiments, and Berthier is so uninteresting that I do not know why I should care about him at all, and yet when I think of it I really have some liking for him.' ' It is because he believes in you,' said the former bishop and reader of men's souls. It was this belief in Napoleon which in time obsessed the Prince of Wagram's mind, which killed his own initiative and was responsible for his blunders in 1809 and at Leipzig, and turned him into a machine which merely echoed the Emperor's commands. 'Monsieur le Maréchal, the Emperor orders.' 'Monsieur, it is not me, it is the Emperor you ought to thank.' These hackneyed phrases typified more than anything else the bounds of the career which the Marshal had deliberately marked out for himself. In Berthier's eyes it was no reproach, but a testimony to his own principles, 'that he never gave an order, never wrote a despatch, which did not in some way emanate from Napoleon.' It was this which, with some appearance of truth, pointing to his notable failures, allowed Napoleon to say of him at St. Helena, 'His character was undecided, not strong enough for a commander-in-chief, but he possessed all the qualities of a good chief of the staff: a complete mastery of the map, great skill in reconnaissance, minute care in the despatch of orders, magnificent aptitude for presenting with the greatest simplicity the most complicated situation of an army.'

2

JOACHIM MURAT, MARSHAL, KING OF NAPLES

STABLE-BOY, seminarist, Marshal, King, Murat holds the unchallenged position of Prince of Gascons: petulant, persevering, ambitious and vain, he surpasses D'Artagnan himself in his overwhelming conceit. The third son of an innkeeper of La Bastide Fortunière in upper Quercy, Joachim Murat was born on March 25, 1767. From his earliest childhood Joachim was a horse-lover and a frequenter of the stables; but his parents had higher aims for their bright, smiling, intelligent darling, and destined him for the priesthood. The young seminarist was highly thought of by the preceptors at the College of Saint Michel at Cahors and the Lazarist Fathers at Toulouse; but neither priest nor mother had truly grasped his dashing character, and one February morning in 1787 Joachim slipped quietly out of the seminary doors and enlisted in the Chasseurs of the Ardennes, who were at the moment billeted in Toulouse. Two years later this promising recruit, having fallen foul of the military authorities, had to leave the service under a cloud. A post as draper's assistant was a poor exchange for the young soldier, who found the cavalry service of the royal army scarcely dashing enough, but the Revolution gave an outlet which Murat was quick to seize. For three years the future King harangued village audiences of Quercy on the iniquities of caste and the equality of all men; so that when, in February, 1792, the Assembly called for volunteers for the 'Garde Constitutionnelle' of Louis XVI, what better choice could the national guard of Montfaucon make than in nominating Joachim Murat, the handsome ex-sergeant of the Chasseurs of the Ardennes?

In Paris, Joachim soon found that the royal road to success lay in denouncing loudly all superior officers of lack of patriotism. Soon there was no more brazen-voiced accuser than Murat. In the course of a year he worked his way out of the 'Garde Constitutionnelle', and by April, 1793, he had attained the rank of captain in the 12th Chasseurs. Meanwhile, he had been selected as aide-de-camp by General d'Ure de Molans: having seen no service, he owed his appointment largely to his conceit and good looks. Blue-eyed, with an aquiline nose and smiling lips; with long chestnut curls falling over his well-poised head; endowed with great physical strength, shown in his strong, supple arms and in the long flat-thighed legs of a horseman, he appeared the most perfect type of the dare-devil, dashing cavalry soldier. The moderate republican general, d'Ure de Molans, was useful to him for a time, but the young Gascon saw that the days of the extremist were close at hand; accordingly, he allied himself with an adventurer called Landrieux, who was raising a body of cut-throats whose object was plunder, not fighting. The Convention, which had licensed Landrieux to raise this corps of patriotic defenders of the country, accepted his nomination of Murat as acting lieutenant-colonel. But they soon fell out, for Murat had the audacity to try and make these patriots fight instead of merely seeking plunder. The consequence of this quarrel was that, early in 1794, he found himself accused as a *ci-devant* noble. Imprisoned at Amiens, and brought before the Committee of Public Safety, in a fit of republican enthusiasm he changed his name to Marat. But this did not save him, and he owed his life to a deputation from his native Quercy, which proved both his humble birth and his high re-publicanism.

The 13th Vendémiaire was the turning-point in Murat's life, for on that day, for the first time, he came in contact with his future chief, the young General Bonaparte, and gained his attention by the masterly way he saved the guns at Sablons from the hands of the Royalists. The future Emperor ever knew when to reward merit, and on being appointed to command the army in Italy he at once selected him as his aide-de-camp. So far he had seen little or no war service. But the campaign of 1796 proved that Bonaparte's judgment was sound, for by the end of the year there was no longer any necessity for Murat to blow his own trumpet. In the short campaign against the Sardinians he showed his talent as a cavalry leader by his judgment in charges at Dego and Mondovi. He had no cause to grumble that he was not appreciated, for his general selected him to take to Paris the news of this victorious campaign and of the triumphant negotiations of Cherasco. He returned from Paris in May as brigadier-general, in time to take part in the crossing of the Mincio and to rob Kilmaine of some of his honours. The commander-in-chief still kept him attached to the headquarter staff, and constantly employed him on special service. His enterprises were numerous and varied - one week at Genoa on a special diplomatic mission, a week or two later leading a forlorn attack on the great fortress of Mantua, then commanding the right wing of the army covering the siege, he showed himself ever resourceful and daring. But during the autumn of 1796 he fell under the heavy displeasure of his chief, for at Milan and Montebello Josephine had shown too great favour to the young cavalry general. Murat accordingly had no scruples in intriguing with Barras against his chief. But his glorious conduct at Rivoli once again brought him back to favour, and Bonaparte entrusted him with an infantry brigade in the advance on Vienna, and later with a delicate independent mission in the Valtelline. But Murat, unlike Lannes, Marmont and Duroc, was not yet indispensable to Bonaparte, and accordingly was left with the Army of Italy when the general returned in triumph to Paris. It was mainly owing to Masséna's enthusiastic report of his service in the Roman campaign, at the close of 1797, that he was selected as one of the supernumerary officers in the Egyptian expedition.

So far, Murat had not yet been able to distinguish himself above his comrades-in-arms. Masséna, Augereau, Serurier, and Laharpe left him far in the rear, but Egypt was to give him the chance of proving his worth, and showing that he was not only a dashing officer, but a cavalry commander of the first rank. He led the cavalry of the advance guard in the march up the Nile, and was present at the battle of the Pyramids and the taking of Cairo. But so far the campaign, instead of bringing him fresh honours, nearly brought him disgrace; for he joined the party of grumblers, and was one of those who were addressed in the famous reprimand, 'I know some generals are mutinous and preach revolt ... let them take care. I am as high above a general as above a drummer and, if necessary, I will as soon have the one shot as the other.'

On July 27, 1798, Murat was appointed governor of the province of Kalioub, which lies north of Cairo; to keep order among his turbulent subjects his whole force consisted of a battalion of infantry, twenty-five cavalrymen, and a three-pounder gun. His governorship was only part of the work Bonaparte required of him, for he was constantly away organising and leading light columns by land or river, harrying the Arabs and disbanded Mamelukes, sweeping the country, collecting vast depots of corn and cattle, remounting the cavalry - proving himself a past master in irregular warfare. So well did he do his work that the commander-in-chief selected him to command the whole of the cavalry in the Syrian expeditionary force.

Thanks to his handling of his horsemen, the march through Palestine occasioned the French but little loss. During the siege of Acre he commanded the covering force, and pushed reconnaissances far and wide. So feared was his name that the whole Turkish army fled before him on the banks of the Jordan, and left their camp and immense booty in the hands of the French. But though he had thus destroyed the relieving force, Acre, victualled by the English fleet, still held out, and Bonaparte had to retreat to Egypt.

It was at Aboukir that Murat consolidated his reputation as a great commander. The Turkish general had neglected to rest the right flank of his first line on the sea, and Murat, seizing his opportunity, fell on the unguarded flank with the full weight of his cavalry, and rolled the unfortunate Turks into the water. Thereafter, by the aid of a battery of artillery, the centre of the second line of the Turkish army was broken, and the French horse dashing into the gap, once again made short work of the enemy, and their leader captured with his own hands the Turkish commander. Bonaparte, in his despatch, did full justice to his subordinate. 'The victory is mainly due to General Murat. I ask you to make him general of division: his brigade of cavalry has achieved the impossible.' Murat himself was much distressed at being wounded in the face, as he feared it might destroy his good looks; however, he soon had the satisfaction of writing to his father: 'The doctors tell me I shall not be in the least disfigured, so tell all the young ladies that even if Murat bas lost some of his good looks, they won't find that he has lost any of his bravery in the war of love.'

His grumbles forgiven, Murat left Egypt among the chosen band of followers of whose fidelity Napoleon was assured; his special mission was to gain over the cavalry to the side of his chief. He it was who, with Leclerc, on the 18th Brumaire, forced his way into the Orangerie at the head of the grenadiers and hurled out the deputies. The First Consul rewarded him amply, appointing him inspector of the Consular Guard, and, later still, in preference to his rival Lannes, gave him in marriage his sister Caroline. Murat had met Caroline Bonaparte at Montebello during the Italian campaign of 1796, and had at once been struck by her beauty. Like many another cavalier, he had a flame in every country, or rather, in every town which he visited. But by 1799 the gay Gascon saw that it was time to finish sowing his wild oats, since destiny was offering him a chance which falls to the lot of few mortals. It was by now clear that the First Consul's star was in the ascendant. Already his family were reaping the fruits of his success. Ambition, pride and love were the cords of the net which drew the willing Murat to Caroline. As brother-in-law to the First Consul, Joachim felt secure against his bitter rival, Lannes. To add point to this success, he knew that the victor of Montebello was straining every nerve to gain this very prize. Moreover, Fortune herself favoured his suit. Bonaparte had offered the hand of Caroline to the great General Moreau, but the future victor of Hohenlinden refused to join himself to the Corsican triumph. To cover his confusion the First Consul was glad to give his sister's hand to one of his most gallant officers, especially as by so doing he once and for all removed the haunting fear of an intrigue between him and Josephine. Accordingly, on January 25, 1800, Murat and Caroline were pronounced man and wife in the temple of the canton of Plailly, by the president of the canton. Though Caroline only brought with her a dot of forty thousand francs, she stood for what was better still, immense possibilities.

Murat's honeymoon was cut short by the Marengo campaign. In April he started, as lieutenant-general in command of the cavalry, to join the Army of the Reserve at Dijon. Once the corps of Lannes had, by the capture of Ivrea, secured the opening into Italy, the cavalry were able to take up their role, and with irresistible weight they swept down the plains of Lombardy, forced the river crossings, and on June 2nd entered Milan. Thence the First Consul despatched his horsemen to seize Piacenza, the important bridge across the Po, the key of the Austrian lines of communication. Murat, with a few troops, crossed the river in some twenty small rowing-boats, and, dashing forward, captured the bridge head on the southern bank, and thus secured not only the peaceful crossing of his force, but the capture of the town and the immense Austrian depots. At Marengo the cavalry acted in separate brigades, and the decisive stroke of the battle fell to the lot of the younger Kellermann, whose brilliant charge decided the day in favour of the French. The despatches only mentioned that 'General Murat's clothes were riddled by bullets.'

So far Murat had always held subordinate commands; his great ambition was to become the commander-in-chief of an independent army. His wife, Caroline, and his sister-in-law, Josephine, were constant in their endeavours to gain this distinction for him from the First Consul. But it was not till the end of 1800 that they succeeded; and then only partially, for in December the lieutenant-general was appointed commander of a corps of observation, whose headquarters were at Milan, and whose duty was to overawe Tuscany and the Papal States. His campaign in central Italy is more noticeable for his endeavours to shake himself free from the control of General Brune, the commander-in-chief of the Army of Italy, than for any very brilliant manoeuvres. Tuscany and the Papal States were easily conquered, and the King of Naples was only too glad to buy peace at Foligno. Italy lay at the feet of the French general, but what was most gratifying of all, after his successful negotiation with the King of Naples, the First Consul tacitly accepted the title which his brother-in-law had assumed of commander-in-chief of the Army of Naples. Murat had the satisfaction of having under his orders Lieutenant-General Soult, three generals of division and four generals of brigade. For the moment his Gascon vanity was satiated, while his Gascon greed was appeased by substantial bribes from all the conquered countries of the Peninsula. The 'commander-in-chief' was joined at Florence in May, 1801, by his wife, Caroline, and his young son, Achille, born in January, whom he found 'charming, already possessed of two teeth'. In the capital of Tuscany Murat gravely delivered to the inhabitants a historical lecture on their science, their civilisation, and the splendour of their state under the Medici. He spent the summer in visiting the watering-places of Italy.

In August the First Consul raised him to the command of the troops of the Cisalpine Republic, and he retained this post for the next two years, and had his headquarters in Milan, making occasional expeditions to Paris and Rome, and on the whole content with his position, save for occasional quarrels with Melzi, the president of the Italian Republic. Their jurisdictions overlapped and the Gascon would play second fiddle to no one save to his great brother-in-law.

In January, 1804, the First Consul recalled Murat to Paris, nominating him commandant of the troops of the first military division and of the National Guard, and Governor of the city. Bonaparte's object was not so much to please his brother-in-law as to strengthen himself. He was concentrating his own family, clan, and all his most faithful followers in readiness for the great event, the proclamation of the Empire. Men like Lannes, whose views were republican, were discreetly kept out of the way on foreign missions; but Murat, as Bonaparte knew, was a pliant tool. As early as 1802 he had hotly favoured the Concordat, and had had his marriage recelebrated by Cardinal Consalvi ; and both Caroline and Joachim in finitely preferred being members of the imperial family of the Emperor of the French to being merely relations of the successful general and First Consul of the French Republic. They were willing also to obey the future Emperor's commands, and to aid him socially by entertaining on a lavish scale, and their residence in Paris, the Hotel Thélusson, became the centre of gorgeous entertainments. While Murat strutted about in sky-blue overalls, covered with gold spangles, invented new uniforms, and bought expensive aigrettes for his busby, his wife showed her rococo taste by furnishing her drawing-room in red satin and gold, and her bedroom in rose-coloured satin and old point lace. They had their award. Five days after the proclamation of the Empire, after a furious scene, Napoleon conceded the title of Imperial Highness to his sister with the bitter words:

'To listen to you, people would think that I had robbed Tyou of the heritage of the late King, our father.' Meanwhile the Governor of Paris had received his Marshal's baton, and in the following February was created Senator, Prince, and Grand Admiral of France.

The rupture of the peace of Amiens did not affect the life of the Governor of Paris; for two years he enjoyed this office, with all its opportunities of ostentation and display. But in August, 1805, the approaching war with Austria caused the Emperor to summon his most brilliant cavalry leader to his side. In that month he despatched him, travelling incognito as Colonel Beaumont, to survey the military roads into Germany, and especially to study the converging roads round Wiirzburg, and the suitability of that town as an advance depôt for an army operating on the Danube. From Wiirzburg Murat travelled hurriedly through Nuremberg, Ratisbon, and Passau, as far as the river Inn, returning via Munich, Ulm, the Black Forest, and Strassburg. Immediately on his return the Emperor appointed him 'Lieutenant of the Empire, and commandant in his absence' of all the troops cantonned along the Rhine, and of such corps of the Grand Army as reach that river before himself. When war actually broke out Murat's duty was to mask, with his cavalry in the Black Forest, the turning movement of the other corps of the Grand Army which were striking at the Austrian rear. Once the turning movement was completed the Prince was entrusted with the command of the left wing the army, which included his own cavalry division an the corps of Lannes and Ney. Excellent as he was cavalry commander in the field, Murat had no head for great combinations. Instead of profiting by the advice of those able soldiers, Lannes and Ney, he spent his time quarrelling with them. He accordingly kept his troops on the wrong side of the Danube, with the result that in spite of Ney's brilliant action at Elchingen, two divisions of the Austrians under the Archduke Ferdinand escaped from Ulm. Prince Murat, however, retrieved his error by his brilliant pursuit of the escaped Austrians, and by hard riding and fighting captured quite half of the Archduke's command.

Impetuosity, perseverance, and dash are undoubted useful traits in the character of a cavalry commander, and of these he had his fair share. But his jealousy and vanity often led him astray. During the advance down the Danube, in his desire to gain the credit of capturing Vienna, he lost touch completely with the Russians and Austrians, who had retreated across the Danube at Krems, and he involved the Emperor in a dangerous position by leaving the unbeaten Russians on the flank of his line of communications. But the Prince quickly made amends for his rashness. The ruse by which he and Lannes captured the bridge below Vienna was discreditable no doubt from the point of view of morality. It was a direct lie to tell the Austrian commander that an armistice had been arranged and the bridge ceded to the French. But the fact remains that Murat saved the Emperor and the French army from the difficult and costly operation of crossing the broad Danube in the face of the Allies. A few days later the Prince's vanity postponed for some time the culminating blow, for although he had so successfully bluffed the enemy, he could not realise that they could deceive him, and believing their tales of an armistice, he allowed the Allies to escape from Napoleon's clutches at Hollabriinn. At Austerlitz the Prince Marshal covered himself with glory. In command of the left wing, ably backed by Lannes, he threw the whole weight of his cavalry on the Russians, demonstrating to the full the efficacy of a well-timed succession of charges on broken infantry, and giving a masterly lesson in the art of re-forming disorganised horsemen, by the use he made of the solid ranks of Lannes' infantry, from behind which he issued again and again in restored order, to fall on the shaken ranks of the enemy. At Austerlitz he was at his best. His old quarrel with Lannes was for the moment forgotten; his lieutenants, Nansouty, d'Hautpoul, and Sébastiani, were too far below him to cause him any jealousy. The action on the left was mainly one of cavalry, in which quickness of eye and decision were everything, where a fault could be retrieved by charging in person at the head of the staff, or by a few fierce words to a regiment slightly demoralised. Rapidity of action and a self-confidence which on the battlefield never felt itself beaten were the cause of Murat's success.

It was the fixed policy of Napoleon to secure the Rhine valley, so that never again would it be possible for the Austrians to threaten France. To gain this end he originated the Confederation of the Rhine, grouping all the small Rhineland states in a confederation of which he himself was the Protector, and binding the rulers of the individual states to his dynasty, either by marriage or by rewards. As part of this scheme the Emperor allotted to Murat and Caroline the duchies of Cleves and Berg, welding them into one province under the title of the Grand Duchy of Berg. Thus the Gascon innkeeper's son became in 1806 Joachim, Prince and Grand Admiral of France, and Grand Duke of Berg. He gained this honour not as Murat, the brilliant cavalry general, but as Prince Joachim, the brother-in-law of the Emperor Napoleon. The Grand Duke and the Grand Duchess did not, however, reside long in their capital Düsseldorf; they infinitely preferred Paris. In their eyes Berg was but a stepping-stone to higher things, a source of profit and a pretext for exalting themselves at the expense of their neighbours. The Grand Duke entrusted the interior management of the Duchy to his old friend Agar, who had served him well in Italy, and who later became Count of Mosburg. Any prosperity which Grand Duke enjoyed was entirely due to the financial ability of Agar. Murat, however, kept foreign affairs in own hands. As Foreign Minister, by simply taking what he wanted, he added considerably to the extent of duchy. But, like all Napoleon's satellites, he constantly found his position humiliating, for in spite of his tears and prayers, he had continually to see his duchy sacrificed to France. It was no use to complain that Napoleon had taken away the fortress of Wesel, which had been handed over to the Grand Duchy by special treaty by the King of Prussia, for, as Queen Hortense wisely asked him, 'Who had really made that treaty? Who had given him duchy, the fortress, and everything?'

In September, 1806, Murat's second and last visit Düsseldorf was brought to an abrupt close by the opening of the Prussian campaign. On the eve of the battle of Jena his cavalry covered forty miles and arrived in time to give the enemy the coup de grâce on the following day, driving them in flight into Weimar. Then followed the famous pursuit across Prussia, in which Murat captured first-class fortresses with cavalry regiments, and divisions of infantry with squadrons of horse, and ended by seizing Blücher and the whole of the Prussian artillery on the shore of the Baltic at Lübeck. But though his cavalry had thus wiped the Prussian army out of existence, the war dragged on, for, as in 1805, the Russians had entered the field. In November the Emperor despatched his brother-in-law to command the French corps which were massing round Warsaw. The Grand Duke read into this order the idea that he was destined to become the King of a revived Poland; accordingly he made a triumphant entry into Warsaw in a fantastic uniform, red leather boots, tunic of cloth of gold, sword-belt glittering with diamonds, and a huge busby of rich fur bedecked with costly plumes. The Poles greeted him with enthusiasm, and Murat hastened to write to the Emperor that 'the Poles desired to become a nation under a foreign King, given them by your Majesty.' While the Grand Duke dreamed of his Polish crown, the climate defeated the French troops, and when the Emperor arrived at the front the Prince had to lay aside his royal aspirations. But in spite of his disappointment he was still too much of a Frenchman and a soldier to allow his personal resentment to overcome his duty to his Emperor, and he continued to hope that by his daring and success he might still win his Polish crown. At Eylau he showed his customary bravery and his magnificent talent as a cavalry leader, when he saved the shattered corps of Augereau by a successful charge of over twelve thousand sabres. At the battle of Heilsberg the celebrated light cavalryman, Lasalle, saved his life, but a few minutes later the Grand Duke was able to cry quits by himself rescuing Lasalle from the midst of a Russian charge. Unfortunately for Murat, the prospective alliance with Russia once and for all compelled Napoleon to lay aside all thought of reviving the kingdom of Poland, and when the would-be King arrived with a Polish guard of honour and his fantastic uniform, he was met by the biting words of the Emperor: 'Go and put on your proper uniform; you look like a clown.' After Tilsit the disappointed Grand Duke returned to Paris, where his equally ambitious wife had been intriguing with Josephine, Talleyrand and Fouché to get her husband nominated Napoleon's successor, in case the accidents of the campaign should remove the Emperor. But Napoleon had no intention of dying without issue. Thanks to his brother-in-law's generosity, Murat was able to neglect his half-million subjects in Berg and spend his revenues right royally in Paris. But early in 1808 his ambition was one again inflamed by the hope of a crown - not a revived kingship in Poland, but the ancient sceptre of Spain. Napoleon had decided that the Pyrenees should no longer exist, and that Portugal and Spain should become French provinces ruled by puppets of his own. Junot already held Portugal; it seemed as if it needed but a vigorous movement to oust the Bourbons from Madrid. Family quarrels had already caused a revolution in Spain. Charles had fled the kingdom, leaving the throne to his son Ferdinand. Both had appealed to Napoleon; consequently there was a decent pretext for sending a French army into Spain. On February 25th Murat was despatched at a few hours' notice, with orders to take over the supreme command of all the French corps which were concentrating in Spain, to seize the fortresses of Pampeluna and St. Sebastian, and to advance with all speed on Madrid, but he was given no clue as to what the Emperor's ulterior object might be. He was ordered, however, to keep the Emperor daily informed of the state of public opinion in Spain. Prince Joachim very soon perceived that King Charles was rejected by every body, that the Prime Minister, the Prince of Peace, was extremely unpopular, and that Ferdinand was weak and irresolute: it seemed as if he would follow the example of the King of Portugal, and would flee to the colonies when the French army approached his capital. The only disquieting feature of the situation was the constant annihilation of small parties of French soldiers and the brutal murder of all stragglers. On March 23rd the French army entered Madrid. All was tranquil. Meanwhile the ex-King Charles had retired to Bayonne, and, by the orders of the Emperor, the Prince of Peace was sent there also, where upon King Ferdinand, fearing that Napoleon might take his father's part, hurried off to France. At Bayonne both the claimants to the Spanish throne surrendered their rights to the Emperor, while at Madrid, Murat, hoping against hope, played the royal part and kept the inhabitants quiet with bull-fights and magnificent fetes. So far the Spaniards, though restless, were waiting to see whether the French were friends, as they protested, or in reality stealthy foes. The crisis came on May 2nd, when the French troops were compelled to evacuate Madrid on account of the fury of the populace at the attempted abduction of the little Prince, Don Francisco. Murat showed to the full his indomitable courage, fighting fiercely, not only for his Emperor, but for the crown which he thought was his. Bitter indeed were his feelings when he received a letter dated that fatal day, May 2nd, informing him that Joseph was to be King of Spain, and that he might choose either Portugal or Naples as his kingdom. In floods of tears he accepted Naples, but so cruel was the blow that his health gave way, and instead of hurrying off to his new kingdom he had to spend the summer drinking the waters at Bareges; his sensitive Gascon feelings had completely broken down under the disappointment, and, for the time being, he was physically and morally a wreck.

Murat was in no hurry to commence his reign, and his subjects showed no great anxiety to see their new ruler. But when King Joachim Napoleon, to give him his new title, arrived at Naples he was received with unexpected warmth. The new monarch, with his striking personality and good looks, at once captivated the hearts of his fickle Southern subjects. Joseph had been prudent and cold, Joachim was ostentatious and fiery. The Neapolitans had never really cared for their Bourbon sovereigns. Some of the noblesse had from interest clung to the old dynasty, but the greater part of the nobility cared little who ruled them so long as their privileges were not interfered with. Among the middle class there was a strong party which had accepted the doctrines of the French Revolution. The lower class were idle and lazy, and willing to serve any sovereign who appealed to them by ostentation. The people who really held the key of the hearts of the mass of the population were the clergy. Joseph, with his liberal ideas, had attempted to free the people from clerical thraldom. Joachim, however, with his Southern instincts, refused to deny himself the use of such a powerful lever, and quickly ingratiated himself with his new subjects. From the moment that he arrived at Naples the new King determined, if not to rule Naples for the Neapolitans, at least, by pretending to do so, to rule Naples for himself and not for Napoleon. It is not, therefore, surprising that before the close of the year 1808 friction arose, which was further increased by the intrigues of Talleyrand and Fouché. These ministers, firmly convinced that Napoleon would never return from the Spanish war, had decided that in the event of his death they would declare Murat his successor rather than establish a regency for the young son of Louis Napoleon, the King of Holland.

In pursuance of the plan of winning his subjects' affections Joachim had at once called to his aid Agar, who had so successfully managed the finances of the Grand Duchy of Berg. The difficulties of finance in Naples were very great, and with Agar the King had to associate the subtle Corsican, Saliceti, who had so powerfully contributed to the rise of Napoleon. Taxation in Naples was heavy, for the Neapolitans had to find the money for the war with their old dynasty, which was threatening them from Sicily, aided by the English fleet. To secure the kingdom against the Sicilians and English, a large Neapolitan army of thirty thousand troops had to be maintained along with an auxiliary force of ten thousand French. Moreover, the Neapolitans had to pay for having a King like Joachim and a Queen Consort like Caroline. The royal household alone required 1,395,000 ducats per annum. To meet this heavy expense the ministers had to devise all sorts of expedients to raise money. Regular taxation, monopolies, mortgages, and loans barely sufficed to provide for the budget. Still the King managed to retain his popularity, and in his own way attempted to ameliorate the lot of his subjects. He introduced the Code Napoleon. He founded a military college, an artillery and engineer college, a naval college, a civil engineer college and a polytechnic school. He also instituted primary schools in every commune, and started an École Normale for the training of teachers. He expanded the staff of the University and established an Observatory, and Botanical Garden at Naples. He attempted to conciliate the Neapolitan noblesse by gradually dismissing his French ministers and officers and appointing Neapolitan nobles in their place. At the same time he abolished feudal dues and customs. He also attempted to develop industries by giving them protection. Above all, by the strict measures of his minister Manhes he established peace in the interior by breaking down the organised system of the freebooters and robbers. As time went on he found that the clergy and monks were too heavy a burden for his kingdom to bear, and, at the expense of his popularity, he had to cut down the numbers of the dioceses and parishes and abolish the religious orders.

From the first the new King grasped the fact that his kingdom would always be heavily taxed, and his throne insecure as long as the Bourbons, backed by the English, held Sicily. His plan of campaign, therefore, was to drive his enemy out of the smaller islands, and thereafter to demand the aid of French troops and make a determined effort against Sicily. In October, 1808, by a well-planned expedition, he captured the island of Capri, and caused the English commander, Sir Hudson Lowe, to capitulate. It was not till the autumn of 1810, however, that he was ready for the great expedition. Relying on the traditional hatred of the people of Messina for the Bourbons, he collected a strong force on the Straits, and waited till the moment when, after a gale, the English fleet had not yet arrived from the roads of Messina. On the evening of September 17th he sent away his advance guard of two thousand men in eighty small boats. Cavaignac, the commander of this force, secured the important villages of Santo Stefano and Santo Paolo. But at the critical moment the commander of the French division, acting according to the Emperor's orders, refused to allow his troops to cross. Before fresh arrangements could be made the English fleet reappeared on the scene, and Cavaignac and his force were thus sacrificed for no purpose. Joachim, as time showed, never forgave the Emperor for the failure of his cherished plan.

By the commencement of 1812, the coming Russian campaign overshadowed all other questions. Murat, who had earnestly begged to be allowed to share the Austrian campaign of 1809, was delighted to serve in person. But as King of Naples he refused to send a division of ten thousand men to reinforce the Grand Army, 'as a French man and a soldier he declared himself to the core a subject of the Emperor, but as King of Naples he aspired to perfect independence.' It was this double attitude which, from the moment Murat became King, clouded the relations between him and Napoleon. But nevertheless, once he rejoined the Emperor at Dantzig, he laid aside all his royal aspirations and became the faithful dashing leader of cavalry.

During the advance on Moscow the cavalry suffered terribly from the difficulties of constant reconnaissances and want of supplies, but in spite of this Murat urged the Emperor not to halt at Smolensk, but to push on, as he believed the Russians were becoming demoralised. Scarce a day passed without some engagement in which the King of Naples showed his audacity and his talent as a leader. Notwithstanding, Napoleon, angry at the constant escape of the Russians, declared that if Murat had only pursued Bagration in Lithuania he would not have escaped. This reproach spurred on the King of Naples to even greater deeds of bravery, and so well was his figure known to the enemy that the Cossacks constantly greeted him with cries of 'Hurrah, hurrah, Murat!' At the battle of Moskowa he and Ney completely overthrew the Russians, and if Napoleon had flung the Guard into the action, the Russian army would have been annihilated. In spite of the losses during the campaign, when the French evacuated Moscow Murat had still ten thousand mounted troops but by the time the army had reached the Beresina there remained only eighteen hundred troopers with horses. When the Emperor deserted the Grand Army, he left the King of Naples in command, with orders to rally the army at Vilna. But Murat saw that it was impossible to re-form the army there, and accordingly ordered a retirement across the Niemen, a line which he soon found it was impossible to hold. On January 10, 1813, came the news that the Prussians had actually gone over to the enemy. It seemed as if Napoleon was lost, and Murat thereupon at once deserted the army, and set out in all haste for Italy, thinking only of how to save his crown.

The King arrived in Naples bent on maintaining his crown and on allowing no interference from the Emperor. But in spite of this he could not decide on any definite line of action. He was afraid the English and Russians would invade his country, but on the other hand his old affection for Napoleon, and a sort of sneaking belief in his ultimate success, prevented him from listening to the insidious advice of the Austrian envoy, whom the far-seeing Metternich had at once sent to Naples. If Napoleon had not in his despatch glorified Prince Eugéne's conduct to the disparagement of the King of Naples, if he had on vouchsafed some reply to the King's persistent letters inquiry whether he still trusted his old comrade and lieutenant, Murat would have thrown himself heart and soul into the mêlée on the side of his old friend. But in April Napoleon quitted Paris for the army in Germany without sending one line in reply to these imploring letters. Meanwhile on April 23rd came a letter from Colonel Coffin suggesting the possibility of effecting an entente between English and Neapolitan Governments, or at any rate a commercial convention. Thereupon Murat sent officers to enter into negotiations with Lord William Bentinck, who represented the English Government in Sicily. All through the summer, the negotiations were continued, but Murat, in spite of the guarantee of the throne of Naples which the English offered, could not break entirely with his Emperor and benefactor. Still Napoleon, in his blindness, instead attempting to conciliate his brother-in-law, allowed articles to his disparagement to appear in the *Moniteur*. Nevertheless Murat at bottom was Napoleon's man. Elated by the Emperor's success at Lützen and Bautzen, although he refused to allow the Neapolitan troops to join the Army of Italy under Prince Eugène, he hurried off in August to join the French army at Dresden. There a reconciliation took place between the brothers-in-law. But after the defeat at Leipzig King Joachim asked and obtained leave to return to his own dominions.

His presence was needed at home, for in Italy also war had gone against the French. Prince Eugène had to fall back on the line of the Adda, and the defection of Tyrol had opened to the Allies the passes into the Peninsula. Murat, in his hurry, had to leave his coach snowed up in Simplon Pass and proceed on horseback to Milan, where he halted but a few hours to write a despatch to the Emperor, which practically foretold his desertion. He declared that if he, instead of Eugène, was entrusted with the defence of Italy, he would at once march north from Naples with forty thousand men. He had indeed never forgotten the slight put upon him by the article in the *Moniteur*, after the Russian campaign, and he was ready to sacrifice even his kingdom if only he could revenge himself on his enemy, Eugène. As Napoleon would not grant him this request, he determined to humiliate Eugène, and, at the same time, to save his crown by negotiating with the enemy. On reaching Naples, he found that his wife, who hitherto had been an unbending partisan of the French, had entirely changed her politics and was now pledged to an Austrian alliance. The King was ever unstable, vanity always governed his conduct: the Queen was always determined, governed solely by a cold, calculating ambition. Negotiations were at once opened with the Austrians. The King protested 'that he desired nothing in the world so much as to make common cause with the allied Powers.' He promised that he would join them with thirty thousand troops, on condition that he was guaranteed the throne of Naples, and that he should have the Roman States in exchange for Sicily. Meanwhile he addressed an order of the day to his army, stating that the Neapolitan troops should only be employed in Italy. This of course did not commit him either to Napoleon or the Austrian alliance. Meanwhile the Emperor had despatched Fouché to try to bind his brother-in-law to France, but that distinguished double-dealer merely advised the Neapolitan King to move northwards to the valley of the Po with all his troops, and there to wait and see whether it would be best to help the French, or to enter France with the Allies, and perhaps the Tuileries as Emperor.

Joachim Napoleon quietly occupied Rome and pushed forward his troops towards the Po, using the French magazines and depots, but still negotiating with the Austrians, and, at the same time, holding out hopes to the purely Italian party. For the national party of the Risorgimento were striving hard to seize this opportunity to unite Italy and drive out the foreigner, and no one seemed more capable of carrying out their policy than the popular King of Naples. The Austrians flattered the hopes of 'young Italy', by declaring in their proclamation that they had only entered Italy to free her from the yoke of the stranger, and to aid the King of Naples by creating an independent kingdom of Italy. Still Murat hesitated on the brink. As late as the 27th of December he wrote to the Emperor proposing that Italy should be formed into two kingdoms, that he should govern all the peninsula south of the Po, and that the rest of the country should be left to Eugène. Three days later the Austrian envoy arrived with the proposals of the Allies. But he could not yet make up his mind, and; moreover, the English had not yet guaranteed him Naples. In January, however, these guarantees were given, and against his will he had to sign a treaty. Scarcely was the writing dry when he began to negotiate with Prince Eugène. He used every artifice to prevent a collision between the French and Neapolitan troops. When the campaign opened, his troops abandoned their position at the first shot, while he himself took good care not to reach the front until the news of Napoleon's abdication arrived.

But Murat's conduct had alienated everybody. The French loathed him for his duplicity; the Allies suspected him of treachery, and the party of the Risorgimento looked on him as the cause of their subjection to the foreigner; for the Austrian victory had not brought Italy unity and independence, but had merely established the fetters of the old regime. During the remainder of 1814 the lot of the King of Naples was most unenviable. The restored Bourbons of France and Spain regarded him as the despoiler of the Bourbon house of

Sicily. Russia had been no party to the guarantee of his kingdom. England desired nothing so much as his expulsion. Austria alone upheld him, for she had been the chief party to the treaty; but Metternich was waiting for him to make some slip which might serve as a pretext for tearing up that treaty. Even the Pope refused the bribe which the King offered him when he proposed to restore the Marches in return for receiving the papal investiture. In despair Murat once again entered into negotiations with the Italian party. A general rising was planned in Lombardy, but failed, as the Austrians received news of the proposed cession of Milan. With cruel cunning they spread the report that the King of Naples had sold the secret. Henceforward Murat had no further hope. Foreigners, Italians, priests, carbonari and freemasons, all had turned against him.

Such was the situation when on March 8, 1815, the King heard that Napoleon had left Elba. As usual he dealt double. He at once sent a message to England that he would be faithful, while at the same time he sent agents to Sicily to try to stir up a revolt against the Bourbons. As soon as the news of Napoleon's reception in France arrived, he set out at the head of forty thousand troops, thinking that all Italy would rise for him. But the Italians mistrusted the fickle King; the Austrian troops were already mobilised, and accordingly, early in May, the Neapolitan army fled homewards before its enemies. King Joachim's popularity was gone. A grant of a constitution roused no enthusiasm among the people. City after city opened its gates to the enemy. Resistance was hopeless, so on the night of May 19th the King of Naples, with a few hundred thousand francs and his diamonds, accompanied by a handful of personal friends, fled by sea to Cannes. But the Emperor refused to receive the turncoat, though at St. Helena he bitterly repented this action, lamenting 'that at Waterloo Murat might have given us the victory. For what did we need? To break three or four English squares. Murat was just the man for the job.' After Waterloo the poor King fled before the White Terror, and for some time lay hid in Corsica. There he was given a safe conduct by the Allies and permission to settle in Austria. But the deposed monarch could not overcome his vanity. He still believed himself indispensable to Naples. Some four hundred Corsicans promised to follow him thither. The filibustering expedition set out in three small ships on the 28th of September. A storm arose and scattered the armada, but in spite of this, on October 7th, the ex-King decided to land at Pizzo. Dressed in full uniform, amid cries of 'Long live our King Joachim,' the unfortunate man landed with twenty-six followers. He was at once arrested, and on October 13th, tried by court martial, condemned to death, and executed a few hours later.

Joachim Murat met his death like a soldier. As he wrote to his wife, his only regret was that he died far off, without seeing his children. Death was what he courted when landing at Pizzo, for he must have known how impossible it was for him to conquer a kingdom with twenty-six men. Still, he preferred to die in the attempt to regain his crown rather than to spend an ignoble old age, a pensioner on the bounty of his enemies. Murat died as he had lived, brave but vain, with his last words calling out, 'Soldiers, do your duty: fire at my heart, but spare my face.'

The King of Naples owed his elevation entirely to his fortunate marriage with the Emperor's sister; otherwise it is certain he would never have reached such exalted rank, for Napoleon really did not like him or trust him, and had a true knowledge of his ability. 'He was a Paladin,' said the Emperor at St. Helena, 'in the field, but in the Cabinet destitute of either decision or judgment. He loved, I may rather say, adored me; he was my right arm; but without me he was nothing. In battle he was perhaps the bravest man in the world; left to himself, he was an imbecile without judgment.' Murat was a cavalry leader pure and simple. His love of horses, his intuitive knowledge of exactly how much he could ask from his horsemen, his reckless bravery, his fine swordsmanship, his dashing manners, captivated the French cavalry and enabled him to 'achieve the impossible.' Contrary to accepted opinion Napoleon believed 'that cavalry, if led by equally brave and resolute men, must always break infantry.' Consequently we find that at Austerlitz, Jena, and Eylau, the decisive stroke of the day was in each case given by immense bodies of some twenty thousand men under the command of Murat, whose genius lay in his ability to manoeuvre these huge bodies of cavalry on the field of battle, and in the tenacity with which he clung to and pursued a beaten enemy. But this was the sum total of his military ability. He had no conception of the use of the other arms of the service, and never gained even the most elementary knowledge of strategy. When trusted with anything like the command of a mixed body of troops he proved an utter failure. Before Ulm he nearly ruined Napoleon's combination by failing to get in contact with the enemy. In the later half of the campaign of 1806 he hopelessly failed to make any headway against the Russians east of the Vistula. In the retreat across the Niemen he proved himself absolutely incapable of reorganising a beaten force. As a king, Murat was full of good intentions towards his people, but his extravagance, his vanity, his indecision cost him his crown. As a man he was generous and extraordinarily brave. In the Russian campaign he used to challenge the Cossacks to single combat, and when he had beaten them he sent them away with some medal or souvenir of himself. He was a good husband, and lived at peace and amity with his wife, and was exceedingly fond of his children. His faults were numerous; he was by nature intensely jealous, especially of those who came between him and Napoleon, and he stooped to anything whereby he might injure his rivals, Lannes and Prince Eugène. His hot Southern blood led him into numerous quarrels.

Although extremely arrogant, at bottom he was a moral coward, and before the Emperor's reproaches he scarce dared to open his mouth. But his great fault, through which he gained and lost his crown, was his vanity. Vanity, working on ambition and an unstable character is the key to all his career. His blatant Jacobinism, his intrigue with Josephine, his overtures to the Director, his underhand treatment of his fellow Marshals, his discontent with his Grand Duchy, his subtle dealings in Spain, his system of government in Naples, his opposition to Napoleon's schemes, his dissimulation and desertion, his almost theatrical bravery, and his very death were due to nothing save extravagant vanity.

3

ANDRÉ MASSÉNA, MARSHAL, DUKE OF RIVOLI, PRINCE OF ESSLING

ANDRÉ MASSÉNA, 'the wiliest of Italians', was born at Nice on May 6, 1758, where his father and mother carried on a considerable business as tanners and soap manufacturers. On his father's death, when André was still but a small boy, his mother at once married again. Thereon André and two of his sisters were adopted by their uncle Augustine, who proposed to give his nephew a place in his business. But André's restless, fiery nature could not brook the idea of a perpetual monotonous existence in the tanyard and soap factory, so at the age of thirteen he ran away from home and shipped as a cabin boy; as such he made several voyages in the Mediterranean, and on one occasion crossed the Atlantic to Cayenne. But, in spite of his love of adventure, the life of a sailor soon began to pall, and on August 18, 1775, at the age of seventeen, he enlisted in the Royal Italian regiment in the French service. There he came under the influence of his uncle Marcel, who was sergeant-major of the regiment; thanks to his advice and care he made rapid strides in his profession, and received a fair education in the regimental school. In later years the Marshal used to say that no step cost him so much trouble or gave him such pleasure as his promotion to corporal; be that as it may, promotion came rapidly, and with less than two years' service he became sergeant on April 15, 1777. For fourteen years Masséna served in the Royal Italians, but at last he retired in disgust. Under the regulations a commission was unattainable for those who were not of noble birth, and the officers of the regiment had taken a strong dislike to the sergeant, whom the colonel constantly held up as an example, telling them, 'Your ignorance of drill is shameful; your inferiors, Masséna, for example, can manoeuvre the battalion far better than any of you.' On his retirement Masséna lived at Nice. To occupy his time and earn a living he joined his cousin Bavastro, and carried on a large smuggling business both by sea and land; he thus gained that intimate knowledge of the defiles and passes of the Maritime Alps which stood him in such good stead in the numerous campaigns of the revolutionary wars, while the necessity for keeping a watch on the preventive men and thus concealing his own movements developed to a great extent his activity, resource, and daring. So successful were his operations that he soon found himself in the position to demand the hand of Mademoiselle Lamarre, daughter of a surgeon, possessed of a considerable dowry. When the revolutionary wars broke out the Massénas were established at Antibes, where they did a fair trade in olive oil and dried fruits; but a respectable humdrum existence could not satisfy the restless nature of the ex-sergeant, and in 1791 he applied for a sub-lieutenancy in the gendarmerie, and it is to be presumed that, on the principle of setting a thief to catch a thief, he would have made an excellent policeman. It was at this moment that the invasion of France by the monarchs of Europe caused all patriotic Frenchmen to obey the summons to arms. Masséna gladly left his shop to serve as adjutant of the volunteers of the Var. His military knowledge, his erect and proud bearing, his keen incisive speech, and absolute self-confidence in all difficulties soon dominated his comrades, and it was as lieutenant-colonel commanding the second battalion that he marched to the frontier to meet the enemy. Lean and spare, below middle height, with a highly expressive Italian face, a good mouth, an aquiline nose, and black sparkling eyes, from the very first Masséna inspired confidence in all who met him; but it was not till he was seen in action that the greatness of his qualities could best be appreciated. As Napoleon said of him at St. Helena, 'Masséna was at his best and most brilliant in the middle of the fire and disorder of battle; the roar of the cannon used to clear his ideas, give him insight, penetration, and gaiety ... In the middle of the dead and dying, among the hail of bullets which swept down all around him, Masséna was always himself giving his orders and making his dispositions with the greatest calmness and good judgment. There you see the true nobility of blood.' In the saddle from morning till night, absolutely insensible to fatigue, ready at any moment to take the responsibility of his actions, he returned from the first campaign in the Riviera as major-general. During the siege of Toulon he commanded the 'Camp de milles fourches', which included the company of artillery commanded by Bonaparte, and distinguished himself by taking the forts of Lartigues and St. Catharine, thus earning his step as lieutenant-general while his future commander was still a major in the artillery. In the campaign of 1794 it was Masséna who conceived and carried out the turning movement which drove the Sardinians from the Col de Tenda, while Bonaparte's share in the action merely consisted of commanding the artillery. As the trusted counsellor of Dumerbion, Kellermann, and Schérer, for the next two years, the lieutenant-general was the inspirer of the successive commanders of the Army of Italy. He it was who, amid the snow and storms, planned and carried out the combinations which gained for Schérer the great winter of victory at Loano, and thus first taught the French the secret, which the English had grasped on the sea and Napoleon was to perfect on land, of breaking the enemy's centre and falling on one wing with overwhelming force. The campaign of 1796 for the time being altered the current of Masséna's military life. Before the young Corsican's eagle gaze even the impetuous Italian quailed, and from being the brain of the officer commanding the army he had to revert to the position of the right arm and faithful interpreter of orders. Two things, however, compensated Masséna for the change of rôle, for Bonaparte gave his subordinate fighting and glory with a lavish hand, and above all winked at, nay, rather encouraged, the amassing of booty; and wealth more even than glory was the desire of Masséna's soul.

At the very commencement of the campaign Masséna committed a fault which almost ruined his career. After defeating the enemy's advance guard near Cairo, hearing by chance that the Austrian officers had left an excellent dinner in a neighbouring inn, he and some of his staff left his division on the top of a high hill and set off to enjoy the good things prepared for the enemy. At daybreak the enemy attempted a surprise on the French position on the hill, and the troops, without their general and staff, were in great danger. Fortunately, Masséna had time to make his way through the Austrian skirmishers and resume his command. He was greeted by hoots and jeers, but with absolute imperturbability he reorganised his forces and checked the enemy. But one battalion was isolated on a spur, from which there seemed no way of escape save under a scorching flank fire. Masséna made his way alone to this detached post, scrambling up the steep slope on his hands and knees, and, when he at last reached the troops, remembering his old smuggling expedients, he showed them how to glissade down the steep part of the hill, and brought them all safely back without a single casualty. This escapade came to Bonaparte's ears, and it was only Masséna's great share in the victory of Montenotte which saved him from a court martial.

Bonaparte, at the commencement of the campaign, had ended a letter of instructions to his lieutenant with the words 'Watchfulness and bluff, that is the card,' and well Massena learned his lesson. Montenotte, the bridge of Lodi, the long struggle at Castiglione, the two fights at Rivoli and the marshes of Arcola proved beyond doubt that of all the young conquerors of Italy's lieutenants, none had the insight, activity, and endurance of Masséna. But empty flattery did not satisfy him, for as early as Lonato, greedy for renown, he considered his success had not been fully recognised. In bitter anger he wrote to Bonaparte: 'I complain of your reports of Lonato and Roveredo, in which you do not render me the justice that I merit. This forgetfulness tears my heart and throws discouragement on my soul. I will recall the fact under compulsion that the victory of Saintes Georges was due to my dispositions, to my activity, to my sangfroid, and to my prevision.' This frank republican letter greatly displeased Bonaparte, who, since Lodi, had cherished visions of a crown, and to realise this desire had begun to issue his praise and rewards irrespective of merit, and to appeal to the private soldier while visiting his displeasure on the officers. But Masséna's brilliant conduct at the second battle of Rivoli, for the moment, blotted out all rancour, for it was Masséna who had saved the day, who had rushed up to the commander of the shaken regiment, bitterly upbraiding him and his officers, showering blows on them with the flat of his sword, and had then galloped off and brought up two tried regiments of his own invincible division and driven back the assailants; from that moment Bonaparte confirmed him in the title of 'the spoilt child of victory'. In 1797 Bonaparte gave his lieutenant a more substantial reward when he chose him to carry the despatches to Paris which reported the preliminary treaty of Leoben; thus it was as the right-hand man of the most distinguished general in Europe that the Italian saw for the first time the capital of his adopted country.

In choosing Masséna to carry to Paris the tidings of peace, it was not only his prestige and renown which influenced Bonaparte. For Paris was in a state of half suppressed excitement, and signs were only too evident that the Directory was unstable; accordingly the wily Corsican, while despatching secret agents to advance his cause, was careful to send as the bearer of the good news a man who was well known to care for no political rewards, and who would be sure to turn a deaf ear to the insidious schemes of those who were plotting to restore the monarchy, or to set up a dictatorship, and were searching for a sovereign or a Caesar as their political views suggested. It was for these reasons and because he was tired of Masséna's greed and avarice that Bonaparte refused to admit him among those chosen to accompany him to Egypt. Massena saw clearly all the secret intrigue of the capital, and found little pleasure in his newly gained dignity of a seat among the Ancients, for he was extremely afraid of a royalist restoration, in which case he feared 'our honourable wounds will become the titles for our proscription'.

Tired of Paris, in 1798, he was glad to accept the command of the French corps occupying Rome when its former commander, Berthier, was called away to join the Egyptian expedition. On his arrival at Rome, to take over his new command, he found himself face to face with a mutiny. The troops were in rags and badly fed, their pay was months in arrears, and meanwhile the civil servants of the Directory were amassing fortunes at the expense of the Pope, the Cardinals, and the Princes of Rome. Discontent was so widespread that the new general at once ordered all troops, save some three thousand, to leave the capital. Unfortunately Massesna's record was not such as to inspire confidence in the purity of his intentions. Instead of obeying, the officers and men held a mass meeting to draft their remonstrance to the Directory. In this document they accused, first of all, the agents who had disgraced the name of France, and ended by saying, 'The final cause of all the discontent is the arrival of General Masséna. The soldiers have not forgotten the extortions and robberies he has committed wherever he has been invested with the command. The Venetian territory, and above all Padua, is a district teeming with proofs of his immorality.' In the face of such public feeling Masséna found nothing for it but to demand a successor and throw up his command.

But with Bonaparte in Egypt and a ring of enemies threatening France from all sides, the Directors, whose hands were as soiled as Masséna's, could ill spare the 'spoilt child of victory'. Accordingly, early in 1799 the general found himself invested with the important command of the Army of Switzerland. This was a task worthy of his genius and he eagerly accepted the post, but refused to abide by the stipulations the Directors desired to enforce on him, as, according to their plan, the Army of Switzerland was to form part of the Army of the Rhine commanded by Joubert. Masséna had obeyed Bonaparte, but he had no intention of playing second fiddle to any other commander, and, after some stormy interviews and letters, he at last had his way. As the year advanced it became more and more evident that on the Army of Switzerland would fall the full brunt of the attack of the coalition, for Joubert was defeated by the Archduke Charles at Stockach and thrown back on the Rhine, Schérer was defeated in Italy at Magnano, and by June the Russians and Austrians had begun to close in on Switzerland. It was clear that, if the French army were driven out of Switzerland, both the Rhine and the Maritime Alps would be turned, and the enemy would be in a strong position from which to invade France. On Masséna, therefore, hung all the hopes of the Directory. Fortunately for France, the general was admirably versed in mountain warfare. Well aware of the difficulty of keeping up communication between the different parts of his line of defence, Masséna skilfully withdrew his outposts, as the enemy pressed on, with the intention of concentrating his troops round Zurich, thereby covering all the possible lines of advance. But early in the summer his difficulties were further increased by the rising of the Swiss peasantry; luckily, however, the Archduke Charles advanced most cautiously, while the Aulic Council at Vienna, unable to grasp the vital point of the problem, stupidly sent its reserve army to Italy to reinforce the Russians under Suvaroff. By June 5th the Archduke had driven in all the outlying French columns, and was in a position to attack the lines of Zurich with his entire force. Thanks, however, to Masséna's courage and presence of mind, the attack was driven off, but so overwhelming were the numbers of the enemy that during the night the French army evacuated Zurich, though only to fall back on a strong position on Mount Albis, a rocky ridge at the north end of the lake, covered on one flank by the lake and on the other by the river Aar. The two armies for the time being lay opposite to each other, too exhausted after the struggle to recommence operations. The Archduke Charles awaited the arrival from Italy of Suvaroff, who was to debouch on the French right by the St. Gothard Pass. But fortune, or rather the Aulic Council at Vienna, once again intervened and saved France. The Archduke Charles was ordered to leave fifty-five thousand Russians under Korsakoff before Zurich and to march northwards and across the Rhine. Protests were useless; the Court of Vienna merely ordered the Archduke to 'perform the immediate execution of its will without further objections'. But even yet disaster threatened the French, for Suvaroff was commencing his advance by the St. Gothard. But Masséna at once grasped the opportunity fortune had placed in his power by opposing him to a commander like Korsakoff, who was so impressed by his own pride that he considered a Russian company equal to an Austrian battalion. On September 26th, by a masterly series of manoeuvres, the main French force surprised Korsakoff and drove him in rout out of Zurich. Suvaroff arrived just in time to find Masséna in victorious array thrust in between himself and his countrymen, and was forced to save himself by a hurried retreat through the most difficult passes of the Alps.

The campaign of Zurich will always be studied as a masterpiece in defensive warfare. The skilful use the French general made of the mountain passes, the methods he employed to check the Archduke's advance on Zurich, the care with which he kept up communications between his different columns, the skilful choice of the positions of Zurich and Mount Albis, his return to the initiative on every opportunity, and his masterly interposition between Korsakoff and Suvaroff, alone entitle him to a high place among the great commanders of history, and Masséna was rightly thanked by the legislature and hailed as the saviour of the country.

Six weeks after the victory of Zurich came the 18th Brumaire, and Napoleon's accession to the consulate. Masséna, a staunch republican, was conscious of the defects of the Directory, but could not give his hearty consent to the coup d'état, for he feared for the liberty of his country. Still, he said, if France desired to entrust her independence and glory to one man she could choose none better than Bonaparte. The latter, on his side, was anxious to retain Masséna's affections, and at once offered him the command of the Army of Italy. But the conqueror of Zurich foresaw that everything was to be sacrificed to the glory of the First Consul, and it was only after great persuasion, profuse promises, and appeals to his patriotism that he undertook the command, with the stipulation that 'I will not take command of an army condemned to rest on the defensive. My former services and successes do not permit me to change the rôle that I have heretofore played in the wars of the Republic.' The First Consul replied by giving Masséna carte blanche to requisition whatever he wanted, and promised him that the Army of Italy should be his first care. But when Masséna arrived at Genoa he discovered, as he had suspected, that Bonaparte's promises were only made to be broken; for he found the troops entrusted to his care the mere shadow of an army, the hospitals full, bands of soldiers, even whole battalions, quitting their posts and trying to escape into France, and the officers and generals absolutely unable to contend with the mass of misery and want. In spite of his able lieutenants, Soult and Suchet, he could make no head against the Austrians in the field, and after some gallant engagements was driven back into Genoa, where, for two months, he held out against famine and the assaults of the enemy. While the wretched inhabitants starved, the troops were fed on 'a miserable ration of a quarter of a pound of horse-flesh and a quarter of a pound of what was called bread - a horrible compound of damaged flour, sawdust, starch, hair-powder, oatmeal, linseed, rancid nuts, and other nasty substances, to which a little solidity was given by the admixture of a small portion of cocoa. Each loaf, moreover, was held together by little bits of wood, without which it would have fallen to powder.' A revolt, threatened by the inhabitants, was checked by Masséna's order that an assemblage of over five persons should be fired on, and the approaches to the principal streets were commanded by guns. Still he refused to surrender, as every day he expected to heat the cannon of the First Consul's army thundering on the Austrian rear. One day the hopes of all were aroused by a distant roar in the mountains, only to be dashed by finding it to be thunder. It was simply the ascendancy of Masséna's personality which prolonged the agony and upheld his authority, and in bitter earnestness the soldiers used to say, 'He will make us eat his boots before he will surrender.'

At last the accumulated horrors shook even his firm spirit, and on June 4th a capitulation was agreed on. The terms were most favourable to the French; but, as Lord Keith, the English admiral, said, 'General, your defence has been so heroic that we can refuse you nothing.' However, the sufferings of Genoa were not in vain, for Masséna had played his part and held the main Austrian force in check for ten days longer than had been demanded of him; thus the First Consul had time to fall on the enemies' line of communication, and it may be truly said that without the siege of Genoa there could have been no Marengo. Masséna had once again demonstrated the importance of the individual in war; as Bonaparte wrote to him during the siege, 'In such a situation as you are, a man like you is worth twenty thousand men.' In spite of this, at St. Helena, the Emperor, ever jealous of his own glory, affected to despise Masséna's generalship and endurance at Genoa, and blamed him for not taking the offensive in the field, forgetting the state of his army and the paucity of his troops. But at the moment he showed his appreciation of his services by giving him the command of the army when he himself retired to Paris after the victory of Marengo. Unfortunately Masséna's avarice and greed were unable to withstand the temptations of the position, and the First Consul had very soon to recall him from Italy and mark his displeasure by placing him on half-pay.

For two years the disgraced general brooded over his wrongs in retirement, and showed his attitude of mind by voting against the Consulate for life and the establishment of the Empire. The gift of a Marshal's baton did little to reconcile him to the Emperor, for, as he scoffingly replied to Thiebault's congratulations, 'Oh, there are fourteen of us.' So uncertain was the Emperor of his Marshal's disposition that, on the outbreak of the war with Austria, Masséna alone of all the greater Marshals held no command. But with the prospect of heavy fighting in Italy the Emperor could not afford to entrust the Italian divisions to a blunderer, and he once again posted Masséna to his old command. The Austrians had occupied the strong position of Caldiero, near the marshes of Arcola, and the French in vain attempted to force them from it, but the success of the Emperor on the Danube at last compelled the Archduke John to fall back on Austria. The Marshal at once commenced a spirited pursuit, and ultimately joined hands with the Grand Army, south of the Danube.

After the treaty of Pressburg Napoleon despatched; Masséna to conquer Naples, which he had given as a kingdom to his brother Joseph. With fifty thousand men the Marshal swept through Italy. In vain the gallant Queen Caroline armed the lazzaroni; Capua opened its gates, Gaeta fell after twelve days' bombardment, and Joseph, entered Naples in triumph. Calabria alone offered a stern resistance, and this resistance the French brought upon themselves by their cruelty to the peasantry, whom they treated as brigands. Unfortunately his success in Naples was once again tarnished by his greed, for the Marshal by selling licences to merchants and conniving at their escape from the custom-house dues, amassed, within a few months of his entering Naples, a sum of three million francs. Napoleon heard of this from his spies, and, writing, to him, demanded a loan of a million francs. The Duke of Rivoli replied that he was the poorest of the Marshals, and had a numerous family to maintain and was heavily in debt, so he regretted that he could send him nothing. Unfortunately, the Emperor knew where he banked in Leghorn, and as he refused to disgorge a third of his illicit profits, the Emperor sent the inspector of the French Treasury and a police commissary to the bank, and demanded that the three millions, which lay at his account there, should be handed over. The seizure was made in legal form; the banker, who lost nothing, was bound to comply with it. Masséna, on hearing of this misfortune, was so furious that he fell ill, but he did not dare to remonstrate, knowing that he was in the wrong, but he never forgave the Emperor: his titles and a pension never consoled him for what he lost at Leghorn, and, in spite of his cautious habits, he was sometimes heard to say, 'I was fighting in his service and he was cruel enough to take away my little savings which I had invested at Leghorn.'

From what he called a military promenade in Italy the Marshal was summoned early in 1807 to the Grand Army in Poland, and was present in command of one of the army corps at Pultusk, Ostralenka, and Friedland. In 1808 he received his title of Duke of Rivoli and a pension of three hundred thousand francs per annum, but in spite of this he absented himself from the court. When Joseph was given the crown of Spain he requested his brother to send Masséna to aid him in his new sphere, but the Emperor, full of mistrust, refused, while the Marshal himself had no great desire to serve in Spain. When it was clear that Austria was going to seize the occasion of the Spanish War once again to fight France, Napoleon hastened to send the veteran Duke of Rivoli to the army on the Danube. At Abensberg and Eckmühl, for the first time since 1797, he fought under the eye of Napoleon himself. 'Activité, activité, vitesse,' wrote the Emperor, and well his lieutenant carried out his orders. Following up the Five Days' Fighting, Masséna led the advance guard to Vienna, and commanded the left wing at Aspern-Essling. Standing in the churchyard at Aspern, with the boughs swept down by grapeshot crashing round him, he was in his element; never had his tenacity, his resource, and skill been seen to such advantage. But in spite of his skill and the courage of his troops, at the end of the first day's fighting his shattered forces were driven out of the heap of smoking ruins which marked all that remained of Aspern. On the morning of the second day he had regained half of the village when news came that the bridge was broken, and that he was to hold off the Austrians while communication with the Isle of Lobau was being established. The enemy, invigorated by the news of the success of their plan for breaking the bridges, strained every nerve to annihilate the French force on the left bank of the river, but Masséna, Lannes, and Napoleon worked marvels with their exhausted troops. The Duke of Rivoli seemed ubiquitous: at one moment on horseback and at another on foot with drawn sword, wherever the enemy pressed he was there animating his troops, directing their fire, hurrying up supports; thus, thanks to his exertions, the Austrians were held off, the cavalry and the artillery safely crossed the bridge, and the veteran Marshal at midnight brought the last of the rearguard safely to the Isle of Lobau, where, exhausted by fatigue, the troops fell asleep in their ranks.

The death of Lannes threw Napoleon back on the Duke of Rivoli, who for the time became his confidant and right-hand man. It was Masséna who commanded at Lobau and made all the arrangements for the crossing before Wagram. The Emperor and his lieutenant were indefatigable in the care with which they made their preparations. On one occasion, wishing to inspect the Austrian position, dressed in sergeants' greatcoats, attended by a single aide-de-camp in the kit of a private, they went alone up the north bank of the island and took their coats off as if they wanted to bathe. The Austrian sentinels, seeing, as they thought, two French soldiers enjoying a wash, took no notice of them, and thus the Emperor and the Marshal were able to determine the exact spot for launching the bridges. On another occasion, while they were riding round the island, the Marshal's horse put its foot into a hole and fell, and injured the rider's leg so that he could not mount again. This unfortunate accident happened a few days before the battle of Wagram, so the Duke of Rivoli went into battle lying in a light calèche, drawn by four white horses, with his doctor beside him changing the compresses on his injured leg every two hours. During the battle Masséna's corps formed the left of the line. While Davout was carrying out his great turning movement, it was the Duke of Rivoli who had to endure the full fury of the Austrians' attack. In the pursuit after the battle he pressed the enemy with his wonted activity. At the last encounter at Znaim he had a narrow escape, for hardly had he got out of his carriage when a cannon-ball struck it, and a moment later another shot killed one of the horses.

After the treaty of Vienna the Marshal, newly created Prince of Essling, retired to rest at his country house at Rueil, but the Emperor could not spare him long. In April, 1810, within eight months, he was once again hurried off on active service, this time to Spain, where Soult had been driven out of Portugal by Sir Arthur Wellesley, and Jourdan and Joseph defeated at Talavera. The Emperor promised the Prince of Essling ninety thousand troops for the invasion of Portugal, and placed under his command Junot and Ney. The Marshal did his best to refuse the post; he knew the difficult character of Ney and the jealousy of Junot, and he pointed out that it would be better to reorganise the army of Portugal under generals appointed by himself. Berthier replied that 'the orders of the Emperor were positive, and left no point in dispute. When the Emperor delegated his authority obedience became a duty; however great might be the pride of the Dukes of Elchingen and Abrantès, they had enough justice to understand that their swords were not in the same line as the sword of the conqueror of Zurich.' Still, the Prince foresaw the future, and appealed to the Emperor himself, but the Emperor was obdurate. 'You are out of humour today, my dear Masséna. You see everything black, yourself and your surroundings. To listen to you one would think you were half dead. Your age? A good reason! How much older are you now than at Essling? Your health? Does not imagination play a great part in your weakness? Are you worse than at Wagram? It is rheumatism that is troubling you. The climate of Portugal is as warm and healthy as Italy, and will put you on your legs ... Set out then with confidence. Be prudent and firm, and the obstacles you fear will fade away; you have surmounted many worse.' Unfortunately for the Marshal, his forebodings were truer than the Emperor's optimism. On arriving at Salaman his troubles began. Delays were inevitable before he could bring into order his unruly team. Junot and Ney were openly contemptuous, Regnier hung back, and was three weeks late in his arrangements. Meanwhile, all that Masséna saw of the enemy, whom the Emperor had in past years stigmatised as the 'slow and clumsy English', confirmed him in his opinion that the campaign was going to prove the most arduous he had ever undertaken.

In spite of everything, operations opened brilliantly for the French. Ciudad Rodrigo and Almeida fell without the English commander making any apparent effort to relieve them. On September 16th the invasion of Portugal commenced. But losses, disease, and garrison duty had already reduced his troops to some seventy thousand men, and the French found 'an enemy behind eve stone'; while, as the Prince of Essling wrote, 'We are marching across a desert; women, children, and old men have all fled; in fact, no guide is to be found anywhere.' Still the English fell back before him, and he was under the impression that they were going to evacuate

Portugal without a blow, although he grasped the fact that it was the immense superiority of the French cavalry which had prevented the 'sepoy general' making any effort to relieve the fortresses. But on September 26th Masséna found that the English had stayed their retreat, and were waiting to fight him on the rocky ridge of Busaco. Unfortunately for his reputation, he made no reconnaissance of the position, and, trusting entirely to the reports of Ney, Regnier, and Junot, who asserted the position was much less formidable than it looked, sustained a heavy reverse. After the battle his lieutenants urged him to abandon the invasion of Portugal; but the veteran refused such timorous advice, and, rousing himself, soon showed the energy which had made his name so famous at Zurich and Rivoli. Turning the position, the French swept down on Portugal, while the English hurriedly fell back before them. What caused Masséna most anxiety was the ominous desertion of the countryside. He was well aware of the bitter hatred of the Portuguese, and knew that his soldiers tortured and hung the wretched inhabitants to force them to reveal hidden stores of provisions, but it was not until October 10th, when the French had arrived within a few miles of the lines of Torres Vedras, that he learned of the vast entrenched camp which the English commander had so secretly prepared for his army and the inhabitants of Portugal. Masséna was furious, and covered with accusations the Portuguese officers on his staff. 'Que diable,' he cried, 'Wellington n'a pas construit des montagnes.' But there had been no treachery, only so well had the secret been kept that hardly even an officer in the English army knew of the existence of the work, and as Wellington wrote to the minister at Lisbon on October 6th, 'I believe that you and the Government do not know where the lines are.' For six weeks the indomitable Marshal lay in front of the position, hoping to tempt the English to attack his army, now reduced to sixty thousand men. But Wellington, who had planned this victorious reply to the axiom that war ought to feed war, grimly sat behind his lines, while the English army, well fed from the sea, watched the French writhe in the toils of hunger. Masséna was now roused, and as his opponent wrote, 'It is certainly astonishing that the enemy have been able to remain in this country so long ... It is an extraordinary instance of what a French army can do.' At last even Masséna had to confess himself beaten and fall back on Santarem. The winter passed in a fruitless endeavour on the part of the Emperor and the Marshal to force Soult, d'Erlon, and Regnier to co-operate for an advance on Lisbon by the left bank of the Tagus. Meanwhile, in spite of every effort, the French army dwindled owing to disease, desertion, and unending fatigue. So dangerous was the country that a despatch could not be sent along the lines of communication without an escort of three hundred men. The whole countryside had been so swept bare of provisions that a Portuguese spy wrote to Wellington saying, 'Heaven forgive me if I wrong them in believing they have eaten my cat.'

By March, 1811, it became clear that the French could no longer maintain themselves at Santarem; but so skilful were Masséna's dispositions that it was three days before Wellington realised that at last the enemy had commenced their retreat. Never had the genius of the Marshal stood higher than in this difficult retirement from Portugal. With his army decimated by hunger and disease, with the victorious enemy always hanging on his heels, with his subordinates in open revolt, and a Marshal of France refusing to obey orders in the face of the enemy, he lost not a single gun, baggage-wagon or invalid. Still, the morale of his army was greatly shaken; as he himself wrote, 'It is sufficient for the enemy to show the heads of a few columns in order to intimidate the officers and make them loudly declare that the whole of Wellington's army is in sight.' When the Marshal at last placed his wearied troops behind the fortress of Ciudad Rodrigo and Almeida, he found his difficulties by no means at an end. The Emperor, who 'judged men only by results', wrote him a letter full of thinly veiled criticism of his operations, while he found that the country round the fortresses was now included in the command of the northern army under Bessières. Accordingly he had to apply to that Marshal for leave to revictual and equip his troops. Meanwhile Wellington proceeded to besiege Almeida.

By the end of April, after a vigorous correspondence with Bessiéres, Masséna had at last reorganised his army and was once again ready to take the field against the English. Reinforced by fifteen hundred cavalry of the Guard under Bessières, at Fuentes d'Onoro he surprised the English forces covering the siege of

Almeida; after a careful reconnaissance at dawn on May 5th he attacked and defeated the English right, and had it not been for the action of Bessières, who spoiled his combination by refusing to allow the Guard to charge save by his orders, the English would have been totally defeated. Masséna wished at all hazards to continue the fight on the morrow, but his principal officers were strongly opposed to it. Overborne by their counsels, after lying in front of the position for three days he withdrew to Ciudad Rodrigo. It was through no fault of his that he was beaten at Fuentes d'Onoro; Wellington himself confessed how closely he had been pressed when he wrote: 'Lord Liverpool was quite right not to move thanks for the battle of Fuentes, though it was the most difficult I was ever concerned in and against the greatest odds. We had nearly three to one against us engaged above four to one of cavalry: and moreover our cavalry had not a gallop in them, while some of that of the enemy were quite fresh and in excellent order. If Bony had been there we should have been beaten.'

Soon after the battle Masséna was superseded by Marmont, and retired to Paris. The meeting with the Emperor was stormy. 'Well, Prince of Essling,' said Napoleon, 'are you no longer Masséna?' Explanations followed, and the Emperor at last promised that once again he should have an opportunity of regaining his glory in Spain. But Fate willed otherwise. After Salamanca, when Marmont was recalled, Masséna set out again for Spain, only to fall ill at Bayonne and to return home and try to restore his shattered health at Nice. In 1813 and 1814 he commanded the eighth military district, composed of the Rhone Valley, but he was getting too old to take strenuous measures and was glad to make submission to the Bourbons.

Very cruelly the new Government placed an affront on the Marshal by refusing to create him a peer of France under the plea that he was an Italian and a foreigner, but in spite of this the Prince remained faithful during the first part of the Hundred Days, and only went over to Napoleon when he found that the capital an army had recognised the Emperor. At Paris the Emperor greeted him with 'Well, Masséna, did you wish to serve as lieutenant to the Duke of Angoulême and fight me ... would you have hurled me back into the sea if I had given you time to assemble your forces?' The old warrior replied: 'Yes, Sire, inasmuch as I believed that you were not recalled by the majority of Frenchmen.' Ill-health prevented the Marshal from actively serving the Emperor. But during the interval between Napoleon's abdication and the second restoration it fell to the Marshal's lot to keep order in Paris as Governor and Commander of the National Guard. The new Government, to punish him for the aid he had given to the Emperor, nominated him one of the judges of Marshal Ney. This was the last occasion the Prince of Essling appeared in public. Suspected as a traitor by the authorities, weighed down by the horror of Ney's death and the assassination of his old friend Brune, and racked by disease, after a lingering painful illness the conqueror of Zurich breathed his last at the age of fifty-nine on April 4, 1817. Even then the ultra royalists could not conceal their hatred of him. The War Minister Clarke Duke of Feltre, his old comrade, now turned furious legitimist, had hitherto withheld the Marshal's new baton, and it was only the threat of Massena's son-in-law, Reille, to place on the coffin the baton the Marshal had received from the Emperor which at last forced the Government to send the emblem. Great soldier as he was, Masséna's escutcheon was stained by many a blot. His avarice was disgusting beyond words, and with avarice went a tendency to underhand dealing, harshness, and malice. During the Wagram campaign the Marshal's coachman and footman drove him day by day in a carriage through all the heat of the fighting. The Emperor complimented these brave men and said that of all the hundred and thirty thousand men engaged they were the bravest. Masséna, after this, felt bound to give them some reward, and said to one of his staff that he was going to give them each four hundred francs. The staff officer replied that a pension of four hundred francs would save them from want in their old age. The Marshal, in a fury, turned on his aide-de-camp, exclaiming, 'Wretch, do you want to ruin me? What, an annuity of four hundred francs! No, no, no, four hundred francs once and for all'; adding to his staff, 'I would sooner see you all shot and get a bullet through my arm than bind myself to give an annuity of four hundred francs to any one.' The Marshal never forgave the aide-de-camp who had thus urged him to spend his money. His harshness was also well known, and the excesses of the French troops in Switzerland, Naples, and Portugal were greatly owing to his callousness; in the campaign in Portugal he actually allowed detachments of soldiers to set out with the express intention of capturing all girls between twelve and twenty for the use of his men. But while oblivious to the sufferings of others, as a father he was affectionate and indulgent. As he said after Wagram of his son Prosper, 'That young scamp has given me more trouble than a whole army corps;' so careful was he of his safety that he refused during the second day of the battle to allow him to take his turn among the other aides-de-camp; but the young Masséna was too spirited to endure this, and Napoleon, hearing of the occurrence, severely reprimanded the Marshal. Staunch republican by profession, blustering and outspoken at times, he was at bottom a true Italian, and knew well how to use the delicate art of flattery. Writing in 1805 to the Minister of War, he thus ends a despatch: 'I made my first campaign with His Majesty, and it was under his orders that I learned what I know of the trade of arms. We were together in the Army of Italy.' Again, when at Fontainebleau he had the misfortune to lose an eye when out pheasant shooting, he attacked Berthier as the culprit, although he knew full well that the Emperor was the only person who had fired a shot.

But in spite of all this meanness and his many defects, he must always be remembered as one of the great soldiers of France, a name at all times to conjure with. Both Napoleon and Wellington have paid their tribute to his talents. At St. Helena the fallen Emperor said that of all his generals the Prince of Essling 'was the first', and the Duke, speaking to Lord Ros of the French commanders, said, 'Masséna gave me more trouble than any of them, because when I expected to find him weak, he generally contrived somehow that I should find him strong.' The Marshal was a born soldier. War was with him an inspiration; being all but illiterate, he never studied it theoretically, but, as one of his detractors admits, 'He was a born general: his courage and tenacity did the rest. In the best days of his military career he saw accurately, decided promptly, and never let himself be cast down by reverses.' It was owing to this obstinacy combined with clear vision that his great successes were gained, and the dogged determination he showed at Zurich, Loano, Rivoli and

Genoa was no whit impaired by success or by old age, as he proved at Essling, Wagram, and before the line of Torres Vedras. Like his great commander, none knew better than the Prince of Essling that fortune must be wooed, and, as Napoleon wrote to him, 'It is not to you, my dear general, that I need to recommend the employment of audacity.' In spite of his ill success in his last campaign, to the end the Prince of Essling worthily upheld his title of 'the spoilt child of victory'.

4

JEAN BAPTISTE JULES BERNADOTTE, MARSHAL, PRINCE OF PONTE CORVO, KING OF SWEDEN

GASCONY has ever been the mother of ambitious men, and many a ruler has she supplied to France. But in 1789 few Gascons even would have believed that ere twenty years had passed one Gascon would be sitting on the Bourbon throne of Naples and a second would be Crown Prince of Sweden, the adopted son of the House of Vasa.

Jean Baptiste Bernadotte, the son of a petty lawyer, was born at Pau on January 26, 1763. At the age of seventeen he enlisted in the Royal Marine regiment and passed the next nine years of his life in garrison towns in Corsica, Dauphine and Provence. His first notable exploit occurred in 1788, when, as sergeant, he commanded a section of the Marines whose duty it was to maintain order at Grenoble during the troubles which preceded the outbreak of the Revolution. The story goes that Bernadotte was responsible for the first shedding of blood. One day, when the mob was threatening to get out of hand, a woman rushed out of the crowd and caught the sergeant a cuff on the face, whereon the fiery Gascon ordered his men to open fire. In a moment the answer came in a shower of bricks. Blood had been shed, and from that moment the people of France declared war to the death on the old regime. Impetuous, generous, warm-hearted and ambitious, for the next three years Jean Baptiste pursued a policy which is typical of his whole career. Ready when at white heat of passion to take the most extreme measures, even to fire on the crowd, in calmer moments full of enthusiasm for the Rights of Man and the well-being of his fellows; spending long hours haranguing his comrades on the iniquity of kingship and the necessity of taking up arms against all of noble birth, yet standing firm by his colonel, because in former days he had done him a kindness, and saving his officers from the mutineers who were threatening to hang them; watching every opportunity to push his own fortunes, Bernadotte pursued his way towards success. Promotion came rapidly: colonel in 1792, the next year general of brigade, and a few months later general of division, he owed his advancement to the way in which he handled his men. Naturally great neither as tactician or as strategist, he could carry out the orders of others and above all impart his fiery nature to his troops; his success on the battlefield was due to his personal magnetism, whereby he inspired others with his own self-confidence. But with all this self-confidence there was blended in his character a curious strain of hesitation. Again and again during his career he let 'I dare not' wait upon 'I would'. Gascon to the backbone, full of craft and wile, with an eye ever on the future, at times he allowed his restless imagination to conjure up dangers instead of forcing it to show him the means to gain his end. When offered the post of general of brigade, and again when appointed general of division, he refused the step because he had divined that Jacobin would persecute Girondist, that ultra-Jacobin would overthrow Jacobin, and that a reaction would sweep away the Revolutionists, and he feared that the generals of the army might share the fate of those who appointed them. After his magnificent attack at Fleurus, he was at last compelled to accept promotion by Kléber, who rode up to him and cried out, 'You must accept the grade of general of brigade here on the field of battle, where you have so truly earned it. If you refuse you are no friend of mine.' Thereon Bernadotte accepted the post, considering that he could, if necessary, prove that he had not received it as a political favour. The years 1794-6 saw Bernadotte on continuous active service with the Army of the Sambre and Meuse, now in the Rhine valley, now in the valley of the Danube. Every engagement from Fleurus to Altenkirchen added more and more to his reputation with the authorities and to his hold on the affection of his men. 'He is the God of armies,' cried his soldiers, as they followed him into the fire-swept zone. His courage, personality and physical beauty captivated all who approached him. Tall, erect, with masses of coal black hair, the great hooked nose of a falcon, and dark flashing eyes indicating Moorish blood in his veins, he could crush the soul out of an incipient revolt with a torrent of cutting words, and in a moment turn the mutineers into the most loyal and devoted of soldiers. During the long revolutionary wars he always kept before him the necessity of preparing for peace, and found time to educate himself in history and political science. It was with the reputation of being one of the best divisional officers of the Army of the Sambre and Meuse, and a political power of no small importance, that, at the end of 1796, Bernadotte was transferred with his division to the Army of Italy, commanded by Bonaparte. From their, very first meeting friction arose. They were like Caesar and Pompey, 'the one would have no superior, the other would endure no equal.' Bonaparte already foresaw the day when France should lie at his feet; he instinctively divined in Bernadotte a possible rival. Bernadotte, accustomed to the adulation of all with whom he came in contact, felt the loss of it in his new command, where soldiers and officers alike could think and speak of nobody save the conqueror of Italy. Yet neither could afford to break with the other, neither could as yet foretell what the future would bring forth, so amid an occasional flourish of compliments, a secret and vindictive war was waged between the two. As commander-in-chief, Bonaparte, for the time being, held the whip hand and could show his dislike by severe reprimands. 'Wherever your division goes, there is nothing but complaints of its want of discipline.' Bernadotte, on his side, anxious to win renown, would appeal to the 'esprit' of his soldiers of the Sambre and Meuse, and would spoil Bonaparte's careful combinations by attempting a frontal attack before the turning movement was effected by the Italian divisions. By the end of the campaign it was clear to everybody that there was no love lost between the two. After Leoben Bonaparte was for the moment the supreme figure in France. As plenipotentiary at Leoben and commander-in-chief of 'the Army of England' he could impose his will on the Directory. Bernadotte, in disgust at seeing the success of his rival, for some time seriously considered withdrawing from public life, or at any rate from France, where his reputation was thus overshadowed. Among various posts, the Directory offered him the command of the Army of Italy, but he refused them all, till at last he consented to accept that of ambassador at Vienna. Vienna was for the time being the pole round which the whole of European politics revolved, and accordingly there was great possibility there of achieving diplomatic renown. But scarcely had the new ambassador arrived at his destination when he heard of Bonaparte's projected expedition to Egypt. He at once determined to return to France. He felt that his return ought to be marked by something which might appeal to the populace. Accordingly he adopted a device at once simple and effective.

Jacobin at heart when his interest did not clash with his principles, he had from his arrival at Vienna determined to show the princes and dignitaries of an effete civilisation that Frenchmen were proud of their Revolution and believed in nothing but the equality of all men; he refused to conform to court regulations and turned his house into a club for the German revolutionists. His attitude was of course resented, and there was considerable feeling in Vienna against the French Embassy. It only required, therefore, a little more bravado and a display of the tricolour on the balcony of the Embassy to induce the mob to attack the house. Immediately this occurred Bernadotte lodged a complaint, threw up his appointment, and withdrew to France as a protest against this 'scoundrelly' attack on the honour of his country and the doctrine of the equality of men.

On his arrival at Paris he found the Directory shaken to its foundation. Sièyes, the inveterate constitution-monger, who saw the necessity of 'a man with a head and a sword', greeted him joyfully; the banishment of Pichegru, the death of Hoche, the disgrace of Moreau, and the absence of Bonaparte had left Bernadotte for the moment the most important of the political soldiers of the Revolution. Acting on Sièyes's advice, Bernadotte refused all posts offered him either in the army or in the Government and awaited developments. Meanwhile he became very intimate with Joseph Bonaparte, who introduced him to his sister-in-law, Désiré Clary. The Clarys were merchants of Marseilles, and Désiré had for some time been engaged to Napoleon Bonaparte, who had jilted her on meeting Josephine. Desire, very bitter at this treatment, accepted Bernadotte, as she said in later life, 'because I was told that he was a man who could hold his own against Napoleon.' This marriage was a masterstroke of policy; it at once gave Bernadotte the support of the Bonaparte family, for Bonaparte in his way was still fond of

Désiré, and at the same time it gave Bernadotte a partner who at bottom hated Napoleon with a rancour equal to his own. After the disasters in Italy and on the Danube, on July 2, 1799, Bernadotte, thinking the time was come, accepted the post of Minister of War. He speedily put in the field a new army of one hundred thousand men, and by his admirable measures for the instruction of conscripts and for the collection of war material he was in no small way responsible, not only for Masséna's victory of Zurich, but, as Napoleon himself confessed, for the triumph of Marengo.

His term of office, however, was short, for his colleagues intrigued against him. Sièyes desired a man who would overthrow the Directory and establish a dictatorship: Barras was coquetting with the Bourbons. Bernadotte himself talked loudly of the safety of the Republic, but had not the courage to jump with Sièyes or to crouch with Barras. Oppressed by doubt, his imagination paralysed his action, and his personality, which only blazed when in movement, became dull. Still trusting his reputation and thinking that he was indispensable to the Directory, he tendered his resignation, hoping, thus to check the intrigues of Sièyes and Barras. To his surprise it was at once accepted, and he found himself a mere nonentity.

On September 14th Bernadotte resigned, on October 9th Napoleon landed at Fréjus. During the Revolution of the 18th Brumaire Bernadotte remained in the background. Desiring the safety of France by the reorganisation of the Directory, hating the idea of a dictatorship, jealous of the success of his rival, he refused to join the stream of generals which hurried to the feet of the conqueror of Italy and Egypt. Bonaparte, who could read his soul like a book, attempted to draw his rival into his net, but, as ever, the Gascon could not make up his mind. At first he was inclined to join in the conspiracy, but at last he refused, and told Bonaparte that, if the Directory commanded him, he would take up arms against those who plotted against the Republic. Still, even on the eventful day he hesitated, and appeared in the morning among the other conspirators at Bonaparte's house, but not in uniform, thinking thus to serve both parties.

During the years which succeeded the establishment of the Consulate, Bernadotte waged an unending subterranean war against

Napoleon. Scarcely a year passed in which his name was not connected with some conspiracy to overthrow the First Consul. Of these Napoleon was well advised, but Bernadotte was too cunning to allow himself to be compromised absolutely. However much he might sympathise with the conspirators and lend them what aid he could, he always refused to sign his name to any document. Accordingly, although on one occasion a bundle of seditious proclamations was found in the boot of his aide-de-camp's carriage, the charge could not be brought home. On another occasion, when it was proved that he had advanced twelve thousand francs to the conspirator Cerrachi, he could prove that it was the price he had paid the artist for a bust. In spite of the fact that no definite proof could be brought against him, the First Consul could easily, if he chose, have produced fraudulent witnesses or have had . him disposed of by a court martial, as he got rid of the Duc d'Enghien. Napoleon waited his time. He was afraid of a Jacobin out break if he made a direct attack against him. Further, Bernadotte had a zealous friend and ally in Joseph Bonaparte. So when pressed to take stern measures against his enemy, Napoleon always refused to do so, partly from policy, partly because of his former love for Désiré, and partly from the horror of a scandal in his family, which might weaken his position when he seized the imperial throne. Accordingly he attempted in every way to conciliate his rebellious subject, and at the same time to place him in positions where he could do no political harm. Together with Brune and Marmont, he made him a Senator. He offered him the command of the Army of Italy, and, when Bernadotte refused and demanded employment at home, he posted him to the command of the division in Brittany, with headquarters at Rennes. But the First Consul found that Rennes, far off as it was, was too close to Paris; accordingly he tried to tempt his Jacobin general by important posts abroad. He proposed in succession the embassy at Constantinople, the captain-generalcy at Guadaloupe, and the governorship of Louisiana, but Bernadotte refused to leave France. At last, early in 1803 Napoleon nominated him minister to the United States. Three times the squadron of frigates got ready to accompany the new minister, but each time the minister postponed his departure. Meanwhile war broke out with England, and Bernadotte was retained in France as general on the unattached list, owing to the efforts of Joseph.

On the establishment of the Empire Napoleon included Bernadotte's name among the number of the Marshals, partly to please his brother Joseph and to maintain the prestige of his family and partly, as in the case of Augereau, Masséna and Jourdan, to win over the staunch republicans and Jacobins to the imperial regime. For the moment the Emperor achieved his object. The ex-Jacobin, proud of his new title and luxuriating in his lately acquired estate of Grosbois, was actually grateful; but still, Gascon-like, he wanted more and complained he had not enough to maintain his proper state. Napoleon, hearing of this from Fouché, exclaimed: 'Take from the public treasury enough to put this right. I want Bernadotte to be content. He is just beginning to say he is full of attachment for my person; this may attach him more.'

But a few days later the Marshal revealed his true feelings when, talking of Napoleon to Lucien, he said, 'There will be no more glory save in his presence and by his side and through his means, and unfortunately all for him.'

Though the Emperor had promoted him to honour, it was no part of his scheme to allow to remain in Paris a man who, as Talleyrand said, 'was capable of securing four cut-throats and making away with Napoleon himself if necessary, a furious beast, a grenadier capable of all and everything, a man to be kept at a distance at all cost.' Accordingly the Marshal very soon found himself sent to replace Mortier in command of the 'Army of Hanover"

For fifteen months Bernadotte administered Hanover, and the subtle courtesy he showed to friend and foe alike made him as usual the adored of all with whom he came in contact. But whatever he did, the Emperor still suspected him, and gave the cue to all, that Bernadotte was not to be trusted and was no soldier. Napoleon always took care that Bernadotte should never have under his command French soldiers. His troops in 1805 were Bavarians; in 1807, Poles; in 1808, a mixture of Dutch and Spaniards; and in 1809, of Poles and Saxons. Berthier, working out the Emperor's ideas, and himself also hating Bernadotte, took care that in the allotment of duties the disagreeable and unimportant tasks should fall to the Marshal. In spite of the inferiority of his troops, Bernadotte as usual distinguished himself in the hour of battle. At Austerlitz, at the critical moment, he saw that unless the centre was heavily supported Napoleon's plan of trapping the Russians must fail, so without waiting orders he detached a division towards the northern slopes of the plateau, and thus materially assisted in winning the day. But though quickwitted and alert on the battlefield, he never shone in strategy. In the movements which led up to a battle he was always slow and inclined to hesitate, and his detractors seized on this fault to declare, with Napoleon's connivance, that he was a traitor to the Emperor and to France. An incident of the campaign of 1806 gave the Marshal's enemies an excellent opening for showing their dislike. Napoleon, thinking he had cornered the whole Prussian army at Jena on the night of October 13th, sent orders to Bernadotte to fall back from Naumburg and get across the Prussian line of retreat. In pursuance of these orders the Marshal left Naumburg at dawn on the morning of the 14th and marched in the direction of Apolda, which he reached, in spite of the badness of the roads, by 4 pm., and thereby captured about a thousand prisoners. But Napoleon had been mistaken in his calculations; the main Prussian force was not at Jena, but at Auerstadt, where it, was most pluckily engaged; and beaten by Davout, who at once sent to ask aid of Bernadotte; but the Marshal, according to Napoleon's definite orders, pursued his way to Apolda. The Emperor, to vent his dislike against Bernadotte and to cover up his own mistake, asserted that he had sent him orders to go to Davout's assistance, but a careful examination of the French despatches proves that no such document existed; in fact, the official despatches completely exonerate Bernadotte. Before the campaign was finished, Napoleon had to give the Marshal the praise he merited, when, aided by Soult and Murat, he at last forced Blucher to surrender with twenty-five thousand men and all the Prussian artillery at Lübeck. At Eylau Bernadotte's ill luck once again pursued him, for the staff officers sent to order him to march to the field of battle were taken by the enemy. This misfortune gave another opportunity to his detractors, and again the Emperor lent his authority to their false accusations. While secretly countenancing every attack on the Marshal, the Emperor, for family reasons, was 10th to come to an open breach. On June 5, 1806, he had created him Prince of Ponte Corvo, a small principality in Italy wedged in between the kingdom of Naples and the Papal States; his reason for so doing he explained in a letter to his brother Joseph, the King of Naples. 'When I gave the title of duke and prince to Bernadotte, it was in consideration of you, for I have in my armies many generals who have served me better and on whose attachment I can count more. But I thought it proper that the brother-in-law of the Queen of Naples should hold a distinguished position in your country.' It was for this reason also that, after the treaty of Tilsit, the Emperor presented the Prince with vast domains in Poland and Hanover.

During the interval between the peace of Tilsit and the outbreak of the war with Austria in 1809, the Prince of Ponte Corvo returned to his duty of administering Hanover. Pursuing his former policy of ingratiating himself with everybody, he renewed his old friendships with all classes, and gained the goodwill of his neighbours in Denmark and Swedish Pomerania, showing a suavity which was in marked contrast to rigid disciplinarians of the school of Davout. Such conduct, however, did not gain the approval of the Emperor, whose policy was, by enforcing the continental system, to squeeze to death the Hanseatic towns, which were England's best customers.

The Marshal was so keenly aware of the displeasure of the Emperor and the hatred of many of his advisers, especially of Berthier, the chief of the staff, that he actually asked to be placed on half pay at the commencement of the campaign of 1809, but the Emperor refused his request. He had determined to end the unceasing struggle between himself and Bernadotte. The battle of Wagram gave him his opportunity. On the first day of the battle, the Marshal had severely criticised, in the hearing of some of his officers, the methods the Emperor had adopted for crossing the Danube and attacking the Archduke Charles, boasting that if he had been in command he would by a scientific manceuvre have compelled the Archduke to lay down his arms almost without a blow. Some enemy told the Emperor of this boast. On the next day Bernadotte's corps was broken by the Austrian cavalry and only saved from absolute annihilation by the personal exertion of the Marshal and his staff, who, by main force, stopped and re-formed the crowd of fugitives. The Emperor arrived on the scene at the moment the Marshal had just succeeded in staying the rout, and sarcastically inquired, 'Is that the scientific manoeuvre by which you were going to make the Archduke lay down his arms?' and before the Marshal could make reply continued, 'I remove you, sir, from the command of the army corps which you handle so badly. Withdraw at once and leave the Grand Army within twenty-four hours; a bungler like you is no good to me.' Such treatment was more than the Marshal's fiery temperament could stand, and accordingly, contrary to all military regulations and etiquette, he issued a bulletin without the authority of the Emperor praising the Saxon troops, and thus magnifying his own importance. The Emperor was furious, and sent a private memorandum to the rest of the Marshals declaring that, 'independently of His Majesty having commanded his army in person, it is for him alone to award the degree of glory each has merited. His Majesty owes the success of his arms to the French troops and to no foreigners ... To Marshal Macdonald and his troops is due the success which the Prince of Ponte Corvo takes to himself.' It seemed as if Bernadotte's career was finished.

The Emperor found he had no longer any reason to fear him, and for the moment determined to crush him completely. So when he heard that Clarke had despatched the Prince to organise the resistance to the English at Flushing, he at once superseded him by Bessières. But the prospect of an alliance by marriage with either Russia or Austria once again caused the Emperor to reflect on the necessity of avoiding scandal and discord in his own family; accordingly he determined to try and propitiate the Marshal by sending him as his envoy to Rome. To a born intriguer like Bernadotte, Rome seemed to spell absolute exile, and accordingly, in the lowest of spirits, he set about to find excuse to delay his journey, little thinking that fortune had turned and was at last about to raise him to those heights of which he had so long dreamed. Long before, in 1804, at the time of the establishment of the Empire, he had secretly visited the famous fortune-teller, Mademoiselle Lenormand, who had told him that he also should be a king and reign, but his kingdom would be across the sea. His boundless ambition, stimulated by Southern superstition, had fed itself on this prophecy, even when the breach with Napoleon seemed to close the door to all hope.

In May, 1809, a revolution in Sweden had deposed the incapable Gustavus IV and set up as King his uncle Charles, Duke of Sudermania. The new King, Charles XIII, was old and childless. Accordingly the question of the succession filled all men's minds. With Russia pressing in on the east and Denmark hostile on the west, it was important to find someone around whom all might rally, by preference a soldier. It was of course obvious that France, the traditional ally of Sweden, dominated Europe. Accordingly the Swedes determined to seek their Crown Prince from the hands of Napoleon. Now, of all the Marshals, Bernadotte had had most to do with the Swedes. At Hamburg he had had constant questions to settle with the Pomeranians. At the time of Blücher's surrender at Lübeck he had treated with great courtesy certain Swedish prisoners. It seemed therefore to the Swedish King's advisers that the Prince of Ponte Corvo, the brother-in-law of King Joseph, the hero of Austerlitz, was the most suitable candidate they could find. Napoleon, however, was furious when he heard that a deputation had arrived to offer the position of Crown Prince of Sweden to Bernadotte. Too diplomatic to refuse to allow the offer to be made, he set to work at once secretly to undermine the Marshal's popularity in Sweden, and while pretending to leave the decision to Bernadotte himself, assured his friends that the Marshal would never dare to accept the responsibility. But Napoleon had miscalculated. Some kind friend informed the Marshal of what the Emperor had said, and, as Bernadotte himself admitted, it was the taunt, 'He will never dare,' which decided him to accept the Swedish offer. Before the Crown Prince elect quitted France the Emperor attempted to place on him the condition that he should never bear arms against him; but Bernadotte, foreseeing the future, refused to give any such promise, and at last the Emperor gave in with the angry words, 'Go, our destinies will soon be accomplished!'

The Crown Prince took with him to Sweden his eldest son, who had curiously, by the whim of his godfather, Napoleon, been named Oscar. But his wife, Désiré, could not tear herself away from Paris, where she had collected a coterie of artists and writers; her salon was greatly frequented by restless intriguers like Talleyrand and Fouché. Woman of pleasure as she was, the gaiety of Paris was the breath of her nostrils. Accordingly the Crown Princess remained behind, as it were the hostage for the Prince's good behaviour, but in reality a spy and secret purveyor of news hostile to Napoleon.

On landing in Sweden the Crown Prince took all by storm. His good looks, his affability, his great prestige and his apparent love for his new country created an enthusiasm almost beyond belief. But while everything seemed so favourable the crafty Gascon from the first foresaw the dangers which beset his path. Napoleon hated him. Russia looked on him with distrust and desired to absorb Sweden. England and the other Powers mistrusted him as the tool of the Emperor. Accordingly, the moment he landed at Gothenburg the Prince clearly defined the line he intended to pursue, exclaiming, 'I refuse to be either the prefect or the custom-house officer of Napoleon.' This decision meant a complete reversal of Swedish foreign policy and a breach with France. Fortunately for Bernadotte the old King, Charles XIII, was only too glad to leave everything to his adopted son. Since it was impossible to make a complete volte face in a moment, the Crown Prince was content to allow the Swedes to taste to the full the misery of trying to enforce the continental system. For he knew what disastrous effect a war with England would have on Swedish trade, and he foresaw that his subjects would soon be glad to accept any policy whereby their sea-borne commerce might be saved. While the Swedes were learning the folly of fighting the mistress of the sea, the Crown Prince had time to make his plans, so that when the moment arrived he might step forward as the saviour of the country. It was quite clear that a breach with France must mean the loss of Pomerania and all hope of regaining the lost provinces on the southern shores of the Baltic. But Bernadotte determined to find in Norway a *quid pro quo* for Pomerania. To force Russia, the hereditary foe of Sweden, to make her hereditary ally, Denmark, grant Norway to Sweden, would be a master-stroke of diplomacy, while an alliance with Russia would guarantee the Swedish frontiers and would bring peace with England, because Russia was on the point of breaking with the continental system. The Swedes would thus gain Norway and recover their sea-borne trade, while the Crown Prince would be acknowledged as the legitimate heir of the royal house of Vasa and no longer regarded as an interloper, a mere puppet of Napoleon.

Success crowned the efforts of the elated Gascon. The Czar, with the prospect of a French invasion at his door, was delighted beyond measure to find in Sweden an ally instead of a foe. In August, 1812, he invited the Crown Prince to Russia and the treaty of Åbö was signed, whereby Russia promised to lend her aid to Sweden to gain Norway as the price of her help against France; a little later a treaty was concluded between England and Sweden. The Crown Prince returned from Åbö full of relief; not only was he now received into the inner circle of legitimate sovereigns, but the Czar had actually volunteered that if Napoleon fell 'I would see with pleasure the destinies of France in your hands.' Alexander had kindled a flame which never died as long as Bernadotte lived. The remainder of his life might be summed up as an effort to gain the crown of France, followed by a period of vain regrets at the failure of his hopes.

On returning to Stockholm the Crown Prince found himself surrounded by a crowd of cosmopolitan admirers, the most important of whom was Madame de Staël, who regarded him as the one man who could restore France to prosperity. His flatterers likened him to Henry IV and harped on the fact that he also came from Béarn. But in France men cursed the traitorous Frenchman who was going to turn his sword against his country, and his name was expunged from the list of the Marshals and from the rolls of the Senate, while the Emperor bitterly regretted that he had not sent him to learn Swedish at Vincennes, the great military prison. When, in accordance with his treaty obligations, early in 1813 the Crown Prince of Sweden landed at Stralsund to take part in the war against Napoleon, his position was a difficult one. The one object of the Allies was to overthrow Napoleon, the one object of the Crown Prince was to become King of France on Napoleon's fall. The Allies therefore had to beat the French troops, but the Crown Prince would ruin his hopes if French soldiers were beaten by the troops under his command. It was clear that Napoleon could only be overcome by the closest co-operation of all the Allies. Accordingly the Czar and the King of Prussia summoned the Crown Prince to a conference at Trachenberg in Silesia and did their best to gratify his pride. The plan of campaign was then arranged, and the Prince returned to command the allied forces in Northern Germany. At St. Helena the Emperor declared that it was Bernadotte who showed the Allies how to win by avoiding all conflict with himself and defeating the Marshals in detail. With great bitterness he added, 'He gave our enemies the key to our policy, the tactics of our armies, and showed them the way to the sacred soil of France.' Be this as it may, his conduct during the campaign justified the suspicion with which he was regarded by friend and foe. Only three times did the Prince's army come in contact with the forces of the Emperor. At Grosbeeren and Dennewitz, where his divisional officers fought and won, the Prince kept discreetly in the rear. At Leipzig he held back so long that the French army very nearly escaped. It was the taunt of his chief of the staff, 'Do you know that the soldiers say you are afraid and do not dare to advance?' which at last forced him into battle. But while thus he offended his allies, he gained no respect from his former countrymen. He had always believed that his presence alone was sufficient to bring over the French troops to his side, but his first attempt ought to have shattered this delusion. At Stettin, during the armistice, he entered the fortress and tried to seduce the governor, an ex-Jacobin and erstwhile friend. As he left the town a cannon was fired and a ball whistled past his ear. He at once sent a flag of truce to demand an explanation for this breach of the etiquette of war, whereon his friend the ex-Jacobin replied, 'It was simply a police affair. We gave the signal that a deserter was escaping and the mainguard fired.' In spite of this warning and many other indications, Bernadotte failed to understand how completely he had lost his influence in France, and while the Allies were advancing on Paris his secret agents were busy, especially in Southern France, trying to win the people to his cause. Keeping well in the rear of the invading armies, he entirely neglected his military duties and passed his time listening to the reports of worthless spies. The result of his intrigues was that he quite lost touch with the trend of events at the front, and when Paris fell, instead of being on the spot, he was far away. The Czar, long disgusted with his delays, no longer pressed his suit, and finding an apparent desire for a Bourbon restoration, accepted the return of that house. So when the Crown Prince came to Paris he found nothing for it but to make his best bow to the Bourbons and slink away home to gain what comfort he could in the conquest of Norway. Thus once again was Sièyes' saying proved correct: 'He is a blackbird who thinks himself an eagle.'

On his return home his Swedish subjects gave their Crown Prince a very warm welcome. They knew of none of his intrigues or tergiversations, they only saw in him the victorious conqueror of Napoleon, who, by his successful campaigns, was bringing peace and prosperity to Sweden, by his diplomacy had acquired Norway, and by his clever huckstering had gained twenty million francs for ceding to France the isle of Guadaloupe, of which Sweden had never taken possession, and another twelve millions for parting with the lost Pomeranian provinces. But in spite of his popularity at home the Crown Prince had much to make him anxious abroad. At the Congress of Vienna a strong party backed the claims of the deposed Gustavus IV, and it was only the generous aid of the Czar which defeated this conspiracy. Further, the attitude of the Powers clearly showed him how precarious was the position of an intruder among the hereditary rulers of Europe. Consequently, when Napoleon returned from Elba the Prince exclaimed: 'The cause of the Bourbons is for ever lost,' and for a moment thought of throwing in his lot with the Emperor. But the sudden defeat of Murat came as a warning, and he hastened to offer the aid of twenty-six thousand troops to the Allies. Though outwardly in accord with them, the Crown Prince secretly hoped for the victory of Napoleon; to his intimates he proclaimed that 'Napoleon was the first captain of all ages, the greatest human being who had ever lived, superior to Hannibal, to Caesar, and even to Moses.' Whereat the Crown Princess, who had at last rejoined her husband in Sweden, replied: 'You ought to exclude Moses, who was the envoy of God, whereas Napoleon is the envoy of the Devil.'

The news of Waterloo once again drove the Prince's ideas into their old current. Surely France must now recognise that he alone could save her; but the second restoration dashed his hopes to the ground. Yet hope springs eternal in the human breast, and Bernadotte, year by year, watched the trend of French politics with an anxious eye. Even as late as the Revolution of 1830 he still thought it was possible that France might call him to be her ruler, and he never lost the chance of doing the Bourbons an ill-turn. In spite of these intrigues, save for an appeal lodged in 1818 against the high-handed conduct of the Quadruple Alliance in interfering between Sweden and Denmark, Bernadotte's European career really ended with the fall of Napoleon. As Charles XIV he ascended the Swedish throne on February 18, 1818, on the death of his adoptive father. As King he pursued the same policy as Crown Prince, alliance with Russia. His internal policy was based on the principle of maintaining his dynasty at all costs. With this object, in Sweden he ruled more or less as a benevolent despot, consulting his States General as little as possible, paying the greatest attention to commerce and industry, and opening up the mines and waterways of the country. In Norway, however, where the Storthing had long enjoyed great powers, he ruled as a liberal constitutional monarch, and with such good fortune did he and his successors pursue their policy that of all the diplomatic expedients arranged at the Congress of Vienna, the cession of Norway to Sweden stood the test of time the longest, and it was not till 1906 that the principle of nationality was at last enforced in Scandinavia.

Though Charles XIV made no attempt to interfere in European politics, the princes of Europe could never shake off their dislike of him, standing as he did as the one survival of Napoleon's system. When the time came for his son Oscar to seek a bride, the Swedish proposals were met with scorn in Denmark and Prussia, and even in Mecklenburg-Anhalt and Hesse-Cassel. As the Austrian envoy at the Swedish court whispered to his English colleague, 'All Europe would see the fall of these people here without regret.' Consequently the Swedish King was driven to seek a bride for his son from Napoleon's family, and eventually the young Prince married the daughter of Eugène Beauharnais, the old ex-Viceroy of Italy, Napoleon's stepson.

Charles XIV, a man of regrets, spent the remainder of his life buried in the memories of the past. He seldom got up till late in the day, dictating his letters and receiving his ministers in bed. When he was dressed, he spent some hours going over his private affairs and revising his investments, for he feared to the end that he might be deprived of his crown. In the evening he entertained the foreign representatives and held his courts, after which he passed the small hours of the night with his particular cronies fighting and re-fighting his battles, and proving how he alone could have saved Europe from the misery of the Napoleonic wars. He died on March 3rd, 1844, at the age of eighty, having given his subjects the precious boon of twenty-five years of peace.

In spite of his brilliant career, Bernadotte must ever remain one of the most pathetic figures in history. He stands convicted as a mere opportunist, a man who never once possessed his soul in peace and who was incapable of understanding his own destiny. So much was this the case that in his latter days the old Jacobin, now a crowned King, really believed he was speaking the truth when he said that along with Lafayette he was the only public man, save the Count of Artois, who had never changed since 1789. He saw no inconsistency between the declaration of his youth, 'that royalty was a monster which must be mutilated in its own interest,' and his speech as an old man to the French ambassador, 'If I were King of France with an army of two or three hundred thousand men I would put my tongue out at your Chamber of Deputies.' He was Gascon to the backbone, and his tongue too often betrayed his most secret and his most transient thoughts. For the moment he would believe and declare that 'Napoleon was not beaten by mere men ... he was greater than all of us ... the greatest captain who has appeared since Julius Cæsar ... If, like Henry IV, he had had a Sully he would have governed empires.' Then, thinking of himself as Sully, he would gravely add, 'Bonaparte was the greatest soldier of our age, but I surpassed him in powers of organisation, of observation and calculation.' Yet with it all he had many of the qualities which go to make a man great. His personal magnetism was irresistible, he had consummate tact, a keen eye for intrigue, a clear vision to pierce the mazes of political tangles, and considerable strength of purpose backed by an intensely fiery nature. Frank and generous, he inclined naturally to a liberal policy, but his innate selfishness too often conquered his generous principles. It was this conflict between his liberal ideas and his personal interest which caused that fatal hesitation which again and again threatened to spoil his career and which made him so immensely inferior to Napoleon. To gain his crown he willingly threw over his religion and became a Lutheran; to keep his crown he was ready to sacrifice his honour. As a Swedish monarch he thought more of the interests of his dynasty than of the interests of his subjects, but he was far too wily to show this in action. Posing as a patriot King and boasting of his love for his adopted country, he ever remained at heart a Frenchman.

When in 1840 the remains of the great Emperor wer transferred to Paris, he mournfully exclaimed to his representative: 'Tell them that I who was once a Marshal of France am now only a King of Sweden.'

5

JEAN DE DIEU NICOLAS SOULT, MARSHAL, DUKE OF DALMATIA

OF all the Marshals of Napoleon, perhaps none is better known to Englishmen than Jean de Dieu Soult. His long service in the Peninsula, ending with the stern fighting in the Pyrenees and the valley of the Garonne, and the prominent part he took in French politics during the years of the Orleanist monarchy, made his name a household word in England. The son of a small notary of St. Amand, a little-known town in the department of the Tarn, Soult was possessed of all the fervour of the South and the cunning and tenacity of a Gascon. Born on March 29, 1769, he early distinguished himself by his precocity and his quickness of perception. Although handicapped by a club-foot he determined to be a soldier, and at the age of sixteen he enlisted in the Royal Infantry regiment. His intelligence marked him out for the rank of sergeant, and in 1791 he was sent as sub-lieutenant and drill instructor to a battalion of volunteers of the Haut Rhin. In spite of his lameness and his slight frame, the young sub-lieutenant was possessed of a physique capable of withstanding the greatest fatigue and hardship, and spurred on by ambition, he never shirked a task which might add to his reputation. Consequently, he was soon chosen captain by his comrades, and once war broke out he speedily rose. At the battle of Kaiserslautern, the storm of the lines of Weissenburg and the siege of Fort Louis, he forced himself to the front by his gallantry and his rapid coup d'œil. But it was the battle of Fieurus which once and for all established his reputation. Soult was by then colonel and chief of the staff to General Lefèbvre. The gallant Marceau's battalions were hurled back in rout by the enemy, and their chief in agony rushed up to Lefèbvre crying out for four battalions of the reserve that he might regain the ground he had lost.

'Give them to me,' he exclaimed, 'or I will blow out my brains.' Soult quietly observed that he would thereby only the more endanger his troops. Marceau, indignant at being rebuked by a young staff officer, roughly asked, 'And who are you?' 'Whoever I am,' replied Soult, 'I am calm, which you are not: do not kill yourself, but lead your men to the charge and you shall have the four battalions as soon as we can spare them.' Scarcely had he uttered these words than the Austrians fell with fury on Lefèbvre's division. For hours the issue hung in the balance, and at last even the stubborn Lefèbvre began to think of retreat. But Soult, calmly casting a rapid glance over the field, called out, 'If I am not mistaken from what I judge of the enemy's second line, the Austrians are preparing to retreat.' A few moments later came the order to advance from Jourdan, the commander-in-chief, and thanks to Soult's soundness of judgment, the divisions of Marceau and Lefèbvre were charging the enemy instead of fighting a rearguard action to cover a rout. After the battle, the generous Marceau sought out Soult. 'Colonel,' said he, 'forgive the past: you have this day given me a lesson I shall never forget. It is you in fact who have gained the battle.' Soult had not long to wait for his reward, for in 1794 he was promoted general of brigade.

During the campaign of 1795 Soult was entrusted with a light column of three battalions of infantry and six squadrons of cavalry, and was constantly employed as an advance or rearguard. On one occasion, while covering the retreat at Herborn, his small force was surrounded by four thousand Austrian cavalry. Summoned to surrender, he indignantly refused, and forming his infantry in two columns with the cavalry in the interval between them, during five hours he beat off repeated charges of the enemies' horse and fought his way back to the main body without losing a single gun or a single colour. Ten days later he added to this triumph by inflicting the loss of two thousand men on the enemy in the mountain combat at Ratte Eig, when both sides struggled to gain the heights knee-deep in snow. During the campaigns of 1796 and 1797, Soult increased his reputation amid the marches and counter-marches and battles in the valleys of the Rhine and the Danube. But it was in Switzerland that he laid most firmly the foundation of his future success, for there he gained the friendship and goodwill of Masséna, and it was the conqueror of Zurich who first called Bonaparte's attention to the sterling qualities of the future Duke of Dalmatia, telling the First Consul that 'for judgment and courage Soult had scarcely a superior.' In 1800 Masséna took his trusty subordinate with him to Italy as lieutenant-general of the centre of the army. During the fierce struggle which ended in the Austrians driving the French into Genoa, the lieutenant-general was seen at his best, exposing his person in a way he seldom did later, and showing that strategic insight and power of organisation for which he was so celebrated. On one occasion, when cornered by Bellegarde, he was summoned to surrender. The Austrian parlementaire pointed out that it was hopeless to continue the struggle as he had neither provisions nor ammunition. To this Soult replied: 'With bayonets and men who know how to use them, one lacks nothing,' and in spite of every effort of the enemy, with the 'white arm' alone he cut his way into Genoa. During the siege he was Masséna's right hand, ever ready with shrewd advice, the soul of every sortie, till unluckily he was wounded at the combat of Monte Cretto, and captured by the Austrians, whose prisoner he remained till after Marengo.

On the establishment of the Consulate, Soult, whose politics rested solely on personal ambition and not on principle, at once divined the aims of Bonaparte. Thanks to Masséna's warm introduction and his own reputation, he found himself cordially received by the First Consul. Honours were showered upon him. He was one of the four trusted commandants of the Consular Guard, and when Napoleon began to organise his forces for the struggle with England, he entrusted Soult with the command of the important army corps at Boulogne. The First Consul could have made no better selection. Under his rough exterior Soult hid great powers of business, a keen perspicacity, and much tact. Quick-witted, with a subtle, restless spirit, he had great strength of character, and his ambition spurred him on to a diligence which knew neither mental nor physical fatigue. But in spite of his cold air and self-restraint, he loved the pleasures of the table, and was passionately fond of women, while his wife exercised a complete domination over him, and before her he quailed like a child. In war he had the keen imagination and quick penetration of a great strategist. His special forte was the planning of vigorous enterprises. But he preferred to direct rather than to lead. Though his courage was undoubted, as he grew older he was chary of risking his person, and had not the dashing qualities of Lannes and Ney. As an administrator he was the equal of Davout. Once entrusted with the command of the army corps at Boulogne, the young general of thirty-five laid aside all thoughts of personal pleasure and ease and set himself to manufacture a fighting machine which should be the most perfect of its time. Never was such attention shown to details of administration and instruction, and the discipline of the corps at Boulogne was the severest that French troops had ever undergone. As might be expected, there were many grumbles, and soon rumours and complaints reached the First Consul, who himself remonstrated with his lieutenant, telling him that the troops would sink under such treatment; but he was greeted with the reply, 'Such as cannot withstand the fatigue which I myself undergo will remain at the depôts: but those who do stand it will be fit to undertake the conquest of the world.' Soult was right in his estimate, for in spite of the demands he made on their endurance, he had won their love and admiration; the weak and the grumblers fell out, and when war was declared his corps marched to the front, a body of picked men with absolute confidence in their leader. In spite of the fact that he had never held an independent command, there was no surprise when he was included among the number of the Marshals, for his brilliant record, his selection as commandant of the Guard, his success at Boulogne, and the favour which the First Consul had long shown to him, had marked him out as one of the coming men. The campaign of 1805 bore witness to the justness of the Emperor's choice. It has often been said, and indeed Wellington himself lent credit to the dictum, that Soult was primarily a strategist and no tactician, but at Austerlitz he showed that calm capacity to read the signs of the conflict, and that knowledge of when and where to strike, which had first brought him to the front in the days of Fleurus. Entrusted with the command of the centre, in spite of the entreaties of his subordinates and even the commands of the Emperor, he refused to open his attack until he saw that the Russian left was hopelessly compromised. Thanks to his clearness of foresight, when once he launched his attack he not only put the issue out of doubt, but completely overwhelmed the Russians. Their left was surrounded and annihilated while the centre and right were driven from the field in complete rout. At the moment when the Marshal was directing the movement which wrested from the enemy the key of the position, Napoleon and his staff arrived on the scene. The Marshal explained his manoeuvre and asked the Emperor for orders. 'Carry on, carry on, my dear Marshal,' said the Emperor; 'you know quite as well as I do how to finish the affair.' Then, stretching out his arms to embrace him, he cried out 'My dear Marshal, you are the finest tactician in Europe.' After the treaty of Pressburg Soult's corps remained as part of the army of occupation in the valley of the Danube, and in 1806 formed one of the corps of the Grand Army during the Prussian War. At Jena he had the satisfaction of playing an important part in the battle, for when Ney's rash advance had compromised the situation, it was he who checked the victorious rush of the enemy. But later the Marshal had bitter cause to repent these triumphs won over his rival. Already the enemy of Berthier, and consequently often misrepresented to the Emperor, Soult now incurred the bitter hatred of Ney; and what the enmity of Berthier and Ney meant he found to his cost during the Peninsular War. Immediately after Jena the Marshal was detached in pursuit of the Prussians, and on the day following defeated Marshal Kalkreuth at Greussen and proceeded to blockade Magdeburg. From Magdeburg he hurried off to join in the pursuit of Blücher, and aided by Bernadotte he cornered the crafty old Prussian at Lübeck. But brilliant as his performance was, he did not gain the credit he deserved, for on the day of the action Murat arrived and took over the command, arrogating to himself all the honours of the surrender. The Marshal was justly indignant, but, bitterly as he resented the injustice, he was too politic to storm at the Emperor like Marshal Lannes. In the terrible campaign in Poland the Marshal added to his laurels. At Eylau, when Augereau had been routed, Davout checked, and Ney and Bernadotte not yet arrived on the field, it was he who warned the Emperor against showing any signs of retreat. 'Beware of doing so, Sire,' he exclaimed, 'let us remain the last on the field and we shall have the honour of the day: from what I have seen I expect the enemy will retreat in the night.' The advice was sound, and the Marshal, during the night following the battle, had the pleasure of being the first to perceive that the enemy was retreating, and it was his aide-de-camp who carried the news to headquarters. Well it was for the Emperor that he accepted Soult's advice, for the terrible carnage in the snow had taken the heart out of the troops, and a retreat would have soon degenerated into a rout. So shaken was the French morale, that when, on the next day, the Emperor rode down the lines, instead of being greeted with cries of 'Long live the Emperor,' he was received with murmurs of 'Peace and France,' and even 'Peace and Bread'. During the final advance Soult had his share of the hard fighting at Heilsberg, but he escaped from the horrors of Friedland, as he had been detached to occupy Königsberg. After the peace of Tilsit, the Marshal's corps was cantonned round Stettin, and it was there that in 1808 he received the title of Duke of Dalmatia. The selection of this name caused the Duke much annoyance, for instead of receiving a title which should recall one of his great exploits, as had Ney, Davout, Lannes, Kellermann, and Masséna, his designation was chosen from a country with which he had not the smallest connection, and thus he found himself on a par with Bessières, Maret and Caulaincourt. What he hankered after was the title of Duke of Austerlitz, but the Emperor refused to share the glories of that day. In spite of the huge dotation he received, the Marshal added this supposed slight to the many grudges he bore his master.

From Stettin the Duke of Dalmatia was summoned in September, 1808, to attend the Conference at Erfurt, and from there he was hurriedly despatched to Spain. The Emperor was much displeased with many of his corps commanders, and so on the arrival of the Duke he ordered him to take over from Marshal Bessières the command of the second corps. Soult was delighted at the prospect of service. Full of zeal, he set out for his new command, and pushing on in spite of all obstacles, he arrived at his headquarters alone on a jaded posthorse twenty-four hours before his aides-de-camp. A few days later he dashed to pieces the semblance of a Spanish army at Gamoral and occupied Burgos, where he was unable to prevent his new command from sacking the town and inflicting every possible horror on the inhabitants. From Burgos the Emperor despatched him to the north-west, and thus it was that the cavalry of Sir John Moore's army surprised Soult's outpost at Sahagun. The Emperor could scarcely believe that an English army had actually dared to advance against his troops, but he at once ordered Soult to co-operate with the divisions he led in person from Madrid, and when he found that the English were bound to escape, he handed over the command to the Marshal. The French suffered almost as much as the English in the terrible pursuit, and it was the tried soldiers of both armies who at last met face to face at Corunna. After the battle Soult wrote to the Emperor that without fresh reinforcements he could effect nothing against the English, but, when later he found that the enemy had evacuated Corunna, he claimed that he had won a victory. With a generosity that must be placed to his credit, he took great care of the grave of his adversary, Sir John Moore, and erected a monument with the inscription, 'Hic cecidit Johannes Moore dux exercitus Britannici in pugna Januarii xvi. 1809, Gallos a duce Dalmatiæ ductos.'

Before leaving for France the Emperor had drawn up a cut and dried plan for the systematic conquest of the whole Peninsula. The pivot of the whole scheme rested on the supposed ability of Soult to overrun Portugal and drive the British out of Lisbon by February 16, 1809. Unfortunately, Napoleon left one factor out of his calculations, and that the most important, namely, the feelings of the Spanish and Portuguese populations. The Duke of Dalmatia very soon perceived the Emperor's mistake, but, anxious not to be accused of shirking his task and of allowing himself to be stopped by what were termed bands of ill-armed peasants, he started on his expedition to conquer the kingdom of Portugal with but three thousand rounds for his guns and five hundred thousand cartridges for his infantry, carried on the backs of mules, for owing to the state of the roads in the north-west corner of the Peninsula wheel traffic was impossible. In spite of the difficulties of transport and the murmurs of many of his officers, the indefatigable Marshal hurled all obstacles aside and with sixteen thousand troops forced his way into Oporto on March 29th, six weeks behind his scheduled time. But there he had to call a halt, for he had not the men nor the material for a further advance on

Lisbon. The situation was by no means reassuring. To reach Oporto he had been obliged to cut himself adrift from his base, and he had no tidings of what was happening in the rest of the Peninsula. During April he set himself to conciliate the people of Portugal and at the same time to try and get into touch with the other French corps in Spain. The Marshal's attempt at conciliation was on the whole successful, but his kindness resulted in an unsuspected turn in the situation. A movement was started among a certain section of the Portuguese nobility and officials to offer the crown of Portugal to the Marshal. The Duke of Dalmatia, greedy and ambitious but ever cautious, was of opinion that though the Emperor might disapprove of the idea, he would accept a fait accompli. Accordingly he secretly sanctioned the movement, and allowed placards to appear in Oporto stating that 'the Prince Regent, by his departure to Brazil, had formally resigned the crown, and that the only salvation of Portugal would be that the Duke of Dalmatia, the most distinguished of the pupils of the great Napoleon, should ascend the vacant throne.' Further, he actually, on April 19th, ordered his chief of the staff to send a circular to commanding officers inviting their co-operation in his seizure of the crown, stating that by so doing they would in no way be disloyal to the Emperor. Luckily for the Marshal, the arrival of Sir Arthur Wellesley and the English army, before the plot could succeed, once and for all blew aside this cloudy attempt at kingship. For the Emperor, on hearing of the affair, although he pardoned the Marshal, saying, 'I remember nothing but Austerlitz,' still wrote in the same despatch 'that it would have been a crime, clear lèse majesté, an attack on the imperial dignity,' and added that it was no wonder that the army grew discontented, since the Marshal was working, not for France, but for himself, and that disobedience to the Marshal's orders was quite justified. For once, then, the Marshal, usually so clever and cautious, had allowed ambition to run away with prudence. Meanwhile the military situation grew day by day more disquieting. In the French army there was a section of the officers ready to declare against the Empire whenever a chance occurred, and one of them, Argenton by name, actually entered into a treasonable negotiation with Sir Arthur Wellesley. It was thanks to the discovery of this plot that the Marshal first got information of his enemies' projected advance.

With thirty thousand English marching against him and Spanish and Portuguese forces across the main line of retreat, it was impossible to expect to hold Oporto, and accordingly the Marshal began preparations for withdrawal. But having secured, as he thought, all the boats on the Douro, he concluded that he could only be attacked by a force ferried across at the river mouth by the boats of the English fleet. Consequently he kept no watch upstream. So complete was the surprise that an hour after the enemy had effected a landing above the town the Marshal, who had been up all night, was still in bed; his staff were quietly breakfasting when an officer galloped up with the news of the crossing. Soult could do nothing else but give the order to retreat by whatever means possible, and it was fortunate for the French that the pursuit was not pushed harder. But once he had grasped the situation he made amends for his previous neglect of supervision and showed himself the Soult of Austerlitz and Eylau. Sacrificing his baggage, his guns, and his military chest, guided by a Spanish pedlar, he made a most astounding march through the rugged region of Tras os Montes. Crossing lofty passes, forcing gorges in the teeth of hostile bands of peasantry and guerillas, by hard fighting and magnificent marching he brought his troops to safety. The campaign of Oporto did not add to the Marshal's reputation; his political ambition was the cause of all the disaster, for it prevented him from supervising his subordinates' operations. It was his fault that there was no proper road for retreat and that he was surprised by the English army. Still, though he had committed great faults, he had shown a surprising ability in extricating himself from their consequences.

When Soult reached Lugo, in Spain, he found his rival Ney, from whom he begged stores and equipments, and with whom he was bound to confer on the general situation. Ney at first magnanimously granted the Marshal's requests. But unfortunately the men of Ney's corps greeted the armed rabble which followed Soult's standards with jeers and execrations, and the quarrel spread from the men to the officers and at last to the Marshals; so fierce were Ney's taunts that Soult actually drew his sword and a duel was with difficulty averted. Thereafter Soult, while promising to co-operate with

Ney in the pacification of Galicia, actually did nothing and seriously compromised his rival, whereon Ney refused to obey any orders given by the Duke of Dalmatia. Such was the situation when a summons from Madrid called the two Marshals to the succour of Joseph, who was threatened by the combined armies of Cuesta and Sir Arthur Wellesley in the valley of the Tagus. The Marshals arrived in time to save Madrid, but not in time to surround the Allies, who escaped south across the Tagus, and the one chance of success the Spanish offered them was lost, since Soult, eager for personal aggrandisement, attacked Albuquerque before Marshal Victor had time to arrive on the scene of action. The consequence of this was far-reaching, for Victor, like Ney, refused in future to work in conjunction with Soult. Moreover, when a council was held to decide on the next operations, and Soult, wisely, no doubt, insisted that at Lisbon lay the key to the situation, all the other Marshals voted against his scheme, as each one determined that he would not be made subordinate to the Duke of Dalmatia. Soult accordingly had to content himself with occupying the valley of the Tagus, while the other Marshals returned to the districts which had been allotted to them before the allied advance on Madrid.

While contemplating this unsatisfactory situation the Duke of Dalmatia was rejoiced to receive a despatch from the Emperor appointing him major-general of the forces in Spain in place of Jourdan and entrusting him with the invasion of Andalusia. Before setting out for the South, Soult had the satisfaction of completely routing the Spaniards at Ocaña. It was early in 1810 that he entered Andalusia and seized Seville, Granada, and Malaga. The Marshal found himself in the congenial position of absolute ruler of the richest provinces of Spain. But though the important towns fell easily, and with them the accumulated riches of centuries, the people remained sullenly hostile, and bands of armed peasantry hung ever on the rear and flanks of the French columns, and stragglers and despatch-riders were found by the roadside with their throats cut. To meet this situation, at the Emperor's orders Soult issued a proclamation setting forth that whereas Joseph Bonaparte was King of Spain and no Spanish Government existed, all Spaniards taken in arms were rebels against his Catholic Majesty and would be immediately shot. The Cortes from Cadiz replied by at once issuing a counter-proclamation stating that for every Spaniard executed and for every house burned three Frenchmen should be hung. Still, in spite of this war of reprisals, the French gradually tightened their grip on Southern Spain, and soon Cadiz remained the only important fortress still in the hands of the enemy. The Marshal found it was impossible to take this important position by storm, and contented himself with masking it by a strong corps under Marshal Victor. Meanwhile he was busily engaged in organising the new government of Andalusia, and so successful were his efforts that neither the Spanish Government at Cadiz or the constant incursions of Spanish and British armies were able to shake his hold on that province. But wise and successful as were his methods, the glory of his rule was darkened by his harshness and greed. The churches and convents were ruthlessly despoiled of their treasures, and many a fine Murillo and Velasquez was despatched to Paris to decorate his salons.

In the eyes of the Duke of Dalmatia, Andalusia was a vast reservoir of wealth which might be used as a base from which a well-equipped force could threaten Lisbon, the real focus of all the opposition to the French domination of the Peninsula. It was in pursuance of this plan that he conciliated the municipal authorities, strengthened the police, and built up huge reserve magazines by a system of imposts so carefully arranged that they should not unduly press on the Spanish population. But unfortunately for the Duke's schemes they ran counter to those of King Joseph. For the Marshal determined to use the wealth of his rich provinces for the special object of an attack on the British power at Lisbon, but Joseph desired that the revenue thus acquired should be sent to assist him to maintain his kingly state. Soult, strong in his position as major-general and backed by the Emperor's approval, refused to listen to the demands of the King, and there began a struggle which did more than anything else to bring about the fall of the Napoleonic kingdom of Spain. In spite of the fact that the Marshal gradually wore down the guerrillas, actually raised and trained large bodies of Spanish troops, built up vast magazines and arsenals at Seville, exploited the lead mines at Linares and the copper mines of the Rio Tinto, established foundries for military accessories, and fitted out privateers, the jealousy of

Joseph brought the Marshal's great schemes to nought. The continual and vexatious demands of the King acted in a most unfortunate way on Soult's character, for this stupid opposition so irritated his hard and egotistical nature that he saw in every scheme not planned by himself a desire to belittle his glory. Unfortunately for his own reputation and the success of the French arms, he allowed this feeling to obscure his judgment, and he refused to give more than a half-hearted co-operation to any measures not actually suggested by himself. Thus it was that, in spite of the commands of the Emperor and the entreaties of Joseph, he refused to make any attempt to co-operate with Masséna in his advance on Portugal until it was too late. Then, when he actually did advance, he showed all his old energy and skill, for in fifty days he mastered four fortresses and invested a fifth, he captured twenty thousand prisoners and killed or dispersed ten thousand men; but he disregarded the main objective, the expulsion of the English from Lisbon, and contented himself with the siege of Badajoz, and thus, while winning a fortress, he lost a kingdom. From want of his co-operation Masséna was forced to retreat, and the grip of the English on the Peninsula was more firmly established than ever.

Badajoz was soon to prove itself a place of ill omen for Soult, for a few months later, when an Anglo-Portuguese army under Beresford laid siege to it, he was forced to come to its rescue. It was in the attempt to relieve this fortress that the terrible battle of Albuera was fought. At the commencement of the fight the Marshal, by a masterly manoeuvre, threw himself across the allied right flank and seized the hill that dominated the position, and it looked as if the allied lines were bound to be crumpled up. But a brigade of English infantry stood firm amid the rout, and with measured volleys checked the victorious advance of the elated French. Soult, by every effort of voice and gesture, attempted to force his veterans to face the foe, but in vain. 'Nothing could conquer that astounding infantry. No sudden burst of undisciplined valour, no nervous enthusiasm weakened the stability of their order: their flashing eyes were bent on the dark columns in their front, their measured tread shook the ground, their dreadful volleys swept away the head of every formation, their deafening shouts overpowered the discordant cries that broke from all parts of the tumultuous crowd as slowly, and with a horrid carnage, it was pushed by the incessant vigour of the attack to the farthest edge of the hill. In vain did the French reserve mix with the struggling multitude to sustain the fight: their efforts only increased the immediate confusion, and the mighty mass, breaking off like a loosened cliff, went headlong down the steep. The rain flowed after in a stream discoloured by blood: and eighteen hundred unwounded men, the remnant of six thousand unconquerable British soldiers, stood triumphant on the fatal hill.' Thus Napier describes the battle of Albuera. So nearly a magnificent victory for the French: turned by British valour into a defeat. But it was not only the valour of the enemy which cost Soult his success, it was his own errors. The commencement of the attack was a magnificent conception, but the Marshal failed to understand the tactics of his enemy, and it was his blind attempt to crush the line with heavy columns which allowed the English musket fire to annihilate his dense masses. After the cessation of the combat he committed another great fault. Though his attack had been beaten back, it was known that the Allies had suffered much more severely than the French, and on the strength of this he claimed a signal victory. But instead of holding his ground he withdrew a day later, whereas if he had shown a confident front Beresford would have been bound to retire, and Badajoz would have been relieved. After the battle of Albuera, Soult was reinforced by the Army of Portugal under Marmont; but discord soon broke out between the two Marshals, the Duke of Dalmatia maintaining that the way to attack Lisbon was from his own base in the south, and the Duke of Ragusa advocating the northern route. After lying together for some time the two armies separated, and Soult moved south to complete his operations against Cadiz and Gibraltar. It was while the Marshal was thus engaged, early in 1812, that the Duke of Wellington suddenly captured Ciudad Rodrigo and Badajoz, and was thus able, after defeating Marmont, at Salamanca, to march in the summer on Madrid. Soult replied to Joseph's summons to come to his help by telling him that his best policy was to join him in Andalusia and make a counterstroke at Lisbon. But the King refused to listen to this wise advice, so the Marshal was obliged to give up all his achievements and go to Joseph's help. Meanwhile the King wrote complaining to the Emperor, but Napoleon replied that Soult was the 'only military head' in Spain, and could not be moved. But after more bickering, early in 1813, Joseph wrote, to say that if the Marshal remained in Spain he himself must leave the country, and the Emperor, anxious to regain his military prestige, so weakened by the Russian campaign, was glad to summon the Duke of Dalmatia to the Grand Army. But Soult's gloomy prophecy was soon fulfilled that 'the loss of Andalusia and the raising of the siege of Cadiz are events that will be felt throughout the whole of Europe. 'The Marshal's service at the head of the Imperial Guard was terminated by the news of the fatal battle of Vittoria; for the Emperor immediately hurried him back to try to prevent the English from forcing the barrier of the Pyrenees.

The Duke of Dalmatia gladly accepted the mission, in spite of the repugnance of the Duchess, who hated Spain, where, as she said, 'nothing is got but blows'. So hearty was her dislike of the country that she actually went to the Emperor saying her husband was too shattered in health for the task. But she met with a stern rebuff: 'Madam,' said Napoleon, 'recollect I am not your husband; if I were, you should conduct yourself very differently.'

The campaign of the Pyrenees bore ample testimony to the wisdom of the confidence the Emperor had placed in the power of his lieutenant. With marvellous sagacity Soult reorganised the scattered relics of the French armies, and within ten days of his arrival at headquarters he was ready to assume the offensive, and actually all but surprised the Duke of Wellington at Sorauren. But great as were his strategical powers and his methods of organisation, he was no match for Wellington on the field of battle, and step by step he was forced back into France. Round Bayonne he showed his complete mastery of the art of war by the admirable way he used his command of the inner lines always to oppose the enemy's attack by superior force. Then, when retreat was inevitable, instead of falling back towards Paris, he withdrew south, thus forcing his adversary to divide up his army; for the English had to detach a strong division to cover their communications at Bordeaux. During the retreat, again and again Soult turned at bay, at Orthez and many another good position; but Wellington ever outmanoeuvred him on the field, and even turned him out of the seemingly impregnable position of Toulouse. Never was a retreat more admirably carried out. Every opportunity afforded by the ground, every advantage of position was seized on, to use to the full the French dash in the attack. No more admirable illustration can be found of the truth that the essence of defence lies in a vigorous local offence. Wellington himself bore testimony to Soult's virtues, maintaining that of the Marshals he was second only to Masséna.

With the Restoration the Marshal at once accepted the change of government and gave his adhesion to the Bourbons. His general reputation and the high place he held in the opinion of Wellington and others caused the King in the December of 1814 to appoint him Minister of War. Such was his position when news arrived of Napoleon's landing at Fréjus. The Duke of Dalmatia did all in his power to organise resistance to the Emperor's advance, but he had many enemies, and the King, listening to their advice, replaced him as minister by Clarke, Duke of Feltre. Soult then retired to his country estate at Ville neuve-l'Etang, near Saint Cloud. On his arrival at Paris, the Emperor at once sent for him, but at first he refused to go to court. Ultimately, finding the Emperor's cause in the ascendant, he cast aside hesitation and threw in his lot with him. It has been said that the Duke betrayed the Bourbons and was privy to the Emperor's return, but this is a calumny. Napoleon at St. Helena said, 'Soult did not betray Louis, nor was he privy to my return. For some days he thought that I was mad, and that I must certainly be lost. Notwithstanding this, appearances were so against him, and without intending it, his acts turned out to be so favourable to my project, that, were I on his jury and deprived of what I know, I should have condemned him for having betrayed Louis. But he really was not privy to it.' The Emperor joyfully accepted the Marshal's adherence and made him one of his new peers, and when war was imminent, on the advice of Davout, he created him major-general and chief of the staff. This selection was unfortunate; good strategist and organiser, he was not the man the Emperor required. Berthier, who had not half his military ability, had made an excellent chief of the staff, because he had the rare quality of effacing his own ideas and acting simply as the recorder and expander of those of

Napoleon. But Soult was accustomed to think for himself, and his mind was unable to attune itself to the mind of the Emperor. Further, from long experience, Berthier was accustomed to fill up gaps in the Emperor's orders in the way he intended, but Soult had never so far worked in close co-operation with Napoleon, and after years of independent command was more accustomed to give orders to his own chief of the staff than to work out minutiae for another. Consequently, all through the Waterloo campaign the staff work was badly done. Orders were faultily drafted, mistakes were made in their despatch, and the Emperor was constantly bewailing the loss of 'that brute Berthier'. A typical example of the friction which arose between the Emperor and his new major-general occurred when, at Waterloo, Napoleon asked Soult if he had sent to Grouchy intelligence of the approach of the Prussians; the Marshal replied, 'Yes, I have sent an officer.' 'One officer!' cried Napoleon, 'ah! if only my poor Berthier had been here, he would have sent six.' To add to these troubles, Soult was unfortunately hated by the officers of the army, who regarded him with grave suspicion. But though the Marshal must bear his share in the disaster of Waterloo, it is only fair to add that the morning of the battle he, and he alone, warned the Emperor of the magnitude of the coming struggle, and entreated him to recall at least a portion of Grouchy's command. The Emperor roughly rejected his advice with the words, 'You think that because Wellington defeated you he must be a great general. I tell you that he is a bad general, that the English are bad troops, and that this will be the affair of a déjeuner.' The Marshal, with the memory of many a battle with these 'poor troops' from Oporto to Toulouse, could only sorrowfully say, 'I hope so.'

On the second Restoration the Duke of Dalmatia found himself included among the proscribed, and for three years he retired to the Duchy of Berg, the home of his wife, during which time he occupied himself in the composition of his Memoirs. But in May, 1819, he was recalled to France, and soon found means of ingratiating himself with the Bourbons. In January, 1820, his Marshal's baton and his other honours were restored to him, and he entered the field of politics. With his vast income, acquired from the spoils of nearly every country in Europe, he maintained his high rank in lordly fashion. A visitor who in 1822 went to see his famous collection of pictures thus describes him: 'We were received by the Marshal, a middle-sized though somewhat corpulent personage of from fifty to sixty years of age, whose dark curling hair rendered somewhat conspicuous the bald patch in the middle of his head, while his sunburnt complexion accorded well with his dark intelligent eye. His plain stock, plain dark coat and loose blue trousers, which, capacious as they were, could not hide his bow-legged form, obviously suggested the soldier rather than the courtier, the Marshal rather than the Duke; though if I had encountered such a figure in London I should rather have guessed him an honest East or West Indian captain.' The Marshal knew well how to win favour with the new Government, and when the reactionaries attempted to restore the ancient position of the Church, no one was more regular in his attendance at Church festivals and processions than the Duke of Dalmatia, who always appeared with an enormous breviary carried before him, though people were unkind enough to say that it would be more to the purpose if he restored some of the vast plunder of the churches and monasteries of Spain.

With the fall of the Bourbon dynasty in 1830 the subtle old soldier at once gave his adherence to the Orleanists, and was appointed Minister of War; and it was thanks to his energy and wisdom that the numerous revolts which threatened the early days of the new régime were stamped out. Soult, like Wellington, hated the idea of civil war, but knew that strong measures were the best means to prevent bloodshed, so when, as at Lyons, it was essential to strike, he took good care to have the necessary force at hand. A year later, when the Commune threatened to raise its head in Paris, he overawed the mob by the sudden mobilisation of eighty thousand troops. The weakness of the Government and the courage and decision the Marshal showed during the émeute caused Louis Philippe on October 18, 1832, to entrust him with the headship of the administration. The Marshal proved how often a strong soldier may be a weak politician, and in 1834 he resigned office. But during his term of office he did not forget the needs of the army, as his measures for recruiting, military pensions, and the training of officers prove. When, again, in 1839 Paris was seething with discontent, the King sent for the

Marshal, and under his iron hand order was easily re-established. But the old soldier was no orator, and was listened to more from respect for his character than the cogency of his arguments, and when the crisis was passed he was soon glad to resign his appointment; and though always taking an active part, and ever ready to give his advice to his sovereign, he never again held office. In 1838 the Duke of Dalmatia visited London as representative of France at the Coronation of Queen Victoria, and once again met his old opponent, the Duke of Wellington. Lady Salisbury thus describes their meeting: 'The Duke and Soult met in the music-room at the Queen's concert for the first time for many years, and shook hands. Soult's appearance is different from what I expected: he is a gentlemanlike old man with rather a benevolent cast of countenance, such as I should have expected in William Penn or Washington: tall and rather stooping, the top of the head bald ... The Duke, though the lines on his face are deeper, has a fresher colour and a brighter eye.'

The Duke of Dalmatia clung to the Orleanist dynasty till the end, and attended the last council held by Louis Philippe. He had a special liking for the Citizen Monarch, who reciprocated this affection, and had in 1847 re-established for the veteran the title of Marshal General of France, a designation held previously only by Turenne, Villars, and Saxe. With the fall of the dynasty he appeared no more in public, and at last, on November 26, 1851, château at St. Amand in his eighty-second year.

'Soult is able but too ambitious.' Thus Napoleon appreciated the Duke of Dalmatia when discussing the characters of his Marshals. But Soult was possessed of a crafty caution which seldom if ever allowed his ambition to hinder the success his ability deserved. Cold and calculating by nature, he knew exactly where to draw the line. The attempt to seize the throne of Portugal was the only occasion on which he seemed to throw caution to the winds, and those who knew him best were so astounded at his lack of circumspection that they could scarcely believe that he himself approved of the proclamations which appeared in Oporto. The hard, crafty nature of the Marshal was responsible for his many enemies among the officers of the army. His own staff never loved him, much as they marvelled at his indefatigable industry and his suppleness of mind, which permitted him to turn with ease from the highest political and strategic problems to the drudgery of administrative details, and bring to bear on all questions the cold, hard light of lucid reasoning. He could attract men to him by sheer admiration of his ability, but he could make no real friends, for those who came in contact with him soon discovered that he only thought of what he could make out of them, and then that he would drop them without the slightest regret. Sprung from the lower ranks of society, the Marshal had all the cunning and avarice of the typical bourgeois, and though he had the capacity to overcome his want of education, he had not the power to eradicate these inherent strains of character. Though not so rapacious as Masséna, the Duke of Dalmatia never withheld his hand when plunder offered itself and his home in Paris was decorated with magnificent objects of art filched from nearly every country in Europe. But though he allowed himself the luxury of taking what seized his fancy, he sternly repressed marauding on the part of his officers and men. Hence it was that, like Suchet, he was able to subdue the provinces committed to his charge and win the respect and obedience of the Spaniards. His methodical mind hated the idea of disorder; administration came to him as Nature's gift. Under his rule Andalusia gained a prosperity she had never before known. But we must remember that his success in this province was due not only to his great gift of administration, but also to his ambition, for it was the driving power of self-interest which supplied the energy which oiled the wheels of his system; for the Marshal hoped with the resources of Andalusia to supply the material and means to drive the English from Lisbon without the co-operation of King Joseph or the other French commanders. In striking contrast to the aversion with which he was regarded by his own fellow countrymen was the feeling of admiration with which he was viewed by his foes, and notably by his English adversaries in the Peninsula. They only saw the results of his great versatility and resource, and his acts of courtesy to those who fell into his power; while the discipline he maintained among his troops stood in striking contrast to the conduct of many of the other French commanders. Moreover, the Marshal was too politic to be cruel, and it was easy to guess that his proclamation against the Spaniards was really the work of the Emperor. That this was the case was borne out by the following letter written by Berthier at Napoleon's dictation: 'Let the Duke of Dalmatia know that I learn with indignation that some of the prisoners taken at Ocafia have been released and their arms restored to them. When I witness such behaviour I ask, "Is this treason or imbecility?" Is it then only French blood that is to flow in Spain without regret and without vengeance?' As a soldier the Marshal stands high among his compeers. In spite of his defeats at Oporto, Albuera, and Toulouse, throughout his career he clearly showed that he had the essential quality of a great commander, the ability to see and the capacity to perform what was possible with the material at hand. His strategic insight was great, he had a magnificent eye for country and the power of calmly surveying a field of battle, but, as Wellington pointed out, he had one great fault, for though 'he knew how to bring his troops to the field, he did not know so well how to use them when he had brought them up.' Thus it was that at Sorauren, after he had surprised Wellington and upset the whole of the English strategic plans, he was unable to win the battle which was necessary to reap the harvest of his labours. But the passage of the Pyrenees, the operations round Bayonne, and the retreat on Toulouse, will always be studied as examples of the most perfect military operations of their type. They show to the full the secret of the Marshal's success as a soldier, the blending of ardour with method and dash with caution. As a politician the Duke of Dalmatia met with little success; his methods were those of a dictator rather than those of a statesman. When the hour of action was passed he invariably showed weakness. But whatever were his faults, it must be laid to his credit that throughout the reign of Louis Philippe he lent all the weight of his great name and reputation to the maintenance of order at home and peace abroad.

6

JEAN LANNES, MARSHAL, DUKE OF MONTEBELLO

JEAN LANNES, the future Duke of Montebello, was born on April 10, 1769, the year which saw the birth of many famous soldiers, Napoleon, Wellington, Ney, and Soult. He was the fourth son of a peasant proprietor of Lectourne, a little town on the slopes of the Pyrenees. His family had long been settled in the commune of Omet, in the department of the Gironde. The first to rise to any sort of distinction was Jean's eldest brother, who showed at an early age such ability that the episcopal authorities of Lectourne educated him, and in due time he became a priest. It was to his brother, the abbé, that the young Jean owed such elements of learning as he possessed. But the pressure of need compelled his father to indenture him at an early age to a dyer in Lectourne. The young apprentice was of middle height, very well built, amazingly active, and able to bear the utmost fatigue. His face was pleasant and expressive, his eyes small and keen. Behind those eyes lay a brain of extraordinary activity, which was controlled by a boundless ambition. Enthiusiastic and passionate, Lannes' spirit could brook but little control. Action was the zest of his life. Administration and control came to him not as Nature's gifts, but as the result of his great common sense, which guided his ambition along the paths which led to success. A nature which could not endure the dullness of the dyer's trade in Lectourne could, however, compel the young soldier during the severest campaigns to give up part of his night's rest to study and to the expansion of his knowledge beyond the elements of reading, writing, and arithmetic, all the learning his brother, the abbé, had had time to impart to him. Even in the later years of his life the successful Marshal strove by midnight toil to educate himself up to the position his military talents had won for him.

Jean Lannes had already had a taste of the soldier's life before the outbreak of the revolutionary wars. But his uncontrollable temper had brought this short military experience to an abrupt end, and he had been compelled to return to his work at Lectourne after being wounded in a duel. His employer had greeted his return with the words, 'There is not the price of a drink to be made in the trade. Return to the army; you may perhaps become captain.' But Jean Lannes did not need such advice to drive him to the path of glory. In June, 1792, the Government of France called for volunteers to resist the coming invasion of the Duke of Brunswick's army. Lannes enlisted in the second battalion of the volunteers of Gers, and was at once elected sub-lieutenant by his fellow-citizens. This promotion he owed partly to his former military experience, partly to his personal magnetism, and partly to his extreme political opinions.

When Spain declared war on France the two battalions of Gers were sent to form part of the Army of the Eastern Pyrenees. There Lannes gained his first practical military experience. Both armies were extremely ill-disciplined, and ill-equipped. Consequently there was a great deal of desultory hand-to-hand fighting, in which the young sub lieutenant distinguished himself by his courage and talent. He enjoyed himself hugely fighting all day and dancing all night, when he could spare the time from his books. When military knowledge was almost entirely absent in the army, promotion came quickly to those who distinguished themselves by courage and zeal. On September 25, 1793, Lannes was promoted lieutenant. A month later, on October 21st, he was made captain of the grenadier company. Two months later, on Christmas Day, at the express desire of his chief, General Davout, he was given command of his battalion, and appointed colonel on the staff and acting adjutant-general. This distinction he gained for his brilliant conduct at Villelongue. Summoned from his bed in hospital to command the advance guard of five hundred men, he moved towards the main redoubt of the Spanish lines, and, refusing to be bluffed by the proposal of an armistice, captured the redoubt by a dashing charge. After the action he once again retired to hospital. His next exploit was the delicate mission entrusted to him by General Dugommier of releasing a great number of French émigrés who had been captured in battle, and who otherwise would have fallen victims to the popular fury. While devoting himself to his military duties he yet found time to fall in love. When in hospital at Perpignan, at the end of 1793, he had met Mademoiselle Méric, the daughter of a wealthy banker of that town; the friendship very soon developed into an ardent passion, and on March 19, 1795, the young couple were united, and the marriage seemed very advantageous for the young soldier of fortune, who was barely twenty-five.

After the treaty of Basle the battalions of Gers were brigaded with the old 53rd (regiment d'Alsace), and formed part of the troops which Schérer took to reinforce the Army of Italy in the summer of 1795. Accordingly, Lannes had the good fortune to take part in the battle of Loano, and once again greatly distinguished himself and was specially mentioned in despatches.

But during the winter of 1795-6 his successful career nearly came to an untimely end, for on the reorganisation of the army, along with many other officers, he was placed on half pay. Fortunately, at the moment he was retiring dejected to France, Bonaparte, assumed command of the Army of Italy. The new general felt he could ill spare a capable officer like Lannes, and consequently he retained him provisionally. The young colonel immediately justified his action. At the critical moment of the Austrian counter-attack at Dego, Lannes cleared the village by a brisk bayonet charge. Thereon Bonaparte gave him command of two battalions of grenadiers and one of carbineers, which formed part of his permanent advance guard under General Dallemagne. From this time onward Lannes had found his proper rôle. As nature had intended Marshal Ney for the command of a rear guard, and Murat for the command of cavalry, so she had equipped Lannes with those qualities which are specially required by the commander of an advance guard. Wiry and strong, he never knew what it was to be tired, and, never sparing himself, he never spared his men; his kind and cheery disposition and his personal magnetism carried all before him. His fiery enthusiasm swept aside all difficulties; his inventive genius ever showed him the way to surmount all obstacles. When danger was most pressing Lannes was there, the first to head the charge, the first to rally the discomfited. Never had Fortune a more zealous wooer. At Lodi he was the first man on the bridge. Later, at the head of three hundred men, he re-established order in Lombardy; at one time especially attached to the headquarter staff, at another hurried off to suppress some outbreak in the rear, at another repelling a determined sortie from Mantua, more and more, day by day, he made himself indispensable to his young chief. At the battle of Bassano, of the five flags wrested from the enemy Lannes captured two with his own hands. Wounded slightly at Bassano and more seriously at Governolo, he yet managed to creep out of hospital in time to take his place beside Bonaparte at Arcola. Early in the battle he received two flesh wounds and had to retire to have them dressed. Scarcely were they bandaged when the news arrived that Augereau's division had received a severe check. Oblivious of his wounds, he leapt on his horse and arrived at the head of his columns in time to see Augereau and Bonaparte, flag in hand, vainly attempting to rally their soldiers, only to be swept off the embankment into the marsh. But Lannes headed his grenadiers, and charging home on the Austrians, swept them back to the bridge-head, receiving in the charge yet another wound.

During the early months of 1797 he commanded a column at Bologna, and was present at the capitulation of Mantua. Thereafter he commanded the advance guard of Victor's army which invaded the Papal States. In front of Ancona he met with a characteristic adventure. Making a reconnaissance with two or three officers and half a dozen troopers, he suddenly found himself in the presence of three hundred of the enemy's cavalry. Their commander at once ordered his men to draw their swords preparatory to a charge. Whereon Lannes rode up to him and told him to order his men to return their swords, dismount, and lead their horses back to their headquarters. The officer obeyed. By sheer force of character Lannes thus dominated the situation and saved the lives of himself and his escort. After the preliminaries of peace at Leoben, Bonaparte employed him on several confidential missions, in which his impetuosity led him at times into difficulties, and the commander-in-chief was forced to write to the French Minister at Genoa, 'I have heard the reply that Lannes made to you. He is hot-headed, but a good fellow, and brave. I must write to him to tell him to be more civil to a minister of the Republic.'

Africa has often proved the grave of great military reputations. Napoleon himself only escaped the usual doom by deserting his army and suddenly appearing as a *deus ex machina* in the stormy field of politics at Paris. But though so fatal to those in supreme command, Africa has sometimes been the school from which the young officers have returned with enhanced reputations. It was from the companions who had stood the test of the fiery trial in Egypt and Syria that Bonaparte later selected his most trusted Marshals.

On May 19, 1798, Lannes sailed for Egypt in the Orient as an unattached general of brigade on the headquarters staff. For his successful action at the head of one of the assaulting columns in Malta he was appointed to the command of a brigade in Kléber's division. He took part in the capture of Alexandria, the march on Cairo, and the battles of Chebrass and the Pyramids; but it was not so much his success in these engagements which enhanced his worth in Bonaparte's eyes, as the fact that Lannes alone of all the general officers in Egypt did not share in the grumbling and depression which threatened to cripple the army after its arrival at Cairo. Soldiers and officers alike had but one desire - to return home. Lannes secretly informed Bonaparte of the plans of those who led the discontent, and, in the words of Murat, 'sold the cocoanut'. Thus he gained the future Emperor as his life-long friend and Murat as his life-long enemy. When in February, 1799, Bonaparte started for Syria, he took with him Lannes in command of Menou's division.

When Bonaparte found that his military reputation was likely to suffer by a more prolonged stay in Egypt, and above all that France was now ready to accept the rule of a dictator, he deserted his army in Egypt, leaving Kléber, whom he hated, in command; he took with him his most trustworthy officers, Lannes, Murat, Marmont, Andréossy, and Berthier, ordering Desaix to follow. The return to France, so longed for by most, was less agreeable to Lannes: while in hospital after the battle of Aboukir he had heard that his wife had given birth to a son whose father he could not be. Consequently one of his first acts on his return was to divorce her. But Bonaparte gave him little time to bewail his misfortune, for he relied on him, with Berthier, Murat, and Marmont, to debauch the army and bring it over to his side. Berthier's business was to win over the general staff,

Murat the cavalry, Marmont the artillery, and Lannes the infantry. Shortly after the coup d'état General Lannes was appointed commandant and inspector of the Consular Guard in preference to Murat. But this was a hollow victory over his rival, for when, after the Marengo campaign, these life-long enemies met in open rivalry for the hand of Caroline Bonaparte, the First Consul's sister, Murat, aided by Josephine, became the accepted suitor, and Lannes had to submit to see his hated rival in quick succession the brother-in-law of Napoleon, a Prince of the Holy Roman Empire, the crowned King of Naples, and, most bitter of all, the confidential friend of his idol.

It was in the Marengo campaign that the general had his first opportunity of distinguishing himself as an independent commander, and winning the renown which the victory of Montebello inseparably connects with his name. When Bonaparte made his famous march into Italy with the Army of the Reserve, he appointed Lannes to command the advance guard. The whole success of the operations depended on the rapidity with which they were carried out, for the First Consul, in his endeavour to get astride the Austrian line of communication, was exposing his flank to the enemy, and the French army, if beaten, had no other line of retreat save the terrible defiles of the Alps. Accordingly, Napoleon's selection of Lannes to command the advance guard is the highest possible testimony to his military ability. The battle of Montebello was Lannes's first independent engagement. In it he showed his genius for war. If he had allowed the Austrians to reoccupy Stradella he would have ruined the whole of Napoleon's scheme of operations, but, though his force was only a third of the enemy's, he remembered the advantage that comes to the assailant; instead of waiting in an entrenched position, he attacked, and by his indomitable courage and tenacity, and his tactical ability, he kept the enemy pinned to his entrenchments until the arrival of fresh troops under Victor enabled him to pulverise his foe. The battle was one of the finest of the campaign. 'The bones,' said Lannes, 'cracked in my division like glass in a hailstorm.'

At Marengo Lannes had to reverse his usual rôle and fight a rear-guard action, for during the early part of the engagement the French were outnumbered by thirty thousand men against eighteen thousand, and yet the general was able to report: 'I carried out my retirement by successive echelons under a devastating fire of artillery, amid successive charges of cavalry. I had not a single gun to cover my retreat, and yet it was carried out in perfect order.' The soldier who in the hour of success was full of impetuosity and élan, in the hour of retreat was able to inspire his troops with stubborn courage and unfailing self-confidence, which did much to secure the victory.

After Marengo came a period of peace. Lannes, as commander of the Consular Guard, had his headquarters in Paris, and, owing to his official position, was constantly in touch with Bonaparte. But, necessary as he was in war time, his companionship during peace was not altogether congenial to the First Consul, and as time went on it became almost distasteful. Although happily married to Mademoiselle Louise Antoinette Guéheneuc, the daughter of a senator, he felt himself aggrieved that Bonaparte had not supported his suit with Caroline, and was extremely jealous of many of the First Consul's friends. The constant bickering between Lannes and Murat never ceased. Moreover Lannes, as an out-and-out republican, treated the First Consul in a frank spirit of camaraderie, relying on his services at Arcola and Montebello. This Bonaparte not unnaturally resented. The increased ceremonial of the court and the prospect of the Concordat were abhorrent to the stern republicans, but necessary to establish the divinity which should at least seem to surround a throne. Relations became so strained that Bonaparte was soon glad to seize on any excuse to dismiss Lannes from his post. Murat and his tool Bessières provided him with a plausible reason. Lannes, by nature happy-go-lucky and no financier, wishing no doubt to please the First Consul, spent his money freely in lavish entertainment at his Paris house, and equipped the guard in most gorgeous uniforms. To meet these expenses he overdrew his account with the military authorities by more than three hundred thousand francs. Murat, hearing of this from Bessières, brought it to the First Consul's notice. Bonaparte at once summoned Lannes, rated him soundly, and commanded him immediately to refund the money. Murat was delighted; he thought that his enemy was certain to be disgraced. In his difficulty Lannes turned to his old friend and former chief, Augereau, who at once lent him the money and refused to take any security. But although he was thus able to refund the money, Bonaparte dismissed him from the command of the Guard. Still, remembering his war service and thinking that he might be useful again later, he did not disgrace him utterly, but at the end of 1801 sent him as ambassador to Portugal.

Lannes's diplomatic career was at first not very successful. English influence was all-powerful at Lisbon and the new envoy had not the talent to counteract it. In the autumn of 1802, thinking himself slighted by the Portuguese authorities, without consulting Talleyrand, he suddenly withdrew from Lisbon and returned to France. But at Orleans he received an angry message from Bonaparte forbidding him to return to Paris. The First Consul meanwhile addressed peremptory messages to the court of Lisbon about the supposed insult offered to his ambassador. Thereon the Portuguese Foreign Minister apologised and Lannes returned. Angry as Bonaparte was at the moment, he confessed later that Lannes' soldierly impetuosity had served the cause of France better than the skilfulness of a consummate diplomat. For from this time onwards French influence began to increase at Lisbon, Lannes was courted by the minister, and the Prince Regent himself stood godfather to his son. The story goes that after the ceremony the Prince Regent took the ambassador into a salon of the palace where the diamonds from Brazil were stored, and then gave him a handful, saying, 'That is for my godson,' then a second handful for the mother, and a third for himself. Whatever the truth of the story, the fact remains that Lannes returned to France a rich man, able not only to repay his loan to Augereau but to indulge in fresh extravagance.

From Lisbon the ambassador was summoned to attend the coronation of the Emperor and to take his place among the Marshals. But he was not yet received back into full favour by the Emperor, and had to return to his embassy at Lisbon. It was not till March 22, 1805, that he was recalled to France to command the right wing of the Army of the Ocean, which, when war broke out between Austria and France, became the Grand Army. The fifth corps under Lannes reached the Rhine at Kehl on September 25th. Napoleon's scheme of operations was, by making vigorous demonstrations in the direction of the Black Forest, to persuade the Austrians that be was advancing in force in that direction, while all the time his wings were sweeping round the Austrian rear and cutting their line of communication on the Danube, in the direction of Ratisbon. The task of deceiving the Austrians was performed to perfection by Murat with the reserve cavalry and Lannes's corps. Immediately after Mack's surrender at Ulm, the Emperor detached Lannes and Murat in pursuit of the Archduke Ferdinand, who had successfully broken through the ring of French troops. Lannes's infantry tramped sturdily behind Murat's cavalry, and fighting proceeded day and night. The soldiers marched thirteen, fourteen, and fifteen hours a day, and captured in five days fifteen thousand men with eleven colours, one hundred and twenty-eight guns, and six hundred limbers and provision wagons.

During the rapid advance down the Danube on Vienna, the fifth corps continued in close support of Murat's cavalry. Vienna capitulated and the Marshals pressed on to seize the bridge before the city. The defence of the bridge had been entrusted to General Auersperg, with seven thousand men. The bridge was commanded by a battery of artillery, and the engineers were preparing to blow it up when Murat, Lannes, and Bertrand arrived. The three general officers quietly walked down to the bridge and shouted out to the Austrian picquets that an armistice had been arranged. Thereon the commander of the picquet proceeded to withdraw his men and sent word to Auersperg. Meanwhile the three officers strolled unconcernedly across, while a considerable way behind them a strong body of Lannes's infantry followed. When the French generals reached the Austrian end they found a sergeant of engineers actually proceeding to fire the fuse. Lannes caught him by the arm and snatched the match from his hand, telling him that it was a crime to blow up the bridge, and that he would be disgraced if he did such a thing. Then the two Marshals ran up to the officers commanding the artillery who, growing restive at the continual advance of the French infantry, were preparing to open fire. Meanwhile Auersperg himself arrived, and the Marshals told him the same tale, affirming that the French were to occupy the bridge-head. Uncertain, like his subordinates, and but half convinced, he allowed himself to be bluffed, and thus Napoleon secured without dispute the crossing of the Danube. The boldness and audacity of the scheme so successfully carried out by Murat and Lannes, difficult as it is to condone from a moral point of view, brings out with great clearness the audacity, sangfroid, and resourcefulness, of both these Marshals.

The successful crossing of the Danube was soon followed by the decisive battle of Austerlitz. The battle was brought on by Napoleon impressing the Allies with the idea that it was possible to slip past the French left flank and surround him, much as he had surrounded Mack at Ulm. For this purpose the right under Davout was drawn back and concealed by skilful use of the ground. The centre under Soult and the left under Lannes were to hold their ground until the Russian left was absolutely compromised, when Soult was to push forward, and, seizing the commanding hill of Pratzen, to cut the Russian force in two, while Lannes and Murat were to fall with all their weight on the isolated Russian right. For once Murat and Lannes laid aside their jealousy and worked hand in hand, and the success of the French left was due to the perfect combination of infantry and cavalry. Of the Russian right, seven thousand five hundred were made prisoners, and two colours and twenty-seven pieces of artillery were captured. But hardly had the battle ceased when bickerings broke out again, and Lannes, thinking Napoleon did not appreciate him, sent in his resignation, which the Emperor, much to his surprise, accepted.

The Marshal spent the greater part of the year 1806 in retirement at his native town of Lectourne, where he was joyfully received by his erstwhile neighbours and friends. He was always popular with his fellow-citizens, not only because of his republican ideas and his unaffected simplicity, but because he never forgot those who at any time had befriended him - a man who had once lent him a thousand francs was presented with a beautiful house and garden; the old soldier who had carried him out of the trenches at St. Jean d'Acre was established as a local postmaster, and received a small property and an annuity, and the Marshal never passed the house without going in, taking a meal with him, and making presents to the wife and children. On one occasion Lannes was attending a big official reception at Auch. On his way, he passed a peasant whom he recognised as one of the playfellows of his boyhood; strongly moved, the Marshal when he arrived at the prefecture, asked the prefect if he might invite one of his friends to the luncheon. The prefect was charmed, but much surprised when an aide-de-camp returned with the peasant, whom Lannes embraced, placed by his side, and soon set at ease.

But war once again caused the Emperor to summon his fiery lieutenant. Lannes took command of the fifth corps on October 5, 1806, and five days later had the satisfaction of beating a strong Prussian force at Saalfeld. From Saalfeld the Marshal pushed on towards Jena, near which town, early on October 13th, his scouts came in contact with a large Prussian force under Hohenlohe. His small force was in considerable danger, but Napoleon at once hurried up all possible reinforcements. The Prussians held an apparently impregnable position on the Landgrafenberg, a precipitous hill which commanded the town. But during the night a local pastor pointed out to the French a track, which led up to the summit, which the Prussians had neglected to occupy. Working all night, the French sappers made a road up which guns could be hauled by hand, and on the morning of the 14th the corps of Lannes, Augereau, and the Guard were safely drawn up on the plateau of the Landgrafenberg, while Ney and Soult continued the line to the north. A heavy mist overhung the field of battle, and Hohenlohe was confident that he was only opposed by the fifth corps, and his surprise was immense when the fog lifted and he found himself confronted by the French army. The battle commenced by Lannes seizing the village of Vierzehn Heiligen. While the Prussians were fully occupied in attempting to hold this village, Napoleon threw his flanks round them, and the battle ended in the annihilation of Hohenlohe's army. In the evening Napoleon learned that on the same day Davout had completely defeated the main Prussian army at Auerstädt. Thereon he sent forward his various corps to seize all the important fortresses of Prussia, and detailed Lannes to support Murat in pursuit of the Prussian troops under Hohenlohe and Blücher, which retreated in the direction of the Oder. If the battle of Jena had been followed by peace, as had happened after Austerlitz in the previous year, it is more than probable that once again Lannes would have thrown up his command, for when the bulletin appeared, the part that his corps had taken was almost entirely neglected. The Marshal's letter to his wife showed that he was vexed beyond words with his treatment by Napoleon, and he started out in the worst of tempers to support Murat. But he was too keen a soldier to let his personal grievances interfere with his active work, and, although he gave vent to his spleen in the usual recriminations, he performed his work to admiration. So hard did he push his infantry, marching sixty miles in forty-eight hours, that he was never more than five miles behind the light cavalry, and it was owing to his effective support that, on October 28th, Murat was able to surround Hohenlohe and force him to surrender at Prinzlow. But, in spite of this, Murat in his despatch never mentioned the name of Lannes. It took all Napoleon's tact to smooth the Marshal's ruffled temper, and it was only the prospect of further action which ultimately prevented him from throwing up his command in high dudgeon.

By the beginning of November the theatre of war was virtually transferred from Prussia to Poland. As after Ulm, so after Jena, the Russians appeared on the scene too late to give effective aid to their allies, but in sufficient time to prevent the war from ending. Napoleon, who always had an intense esteem for the Marshal's common sense and military ability, asked him at this time to furnish a confidential report on the possibilities of Poland as a theatre of war, and the Marshal, with his keen insight into character, replied, 'I am convinced that if you attempt to make the Poles rise on our behalf, within a fortnight they will be more against us than for us.'

The French troops crossed the Vistula at Warsaw, and encountered 'the fifth element, mud'. Led by Murat, unable to make headway in mud up to their knees, baffled by the Fabian tactics of the Russians, and lacking the mighty brain of their Emperor, the Marshals fought without co-operation, each for his own glory. Lannes was as bad as the rest, showing in his refusal to give due praise to his brother generals for their help at Pultusk the same petty spirit of which he had complained in Murat. During the long winter weeks spent in cantonments along the Vistula, the Marshal was ill with fever, in hospital at Warsaw, and was not able to return to the head of his corps in time for the bloody battle of Eylau. During May he commanded the covering force at the siege of Dantzig, and was summoned thence to take part in the last phase of the campaign. The Russian General, Bennigsen, allowed himself to be outgeneralled by Napoleon, and the French were soon nearer Königsberg than the Russians. Bennigsen made desperate efforts to retrieve his mistake, and on June 13th actually managed to throw himself across the Alle at Friedland, just at the moment that Lannes arrived on the scene. The Marshal at once saw his opportunity. The Russians were drawn up with the Alle at their backs, so that retreat was impossible, and only victory could save them. The Marshal's design, therefore, was to hold the enemy till the main French army arrived. Bennigsen made the most determined efforts to throw him off, attempting to crush him by superior weight of horsemen and artillery. But the Marshal held on to him grimly, and by magnificent handling of Oudinot's grenadiers, the Saxon horse, and Grouchy's dragoons, he maintained his position in spite of all the Russian efforts during the night of June 13th. On the morning of the 14th, with ten thousand troops opposed to forty thousand, he fought for four hours without giving ground, skilfully availing himself of every bit of wood and cover, till at last reinforcements arrived. When the main French columns were deployed, Lannes, with the remnant of his indomitable corps, had a brief period of rest. But during the last phase of the battle the enemy made a desperate effort to break out of the trap through his shattered corps, and once again the Marshal led his troops with invincible élan, and drove the Russians right into the death-trap of Friedland.

Tilsit followed, and Napoleon showered honours on his trusty lieutenants. On June 30, 1807, he gave to Lannes the principality of Sievers in the department of Kalish, and on March 19, 1808, he conferred on him a greater honour when he created him Duke of Montebello in memory of his famous victory.

The Duke of Montebello spent his days of peace for the most part at Lectourne. He was summoned thence in October, 1808, to accompany the Emperor to Erfurt, and there the Czar Alexander made a special hero of his old adversary of Austerlitz, Pultusk, and Friedland, and presented him with the grand cordon of the Order of St. Andrew.

The period between Tilsit and Erfurt gave Lannes the last peaceful days that he ever spent, for from Erfurt be was hurried off again to war, this time to Spain. As usual when there was hard fighting in prospect, Napoleon knew that he could ill afford to do without his most trusty and able lieutenant. But Lannes had but little enthusiasm for the Spanish War. His reputation stood so high that there was little chance of enhancing it, and by now the fire-eating republican soldier was settling down into a quiet country gentleman, who preferred the domestic circle and the pleasure of playing the grand seigneur before an audience of friends to the stir of the camp and the pomp of the court. But he was too well drilled in soldier instincts to refuse to serve when summoned by his chief, and accordingly, much against his will, he set out on what he expected to be a short inglorious campaign of a couple of months against a disorganised provincial militia.

Lannes accompanied the Emperor on his journey to Spain, attached to the headquarter staff without any definite command, for the Emperor knew that all was not well with the armies there, but he could not, until he had himself looked into the question, decide where he could use to the best advantage the great administrative and tactical ability of the Duke of Montebello. During the hurried crossing of the mountains of Tolosa the Marshal had the misfortune to be thrown from his horse. So severe were the injuries he received that it seemed impossible to take him beyond Vittoria, but Larrey, the Emperor's surgeon, ordered him to be wrapped in the bloody skin of a newly killed sheep; so successful was the prescription that the Marshal was soon able to follow the Emperor and rejoin headquarters. On his arrival the Emperor sent him to take over Moncey's corps of thirty-five thousand men, with orders to attack Castaños's forty-nine thousand at Tudela, while Ney, with twelve thousand, worked round the Spanish rear. On the morning of November 28th Lannes attacked the Spaniards at Tudela and won an easy victory, for the Aragonese, under Palafox, thought only of Saragossa, and the Valencians and Andalusians, under Castaños, of their line of retreat to the south. Lannes, seeing the exaggerated length of the Spanish position, at once divined the reason, and drove home an overwhelming attack against their weak centre. Successful as the battle was, it had not the far-reaching effects Napoleon had desired, for, owing to the mountainous nature of the ground, Ney was unable to get across the Spanish line of retreat; however, the enemy lost four thousand men at Tudela and, what was more important, all their artillery.

The battle of Tudela opened the road to Madrid. But when Napoleon arrived there, instead of driving the remnants of the Spanish armies before him and sweeping down to Seville, he found that there was a pressing danger in the north. To give the scattered Spaniards a chance of rallying, Sir John Moore was making a bold advance on Madrid, and was close to Salamanca. Napoleon at once ordered Lannes to hand over his corps to Moncey and to join headquarters. The corps of Ney and a part of Victor's corps were sent off to oppose the English, and on December 28th Napoleon and the Duke of Montebello set out to overtake them. The weather was awful, and the passage of the mountain passes in face of the blizzards of snow tried the endurance of the troops to the uttermost. Lannes, in spite of the fact that he had not entirely recovered from his fall, joined Napoleon in setting an example to the troops. At the head of the column marched the Emperor with one arm linked to Lannes and the other to Duroc. When completely worn out by the unaccustomed efforts and by the weight of their riding boots, the Emperor and Lannes at times took a brief rest on the limber of a gun carriage, and then got down and marched again.

When Napoleon handed over the pursuit to Soult, he despatched the Duke of Montebello to take command of the corps of Junot and Moncey at Saragossa. On his arrival, on January 22, 1809, the Marshal found that the garrison of Saragossa was in much better heart than the besiegers, for on the west the third corps, owing to illness and fatigue, numbered barely thirteen thousand, and Gazan's division across the Ebro, before the eastern suburb, was scarcely seven thousand strong, while the total strength of the garrison was almost sixty thousand. Consequently Junot and Gazan were seriously contemplating raising the siege. Lannes's first duty was to restore the morale of the troops; to reprimand the general officers, who had been slack in their duty; to set an example to them by his fiery diligence, which refused to let him go to bed once during the whole of the first week he was before Saragossa; to restore the courage of the troops by daily exposing his life in the trenches, and, when necessary, reconnoitring in person with the utmost sangfroid right up to the Spanish positions; supervising hospitals, reorganising commissariat, planning with the engineer officers new methods of sap - in a word, to be everywhere and to do everything. Nothing can more clearly illustrate Napoleon's dictum, 'A la guerre les hommes ne sont rien, c'est un homme qui est tout.' Within five days of Lannes's taking over command the whole complexion of the situation had altered. The French were making the most resolute assaults with irresistible élan, carrying out the most difficult street-fighting with the greatest zest, sapping, mining, and blowing up convents and fortified posts, fighting above ground and below ground, suffering the most terrible losses, yet ever eager to fight again. By February 11th, thanks to the new morale of the troops, and to the fact that dysentery and enteric were playing havoc in the garrison, Lannes had captured house by house the western half of the town, and had arrived at the Corso. But once again murmurings broke out among the French troops, who had by now lost a fourth of their numbers, and at the same time a strong force of Spaniards under Palafox's brothers threatened to overwhelm Suchet, who was covering the siege. Lannes proved superior to all difficulties; by his fiery speeches and tact he reanimated both officers and men, pointing out to them the triumph they had already won in penning in fifty thousand Spaniards with a mere handful. Then, hurrying off with reinforcements for Suchet, he dug the covering force into an entrenched position on the heights of Villa Mayor, and four days later was back at Saragossa in time to superintend the attack across the Corso. On February 18th the French captured the suburb on the left bank of the river, and thus placed the inner town between two fires.

Disease and the success of their enemies had taken all the heart out of the Spanish defence, and on February 20th Palafox surrendered. Between December 21st and February 21st the Spanish losses had been fifty-four thousand dead from wounds and disease, and Saragossa itself was but a heap of crumbling ruins. Lannes did all in his power to alleviate the sufferings of the unfortunate inhabitants, yet in spite of all his efforts another ten thousand died within the next month. Unfortunately also for his reputation the Marshal, acting on distinct orders from Napoleon, treated his military prisoners with extreme severity and executed two of the most prominent. The great strain of the siege told heavily on the health of the Marshal, who had never completely recovered from his accident near Tolosa; accordingly, after refitting the corps under his command, he handed them over to Mortier and Junot, and at the end of March set out for Lectourne. But his stay there was short, for Napoleon, with the Spanish and Austrian wars on his hands, could not afford to do without his assistance.

By April 25th Lannes found himself once again at the post of danger, but this time on the Danube, at the battle of Abensberg. As he himself said, the first rumour of war always made him shiver, but as soon as he had taken the first step forward he had no thought but for his profession. But, much as he would have liked to dally at Lectourne, and much as he grumbled at Napoleon's overweening ambition, once at the front he was the dashing soldier of the first Italian campaign. He arrived in time to take his share in the five days' fighting at Abensberg, Landshut, Eckmühl, and Ratisbon. At Ratisbon he had an opportunity of showing that time had had no effect on his spirit; after two storming parties had been swept away, he called for volunteers for a third attempt: none stepped forward, and he himself rushed to seize a ladder. His staff held him back; but the lesson was not in vain: volunteers crowded to seize the scaling ladders, led by two of the Marshal's aides-de-camp, and soon the walls of Ratisbon were crowned with French soldiers and the town was won.

Napoleon himself accompanied Lannes on the march to Vienna, and the Marshal was perfectly happy. Murat was absent, and there was no evil influence to cloud his friendship with his great chief. Once again Vienna succumbed without a shot, but this time the Austrians took care that there was no bridge over which Napoleon might cross the Danube. Accordingly, the Emperor determined to bridge the river below Vienna, making use of the Isle of Lobau, which lay two-thirds of the way across. The bridge from the south bank to Lobau was built under the personal supervision of the Emperor and Lannes, and on one occasion when they were reconnoitring in person they both fell into the river and the Marshal, who was out of his depth, was pulled out by the Emperor himself.

By May 20th the French army was concentrated in Lobau, and on May 21st a crossing was effected by several bridges, and assured by Masséna occupying the village of Aspern and Lannes that of Essling. By the morning of the 22nd the mass of the French army had reached the north bank of the river. Napoleon, who perceived that the Austrian line was too extended to be strong, gave the command of the centre to Lannes with orders to sally, forth from between the villages of Aspern and Essling and break the enemy's centre. In spite of a devastating artillery fire, the Marshal carried out his orders to perfection, making skilful use of his infantry and cavalry. He had actually forced back the Austrians when he was recalled by Napoleon, who had just heard that the enemy had succeeded in breaking the bridge by sending huge masses of timber down the swollen river. Lannes retreated slowly on Essling, his troops suffering severely from the re-formed Austrian batteries. While thus holding the foe in check the Marshal was struck on the knee by a cannon ball which ricocheted off the ground just in front of him.

He was removed to the rear, and the doctors decided that it was necessary to amputate the right leg. The Marshal bore the operation well. He was moved to Vienna, and sent for the celebrated mechanician, Mesler, to make him a false leg, but unfortunately the hot weather affected the wound and mortification set in. The Emperor, in spite of his anxieties, came daily to visit him, and the dying hero had the last consolation of seeing how much he was valued by his august master and friend. The end came soon. On May 30th the Duke of Montebello died, and Napoleon, on hearing the news, with tears in his eyes cried out, 'What a loss for France and for me!'

The death of Lannes removed the first of Napoleon's chosen Paladins, and, in the opinion of the Emperor himself, perhaps the greatest soldier of them all. At St. Helena the fallen Emperor thus appraised his old comrade: 'Lannes was a man of extraordinary bravery. Calm under fire, he possessed a sure and penetrating coup d'œil; he had great experience in war. As a general he was infinitely superior to Moreau and Soult.' But high as this eulogy is, the fact remains that Lannes was lucky in the time of his death: Fortune had not yet set her face against Napoleon's arms, and he was spared the terrors of the Russian retreat, the terrible fighting at Leipzig, and the gloom and misery of the winter campaign in France. That Lannes would have emerged superior to these trials his previous career affords strong reason to presume. Yet, brilliant as were his actions at Montebello, Saalfeld, Pultusk, and Tudela, masterly as were his operations at the siege of Saragossa, they only prove the Marshal's command of the technique of tactics. As Davout has pointed out, the Duke of Montebello had never an opportunity of showing his ability in the field of grand tactics or in the higher conceptions of strategy; he was a past master in the art of manœuvring twenty-five thousand infantry, but he had never the opportunity of devising and carrying out a complete campaign, involving the handling of hundreds of thousands of men and the successful solution of problems both military and political. 'The Roland of the French Army' had by nature many qualities which go to form a great soldier. His bravery was undoubted; before Ney he was called 'the Bravest of the Brave'. He had personal qualities which inspired his troops with his own courage and élan. He had the military eye, and a mind of extraordinary activity, which worked best when under the pressure of necessity and danger. He was physically strong and able to endure fatigue, and he had great capacity for taking pains. But his temper was often at fault, causing him to burst into fits of uncontrollable rage, while from jealousy he was apt to sulk and refuse to co-operate with his fellows. If an officer failed to grasp his meaning he would storm at him, and attempt himself to carry out the task. But on one occasion he heard the Emperor cry out, 'That devil Lannes possesses all the qualities of a great commander, but he will never be one, because he cannot master his temper, and is constantly bickering with his subalterns, the greatest fault that a commander can make.' From that day forward Lannes made the resolution to command his temper, and, in spite of his nature, his self-control became extraordinary. But though he conquered this weakness, he never overcame his jealousy of his fellow Marshals and generals. Again and again he threw up his command because he thought he was slighted or that others were preferred to him. At times he broke out into violent tirades against the Emperor himself, and on one occasion, in his jealousy, told him that Murat, his brother-in-law, was 'a mountebank, a tight-rope dancer'. Napoleon remonstrated with him, exclaiming, 'It is I alone who give you both glory and success.' Lannes, livid with anger, retaliated, 'Yes, yes, because you have marched up to your ankles in gore on this bloody field, you think yourself a great man; and your emplumed brother-in-law crows on his own dunghill ... Twelve thousand corpses lying on the plain to keep the field for your honour ... and yet to deny me - to me, Lannes - my due share in the honours of the day!' On the day before his death he could not resist humiliating his hated enemy, Bessières, whom Napoleon had put under his command, and he actually insulted him on the field of battle by sending a junior aide-de-camp to tell the Marshal 'to charge home', implying that he was shirking his duty.

As a man, Lannes was warm-hearted and beloved by his family, his staff, and his men. Rough diamond as he was, he was truly one of nature's gentlemen. He never forgot a friend, though he seldom if ever forgave an enemy. His sympathies were essentially democratic; himself one of the people, he believed thoroughly in republican ideas. Outspoken to a fault, he would flare out against Napoleon himself, but one kind word from his great chief would cause him to forget all his bitterness. His impetuosity and his republican ideals of equality were, naturally, extremely offensive on occasions to the Emperor and the new nobility, and Lannes, in spite of all his efforts, was too genuine to conceal his hatred of all flunkeyism. It was this Gascon self-confidence, blended with singular amiability of character, which, while it offended the court, attached to the Marshal his soldiers and the provincial society of Lectourne, where even to this day the name of the Duke of Montebello is held in the most affectionate esteem and regard.

7

MICHEL NEY, MARSHAL, DUKE OF ELCHINGEN, PRINCE OF MOSKOWA

'Go on, Ney; I am satisfied with you; you will make your way.' So spoke a captain of hussars to a young recruit who had attracted his attention. The captain little thought that the zealous stripling would one day become a Marshal of France, the Prince of Moskowa, and famed throughout Europe as the 'Bravest of the Brave'. Still, the youth had presentiments of future greatness. Born on January 10, 1769, the son of a poor cooper, of Sarrelouis, more German than French, Michel Ney, at the age of fifteen, was possessed with the idea that he was destined for distinction. His father and mother tried to persuade him to become a miner, but nothing would please the high-spirited boy save the life of a soldier. Accordingly on February 1, 1787, he tramped off to Metz and enlisted as a private in the regiment known as the Colonel General's Hussars. Physically strong, unusually active, by nature a horseman, he soon attracted the attention of his comrades by his skill in menage and his command of the sabre, and was chosen to represent his regiment in a duel against the fencing master of another regiment of the garrison. Unfortunately for Ney, the authorities got wind of the affair in time to prevent any decision being arrived at, and the young soldier was punished for breaking regulations by a term of imprisonment; but no sooner was he released than he again challenged his opponent. This time there was no interference, and Ney so severely wounded his adversary that he was unable to continue his profession. Though he thus early in his career distinguished himself by his bravery, tenacity, and disregard of rules, it must not for a moment be thought that he was a mere swashbuckler. With the determination to rise firmly before his eyes, he set about, from the day he enlisted, to learn thoroughly the rudiments of his profession, and to acquire a knowledge of French and the faculty of reading and writing; thus he was able to pass the necessary tests, and quickly gained the rank of sergeant. Ney was fortunate in that he had not to spend long years as a non-commissioned officer with no obvious future before him. The Revolution gave him the opportunity so long desired by Masséna and others, and it was as lieutenant that he started on active service with Dumouriez's army in 1793. Once on active service it was not long before his great qualities made themselves recognised. Though absolutely uncultivated, save for the smattering of reading and writing which he had picked up in the regimental school, and to outward appearances rather heavy and stupid, in the midst of danger he showed an energy, a quickness of intuition, and a clearness of understanding which hurled aside the most formidable obstacles. Physical fear he never knew; as he said, when asked if he ever felt afraid, 'No, I never had time.' In his earliest engagements at Neerwinden and in the north of France, he foreshadowed his future career by the extraordinary bravery and resource he showed in handling his squadron of cavalry during the retreat, on one occasion, with some twenty hussars, completely routing three hundred of the enemy's horse. This achievement attracted the attention of General Kléber, who sent for Captain Ney and entrusted him with the formation of a body of franc-tireurs of all arms. The franc-tireurs were really recognised brigands. They received no pay or arms and lived entirely on plunder, but were extremely useful for scouting and reconnaissance, and collected a great deal of information under a dashing officer. From this congenial work Ney was summoned in 1796 to command the cavalry of General Coland's division in the Army of the Sambre and Meuse. There he distinguished himself by capturing Würzburg and two thousand of the enemy with a squadron of one hundred hussars. After this exploit General Kléber refused to listen to his remonstrances and insisted on his accepting his promotion as general of brigade. At the commencement of the campaign of 1797 Ney had the misfortune to be taken prisoner at Giessen. While covering the retreat with his cavalry, he saw a horse artillery gun deserted by its men. Galloping back by himself, he attempted to save the piece, but the enemy's horse swept down and captured him. His captivity was not long: his exchange was soon effected, and he returned to France in time to join in the agitation against the party of the Clicheans, the only occasion he actively interfered in politics.

On the re-opening of the war in 1799 Ney was sent to command the cavalry of the Army of the Rhine. The campaign was notable for an exploit which admirably illustrates the secret of his success as a soldier. The town of Mannheim, held by a large Austrian garrison, was the key of Southern Germany. The French army was separated from this fortress by the broad Rhine. The enemy was confident that any attempt on the fortress must be preceded by the passage of the river by the whole French army. But Ney, hearing that the enemy's troops were cantonned in the villages surrounding the town, saw that if a small French force could be smuggled across by night, it might be possible to seize the town by a coup-de-main. The most important thing to ascertain was the exact position of the cantonments of the troops outside the fortress and of the various guards and sentinels inside the town. So important did he consider this information that he determined to cross the river himself and reconnoitre the position in person. Accordingly, general of division as he was, he disguised himself as a Prussian, and trusting to his early knowledge of German, he crossed the river secretly, and carefully noted all the enemy's preparations, running the risk of being found out and shot as a spy. The following evening, with a weak detachment, he again crossed the river, attacked the enemy's guards with the bayonet, drove back a sortie of the garrison, and entered the town pell-mell with the flying enemy; and under cover of the darkness, which hid the paucity of his troops, he bluffed the enemy into surrender. The year 1800 brought him further glory under Masséna and Moreau, and he became known throughout the armies of France as the 'Indefatigable'.

After the Treaty of Lunéville, the First Consul summoned Ney to Paris, and won his affection by the warmth with which he received him. On his departure Bonaparte presented him with a sword. 'Receive this weapon,' he said, 'as a souvenir of the friendship and esteem I have towards you. It belonged to a pasha who met his death bravely on the field of Aboukir.' The sword became Ney's most treasured possession : he was never tired of handling it, and he never let it go out of his sight; but he little thought what ill luck it would bring him later, for it was this famous sword which, in 1815, revealed to the police his hiding-place, and thus indirectly led him to death. The relations between Ney and the First Consul soon became closer. The general married a great friend of Hortense Beauharnais, Mademoiselle Auguie, the daughter of Marie Antoinette's lady in waiting. Sure of his devotion and perceiving the sternness with which he obeyed orders, in 1802 the First Consul entrusted him with the subjugation of Switzerland. The Swiss army fled before him, and a deputation, charged to make their submission to France, arrived in his camp with the keys of the principal towns. The general met them, listened courteously to their words of submission, then with a wave of the hand refused the keys. With that insight which later led him to warn Napoleon against attempting to trample on the people of Spain and Russia, he replied to the deputation, 'It is not the keys I demand: my cannon can force your gates; bring me hearts full of submission, worthy of the friendship of France.' Soon afterwards, with Soult and Davout, Ney was honoured with the command of one of the corps in the army which the First Consul was assembling for the invasion of England. In selecting him for this important post Napoleon showed that power of discrimination which contributed so greatly to his success. For, save in the raid into Switzerland, Ney had not yet been called upon to deal with complicated questions of administration and finance. His reputation rested purely on his extraordinary dash and bravery in the face of the enemy and his power of using to the full the élan which lies latent in all French armies. For when not in touch with the enemy he was notoriously indolent. He never made any attempt to learn the abstract science of war, and until stirred by danger his character seemed to slumber. Others judged him as the Emperor did at St. Helena when he said, 'He was the bravest of men; there terminated all his faculties.' But, in spite of this limitation in his character, Napoleon employed him again and again in positions of responsibility, for he knew that Ney's word once passed was never broken, that his devotion to France and to its ruler was steadfast, that in spite of his peevishness and his fierce outbursts of temper and bitter tirades, when it came to deeds there would be no wavering. Consequently the First Consul availed himself gladly of his great reputation for bravery, considering that hero worship did more to turn the young recruits into soldiers than the greatest organising and administrative talents. Moreover, Napoleon kept an eye on the composition of the staff of his Marshals and generals, and he knew that Ney had in Jomini, the chief of his staff, a man of admirable talent and sagacity, who would turn in their proper direction the sledge-hammer blows of the 'Bravest of the Brave'.

With the creation of the Empire Ney was included among the Paladins of the new Charlemagne and received hi Marshal's baton, the Grand Cross of the Legion of Honour, and the Order of the Christ of Portugal. But the new Marshal cared little for the life of a courtier, much as he prized his military distinctions. Banquets and feasting offered little attraction to the hero, and he despised riches and rank. 'Gentlemen,' said he one day to his aides-de-camp, who were boasting of their families and rich appointments, 'Gentlemen, I am more fortunate than you: I got nothing from my family, and I esteemed myself rich at Metz when I had two loaves of bread on the table.' Accordingly, no young subaltern thirsting for glory was happier than Marshal Ney when, in August, 1805, the order came to march on Austria. The campaign, so suddenly commenced, brought the Marshal the hard fighting and the glory he loved so well. In the operations round Ulm, he surpassed himself by the tenacity with which he stuck to the enemy, and, thanks to the skill of Jomini, his errors only added to his fame, and the combat of Etchingen became immortal when Napoleon selected this name as a title for the Marshal when he created him Duke. During the fighting which penned the Austrians into Ulm, two sides of the Marshal's character were clearly seen - his extraordinary bravery and his jealousy. The Emperor, anxious for the complete success of his plans, despatched an officer to command Ney to avoid incurring a repulse and to await reinforcements. The aide-de-camp found him in the faubourg of the town amongst the skirmishers. He delivered his message, whereupon the Marshal replied, 'Tell the Emperor that I share the glory with no one; I have already provided for a flank attack.' In September, 1806, Ney was ordered to march to Würzburg to join the Grand Army for the war against Prussia. The campaign gave him just those opportunities which he knew so well how to seize, and before the end of the war the Emperor had changed his sobriquet from the 'Indefatigable' to the 'Bravest of the Brave'. But glorious as his conduct was, his rash impetuosity more than once seriously compromised Napoleon's plans. At Jena his rashness and his jealousy of his fellow Marshals caused him to advance before the other corps had taken up their positions. His isolated attack was defeated by the Prussians, and it took the united efforts of Lannes and Soult to rally his shattered battalions and snatch victory from the enemy. But his personal bravery at Jena, his brilliant pursuit of the enemy, the audacity with which he bluffed fourteen thousand Prussians to surrender at Erfurt, and his capture of twenty-three thousand prisoners and eight hundred cannon at the great fortress of Magdeburg made ample amends for his errors.

But glorious as was his success, his impetuosity soon brought him into further disgrace. Detached from the main army on the Lower Vistula in the spring of 1807, he advanced against a mixed force of Prussians and Russians before Napoleon had completed all his plans. The Emperor was furious, and Berthier was ordered to write that 'The Emperor has, in forming his plans, no need of advice or of any one acting on his own responsibility: no one knows his thoughts; it is our duty to obey.' But to obey orders when in contact with the enemy was just what the fiery soldier was unable to do, and the Emperor, recognising this full well, ordered his chief of the staff to write that 'His Majesty believes that the position of the enemy is due to the rash manoeuvre made by Marshal Ney.' When the main advance commenced the Marshal was summoned to rejoin the Grand Army. He did not arrive in time to take any prominent share in the bloody battle of Eylau; in spite of every exertion, his corps only reached the field of battle as darkness set in. The sight of the awful carnage affected even the warworn Marshal, and made him exclaim, 'What a massacre!' and, as he added, 'without any issue.' Friedland was a battle after Ney's own heart. He arrived on the field at the moment Napoleon was opening his grand attack, and with his corps he was ordered to assault the enemy's left. Hurling division after division, by hand-to-hand fighting he drove the enemy back from their lines, and flung them into the trap of Friedland, there to fall by hundreds under the fierce fire of the French massed batteries. It was his sangfroid which was responsible for the devotion with which the soldiers rushed against the enemy. At the beginning of the action some of the younger grenadiers kept bobbing their heads under the hail of bullets which almost darkened the air. 'Comrades,' called out the Marshal, who was on horseback, 'the enemy are firing in the air; here am I higher than the top of your busbies, and they don't hurt me.'

After the peace of Tilsit, Ney, soon Duke of Elchingen, had a year's repose from war, but in 1808 he was one of those summoned to retrieve the errors arising from Napoleon's mistaken calculation of the Spanish problem. The selection was an unfortunate one. Accustomed to the ordinary warfare of Central Europe, at his best in the mêlée of battle, in Spain, where organised resistance was seldom met, where the foe vanished at the first contact, the Marshal showed a hesitation and vacillation strangely in contrast with his dashing conduct on the battlefield. Fine soldier as he was, he lacked the essentials of the successful general - imagination and moral courage. He was unable to discern in his mind's eye what lay on the other side of a hill, and the blank which this lack of imagination caused in his mind affected his nerves, and made him irresolute and irritable. Moreover, in Spain, the success of the Emperor's plans depended on the loyal co-operation of Marshal with Marshal. But unfortunately Ney, obsessed by jealousy, was most difficult to work with; as Napoleon himself said, 'No one knew what it was to deal with two men like Ney and Soult.' From the very outset of his career in Spain he showed a lack of strategic insight and a want of rapidity of movement. Thus it was that he was unable to assist Lannes in the operations which the Emperor had planned for the annihilation of the Spaniards at Tudela. His heart was not in the work, and he made no attempt to hide this from Napoleon. When the Emperor before leaving Spain reviewed his troops, and told him that 'Romana would be accounted for in a fortnight; the English are beaten and will make no more effort; that all will be quiet here in three months,' the Duke of Elchingen boldly told him, 'The men of this country are obstinate, and the women and children fight; I see no end to the war.' It was with gloomy forebodings, therefore, that he saw the Emperor ride off to France. But what increased his dislike of the whole situation was that his operations were made subservient to those of Soult, his old enemy and rival. The hatred which existed between the two was of long standing, and had burned fiercely ever since the days of Jena, when Soult had been mainly instrumental in retrieving the disaster threatened by Ney's impetuosity. It came to a head when, after the Duke of Dalmatia's expulsion from Portugal, the armies of the two Marshals met at Lugo. Soult's corps arrived without cannon or baggage, a mere armed rabble, and Ney's men jeered at the disorganised battalions. The Marshals themselves took sides with their men. Matters were not improved when Joseph sent orders that Ney was to consider himself under Soult, and, though Napoleon himself confirmed the decision, it brought no peace between the rival commanders. All through the Talavera campaign there was perpetual discord, and it was Ney's hesitation, arising from vacillation or jealousy, which prevented Soult from cutting off the English retreat across the Tagus.

After the battle of Wagram, Masséna was despatched to Spain to command the Army of Portugal. The Duke of Elchingen showed to his new chief the same spirit of disobedience and hatred of control. At times slack and supine in his arrangements, as in the preparations for the siege of Ciudad Rodrigo and in his want of energy after the siege of Almeida, at other times upsetting his superiors' plans by his reckless impetuosity, he was a subordinate whom no one cared to command. Still, when it came to actual contact with the foe, no officer was able to extract so much from his men, and his defeat of Crawford's division on the Coa and his dash at Busaco were quite up to his great reputation. Before the lines of Torres Vedras his ill-humour broke out again. He bitterly opposed the idea of an assault, and he grumbled at being kept before the position. In fact, nothing that his chief could order was right. It was to a great extent owing to the conduct of the Duke of Elchingen that Masséna was at last compelled to retreat. As he wrote to Berthier, 'I have done all I could to keep the army out of Spain as long as possible . . . but I have been continually opposed, I make bold to say, by the commanders of the corps d'armée, who have roused such a spirit amongst officers and men that it would be dangerous to hold our present position any longer.' When, however, the retreat was at last ordered, Ney showed to the full his immense tactical ability. Although the army was greatly demoralised during the retreat through Portugal, he never lost a single gun or baggage wagon. As Napier wrote, 'Day after day Ney - the indomitable Ney - offered battle with the rear guard, and a stream of fire ran along the wasted valleys of Portugal, from the Tagus to the, Mondego, from the Mondego to the Coa.' As often as Wellington with his forty thousand men overtook the Marshal with his ten thousand, he was baffled by the tactical cleverness with which his adversary compelled him to deploy his whole force, only to find before him a vanishing rear guard. But while displaying such brilliant ability, the Duke of Elchingen would take no orders from his superior, and when Masséna told him to cover Almeida and Ciudad Rodrigo, he flatly refused and marched off in the opposite direction. Thereon the Prince of Essling was compelled to remove him from his command, and wrote to Berthier, 'I have been reduced to an extremity which I have earnestly endeavoured to avoid. The Marshal, the Duke of Etchingen, has arrived at the climax of disobedience. I have given the sixth corps to Count Loison, senior general of division. It is grievous for an old soldier who has commanded armies for so many years to arrive at such a pass with one of his comrades. The Duke of Elchingen since my arrival has not ceased to thwart me in my military operations . . . His character is well known, I will say no more.' Thus Ney returned to France in disgrace with his comrades, and hated by his enemies owing to the licence he allowed his soldiers.

The Emperor, however, much as he insisted on blind obedience to his own orders, soon forgave the Duke of Elchingen, and heaped his wrath on the unfortunate Masséna, whom he held responsible for the failure of the campaign in Portugal. Accordingly, when in 1812 he planned his Russian campaign, he entrusted Ney with the command of the third corps. Under the personal eye of Napoleon, the Duke of Elchingen was a different man to the Ney of Spain. At Smolensk he showed his old brilliancy, and after the battle he opposed the further advance into Russia, maintaining that so far the Russians had never been beaten but only dislodged, that the peasants were hostile, and once again reminding the Emperor of his failure in Spain. It was with great disapprobation that he heard Napoleon accept Caulaincourt's advice, and determine to advance to Moscow. 'Pray heaven,' he said, 'that the blarney of the ambassador general may not be more injurious to the army than the most bloody battle.' Gloomy as were his forebodings, they had no effect on his conduct when he met the enemy, and he won for himself the title of Prince of Moskowa in the hard-fought battle outside the walls of Moscow. But it is the retreat that has made his name so glorious. After the first few days he was entrusted with command of the rear guard, and as demoralisation set in he alone was able to keep the soldiers to their duty. At Krasnoi his feeble corps of six thousand men was surrounded by thirty thousand Russians. The main body was beyond recall. When summoned to lay down his arms, he replied, 'A Marshal of France never surrenders,' and closing his shattered columns, he charged the enemy's batteries and drove them from the field. For three days he struggled on surrounded by the foe. On one occasion when the enemy suddenly appeared in force where least expected, his men fell back in dismay, but the Marshal with admirable presence of mind ordered the charge to be beaten, shouting out, 'Comrades, now is the moment: forward! they are ours.' At last, with but fifteen hundred men left, be regained the main body near Orcha. When Napoleon heard of their arrival, he rushed to meet the Marshal, exclaiming, 'I have three hundred million francs in my coffers at the Tuileries; I would willingly have given them to save Marshal Ney.' He embraced the Duke, saying 'he had no regret for the troops which were lost, because they had preserved his dear cousin the Duke of Elchingen.' At the crossing of the Beresina, Ney once again covered himself with glory, and through the remainder of the terrible retreat he commanded the rear guard, and was the last man to cross the Niemen at Kovno and reach German soil. General Dumas, one of the officers of the general staff, relates how he was resting in an inn at Gumbinnen, when one evening a man entered clad in a long brown cloak, wearing a long beard, his face blackened with powder, his whiskers half burned by fire, but his eyes sparkling with brilliant lustre. 'Well, here I am at last,' he said. 'What, General Dumas, do you not know me?' 'No, who are you?' 'I am the rear guard of the Grand Army - Marshal Ney. I have fired the last musket on the bridge of Kovno: I have thrown into the Niemen the last of our arms, and I have walked hither, as you see, across the forests.'

The campaign of 1813 saw the Duke of Elchingen once again at the Emperor's side. At Lützen, his corps of conscripts fought nobly: five times the gallant Ney led them to the attack; five times they responded to the call of their leader. As he himself said, 'I doubt if I could have done the same thing with the old grenadiers of the Guard ... The docility and perhaps inexperience of those brave boys served me better than the tried courage of veterans. The French infantry can never be too young.' But at Bautzen he showed another phase of his character. Entrusted with sixty thousand men with orders to make a vast turning movement, his timidity spoiled the Emperor's careful plans. So hesitating and uncertain were his dispositions that the Allies had ample time to meet his attack and quietly withdrew without being compromised, leaving not a cannon or a prisoner in the hands of the French. Well might the Emperor cry out, 'What, after such a butchery no results? No prisoners?' But in spite of Ney's lack of strategic skill and his well-known vacillation when confronted with problems he did not understand, Napoleon was forced to employ him on an independent command. After Oudinot was beaten at Grosbeeren, he despatched him to take command of the army opposed to the mixed force of the Allies under Bernadotte, which was threatening his communications from the direction of Berlin. But Ney was no more successful than Oudinot. His dispositions were even worse than those of the Duke of Reggio, and at Dennewitz, night alone saved his force from absolute annihilation, while he had to confess to nine hundred killed and wounded and fifteen thousand taken prisoners. He but wrote the truth in his despatch to the Emperor, 'I have been totally beaten, and still do not know whether my army has reassembled.' At Leipzig also he was responsible for the want of success during the first day of the battle, and spent the time in useless marching and counter-marching; in this case, however, the faulty orders he received were largely responsible for his errors. But all through the campaign he felt the want of the clear counsel of the born strategist Jomini, his former chief of the staff, who had gone over to the Allies.

During the winter campaign in 1814 in France no one fought more fiercely and stubbornly than the Duke of Elchingen. When the end came and Paris had surrendered, he was one of those who at Fontainebleau refused to march on Paris, in spite of the cries of the Guard 'To Paris!' Angered by the tenacity with which the Marshals protested against the folly of such a march, the Emperor at last exclaimed, 'The army will obey me.' 'No,' replied Ney, 'it will obey its commanders.' Macdonald, who had just arrived with his weary troops, backed him up, exclaiming, 'We have had enough of war without kindling a civil war.' Thereon Napoleon was induced to sign a proclamation offering to abdicate; and Caulaincourt, Macdonald, and Ney set out for Paris to try and get terms from the Czar. Once in the capital the Marshal seemed to despair of his commission. Feeble and irresolute, he was easily gained over by Talleyrand, and at once made his formal adhesion to the provisional government. When the commissioners returned to the Emperor, he saw but too clearly that his day was done. 'Oh,' he exclaimed, 'you want repose; have it then; alas you know not how many disappointments and dangers await you on your beds of down.'

The Emperor's prophecy was but too true. Though honours were showered upon him, the peace which followed the restoration of the Bourbons brought but little satisfaction and enjoyment to the Duke of Elchingen. Accustomed to the bustle and hurry of a soldier's life, he was too old to acquire the tastes of a life of tranquillity. Books brought him no satisfaction, since he could scarcely read; society frightened him, and his plain manners and blunt speech shocked the salons of Paris and grated on the nerves of the courtiers. By nature ascetic, he hated dissipation. Moreover, his family life was by no means happy. His wife, ambitious, fond of luxury and pleasure, was unable to share his pursuits and tastes, and worried her husband with childish complaints of loss of prestige at the new court. Consequently the blunt old soldier was only too glad to leave her at his hotel in Paris, and bury himself in his estate in the country, where field sports offered him a recreation he could appreciate, and his old comrades and country neighbours afforded him a society at least congenial.

From this peaceful life at Coudreaux the Marshal was suddenly summoned on March 6, 1815, to Paris. On arriving there he was met by his lawyer, who informed him of Napoleon's descent on Fréjus. 'It is a great misfortune,' he said; 'what is the Government doing? Who are they going to send against that man?' Then he hurried off to the Minister of War to receive his instructions. He was ordered to Besançon to take command of the troops there, and to help oppose Napoleon's advance on Paris. Before starting for his headquarters he went to pay his respects to the King, and expressed his indignation at the Emperor's action, promising 'to bring him back in an iron cage'. On arriving at his command he found everything in confusion, and the soldiers ready at any moment to declare for the Emperor. Ney had but one thought, and that to save the King. In reply to a friend who told him that the soldiers could not fight the Emperor, he replied, 'They shall fight; I will begin the action myself, and run my sword to the hilt in the breast of the first who hesitates to follow my example.' But when he arrived, on the evening of the 13th, at Lons la Saulnier he was met by the news that on all sides the troops were deserting, and that the Duke of Orleans and Monsieur had been compelled to withdraw from Lyons. That same evening emissaries arrived from Napoleon alleging that all the Marshals had promised to go over, and that the Congress of Vienna had approved of the overthrow of the Bourbons, assuring the Marshal that the Emperor would receive him as on the day after the battle of Moskowa. While but half convinced by these specious arguments and a prey to doubt, news arrived that his vanguard at Bourg had deserted, and that the inhabitants of Châlons-sur-Saône had seized his artillery. In his agony he exclaimed to the emissaries, 'It is impossible for me to stop the water of the ocean with my own hand.' On the morrow he called the generals of division to give him counsel; one of them was Bourmont, a double-dyed traitor who deserted Napoleon on the eve of Waterloo; the other was the stern old republican warrior Lecourbe. They could give him but little advice, so at last the fatal decision was made, and Ney called his troops together and read the proclamation drawn up by Napoleon.

Scarcely had he done so than he began to perceive the enormity of his action. Meanwhile he wrote an impassioned letter to Napoleon urging him to seek no more wars of conquest. It might suit the Emperor's policy to cause the Marshal to desert those to whom he had sworn allegiance, but he mistrusted men who broke their word, and though he received Ney with outward cordiality, he saw but little of the 'black beast', as he called him, during the Hundred Days, for the Duke of Elchingen, full of remorse and shame, hid himself at Coudreaux. It was not till the end of May that Napoleon summoned him to Paris, and greeted him with the words, 'I thought you had become an émigré.' 'I ought to have done it long ago,' replied the Marshal; 'now it is too late.' Still the Emperor kept him without employment till on June 11th he sent him to inspect the troops around Lille, and from there summoned him to join the army before Charleroi on the afternoon of June 15th. Immediately on his arrival he was put in command of the left wing of the army, composed of Reille and D'Erlon's corps, and received verbal orders to push northwards and occupy Quatre Bras. The Marshal's task was not an enviable one. He had to improvise a staff and make himself acquainted with his subordinates and at the same time try and elucidate the contradictory orders of his old enemy Soult, now chief of the staff to the Emperor. Accordingly, when on the evening of the 15th his advance guard found Quatre Bras held by the enemy, he decided to make no attack that night. But on the morning of the 16th he made a still greater error. For not only did he neglect to make a reconnaissance, which would have showed him that he was opposed by a mere handful of troops, but, slothful as ever, he omitted to give orders for the proper concentration of his divisions, which were strung out along sixteen miles of road. A day begun thus badly was bound to bring difficulties. But these difficulties were enormously increased in the afternoon. After three despatches ordering him to carry Quatre Bras with all his force, he received a fourth written by Soult at Napoleon's order telling him to move to the right to support Grouchy in his attack on the Prussians, ending with the words, 'The fate of France is in your hands, therefore do not hesitate to move according to the Emperor's commands.' To add further to his difficulties, d'Erlon's corps was detached from his command without his knowledge. In this distracted condition, the Marshal lost all control over himself, calling out, 'Ah, those English balls! I wish they were all in my belly!' Thus it was, mad with rage, that he rode up to Kellermann, calling out, 'We must make a supreme effort. Take your cavalry and fling yourself upon the English centre. Crush them - ride them down!' But it was too late. Wellington himself with thirty thousand men now held Quatre Bras.

The Marshal had himself to thank for his want of success, for if he had been less slothful in the morning, the battle would have been won before the contradictory orders could have had any effect on his plans. On the morning of the 17th the dispirited Prince of Moskowa took no steps to find out what his enemy was doing, although he received orders from the Emperor at ten o'clock to occupy Quatre Bras if there was only a rear guard there. Accordingly the English had ample time to retreat. When Napoleon hurried up in pursuit at 2 p.m. he greeted his lieutenant with the bitter reproach, 'You have ruined France!' But though the Emperor recognised that he was no longer the Ney of former days, he still retained him in his command. At Waterloo the Marshal showed his old dash on the battlefield. The left wing was hurled against the Allies with a vehemence that recalled the Prince of Moskowa's conduct in the Russian campaign. But, impetuous as ever, finding he could not crush the stubborn foe with his infantry, he rushed back and prematurely ordered up 5,000 of the cavalry of the Guard. 'He has compromised us again,' growled his old enemy Soult, 'as he did at Jena.' 'It is too early by an hour,' exclaimed the Emperor, 'but we must support him now that he has done it.' The mistake was fatal to Napoleon's plans. In vain the French cavalry charged the English squares, still unshaken by artillery and infantry fire. Meanwhile the Prussians appeared on the allied left. The Emperor staked his last card, and ordered the Guard to make one last effort to crush the English infantry. Sword in hand the gallant Prince of Moskowa led the magnificent veterans to the attack. But the fire of the English lines swept them down by hundreds. A shout arose, 'La garde recule.' Ney, the indomitable, in vain seeking death, was swept away by the mass, his clothing in rags, foaming at the mouth, his broken sword in his hand, rushing from corps to corps, trying to rally the runaways with taunts of 'Cowards, have you forgotten how to die?' At one moment he passed d'Erlon as they were swept along in the rush, and screamed out to him, 'If you and I come out of this alive, d'Erlon, we shall be hanged.' Well it had been for him if he could have found the death he so eagerly sought. Five horses were shot under him, his clothes were riddled with bullets, but he was reserved for a sinister fate.

The Marshal returned to Paris and witnessed the capitulation and second abdication. Thereafter he had thoughts of withdrawing to Switzerland or to America. But unfortunately he considered himself safe under the terms of the capitulation, and, anxious to clear his name for the sake of his children, he remained hidden at the château of Bessonis, near Aurillac, waiting to see what the attitude of the Government would be. There he was discovered by a zealous police official, who caught sight of the Egyptian sabre Napoleon had presented to him in 1801. He was at once arrested and taken to Paris. The military court appointed to try him declared itself unable to try a peer of France. Accordingly the House of Peers was ordered to proceed with his trial, and found him guilty by a majority of one hundred and sixty-nine to nineteen. The Marshal's lawyers tried to get him off by the subterfuge that he was no longer a Frenchman, since his native town, Sarrelouis, had been taken from France. But Ney would hear of no such excuse. 'I am a Frenchman,' he cried, 'and will die a Frenchman.' Early on the following day, December 7, 1815, the sentence was read to the prisoner. The officer entrusted with this melancholy duty commenced to read his titles, Prince of Moskowa, Duke of Elchingen, &c. But the Marshal cut him short: 'Why cannot you simply say 'Michel Ney, once a French soldier and soon to be a heap of dust'?' At eight o'clock in the morning the Marshal, with a firm step, was conveyed to the place of execution. To the officer who prepared to bandage his eyes he said, 'Are you ignorant that for twenty-five years I have been accustomed to face both ball and bullet?' Then, taking off his hat, he said, 'I declare before God and man that I have never betrayed my country. May my death render her happy. Vive la France!' Then, turning to the soldiers, he gave the word, 'Soldiers, fire!'

Thus, in his forty-seventh year, the Prince of Moskowa, a peasant's son, but now immortal as the 'Bravest of the Brave', expiated his error. Pity it was that he had not the courage of his gallant subordinate at Lons la Saulnier, who had broken his sword in pieces with the words, 'It is easier for a man of honour to break iron than to infringe his word.' Looking backward, and calmly reading the evidence of the trial, it is clear that Ney set out in March, 1815, with every intention to remain faithful to the King. But his moral courage failed him; and the glamour of his old life, and the contact with the iron will of the great Corsican, broke down his principles. To some the punishment meted out to him seemed hard; but when the Emperor heard of his execution he said that he only got his deserts. 'No one should break his word. I despise traitors. Ney has dishonoured himself.' And the Duke of Wellington refused to plead for the Marshal, for he said 'it was absolutely necessary to make an example.' But the clearest proof of the justice of the penalty was the fact that from the fatal day at Lons la Saulnier the Marshal was never himself again, and he who, during those terrible days in Russia, had been able to sleep like a little child, never could sleep in peace.

Among the Marshals of Napoleon, Ney, with his title of the 'Bravest of the Brave', and his magnificent record of hard fighting, will always appeal to those who love romance. But, great fighter as he was, he was not a great general. At times, at St. Helena, Napoleon, remembering his mistakes at Quatre Bras and Waterloo, used to say that he ought not to have made him a Marshal, for he only had the courage and honesty of a hussar, forgetting his words in Russia, 'I have three hundred millions francs in my coffers at the Tuileries; I would willingly have given them to save Marshal Ney.' But, cruel as it may seem, perhaps the Emperor expressed his real opinion of him when he said, 'He was precious on the battlefield, but too immoral and too stupid to succeed.' In action he was always master of himself, but as Jomini, his old chief of the staff, wrote of him, 'Ney's best qualities, his heroic valour, his rapid coup d'oeil, and his energy, diminished in the same proportion that the extent of his command increased his responsibility. Admirable on the battlefield, he displayed less assurance not only in council, but whenever he was not actually face to face with the enemy.' In a word, he lacked that marked intellectual capacity which is the chief characteristic of great soldiers like Hannibal, Caesar, Napoleon, and Wellington.

8

LOUIS NICOLAS DAVOUT, MARSHAL, DUKE OF AUERSTÄDT, PRINCE OF ECKMÜHL

There was an old saying in Burgundy that 'when a Davout comes into the world, another sword has leaped from the scabbard'; but so finely tempered a weapon as Louis Nicolas had never before been produced by the warrior nobles of Annoux, though the line stretched back in unbroken descent to the days of the first Crusades. Born at Auxerre on May 18, 1770, the future Marshal was destined for the service, and at the age of fifteen entered the Royal Military School at Paris. In the fatal year 1789 he received his commission in the Royal Champagne regiment of cavalry stationed at Hesdin, but his period of service with the royal army was short. From his boyhood, young Davout was one of those whom it was impossible to drive, who, while they submit to no authority, are as clay in the hands of the master mind who can gain their affections. His turbulent spirit had early become captivated by the specious revolutionary logic of a brilliant young lawyer, Turreau, who, a few years later, became his stepfather. Full of burning zeal for his new political tenets, chafing under the dull routine of garrison life, despising his mediocre companions, the young sub-lieutenant soon found himself in trouble, and was dismissed the service for the part he took in aiding the revolutionaries in their attempts to seduce the privates and non-commissioned officers from their allegiance to their sovereign. His return to civil life was but brief, for, when in 1791 the Prussian invasion summoned the country to arms, Louis Nicolas enlisted in the Volunteers of the Yonne, and owing to his former military training was at once elected lieutenant-colonel.

The Volunteers of the Yonne formed part of the corps opposed to the Austrians in the Low Countries, and owing to the stern discipline of their lieutenant-colonel, became distinguished as the most reliable of all the volunteers raised in 1791. Davout adopted the same plan which proved so effective among the Scotch regiments during the eighteenth century: keeping in close communication with the local authorities of the Yonne, and rewarding or punishing his men by posting their names with their records in the various cantons from which they were drawn. After fighting bravely under Dumouriez, it fell to the lot of the battalion to attempt to capture that general, when, after the battle of Neerwinden, he tried to betray his army to the Austrians. Soon after this the lieutenant-colonel had to throw up his command when the Convention decreed that no ci-devant noble could hold a commission; but Davout's record was so strongly republican that his friend Turreau had little difficulty in getting him reinstated in his rank, and sent to command a brigade of cavalry in the Army of the Moselle. Except for two years during which he was at home on parole, after the capture of Mannheim, the general was on active service in the Rhine valley till the peace of Campo Formio in 1797. During these years he steadily added to his reputation as a stern commander and a stubborn fighter, and as such attracted the attention of Desaix, who introduced him early in 1798 to Bonaparte. The future Emperor saw at a glance that this small, stout, bald-headed young man had qualities which few others possessed. Accordingly he took him with him to Egypt. Like all who met the young Napoleon, Davout fell entirely beneath his spell. In spite of the fact that he was not included among the few friends whom Bonaparte selected to return with him in 1800, his enthusiasm for the First Consul increased day by day. Returning to France with Desaix, just before the Marengo campaign, he at once hastened to Paris to congratulate the new head of the Government. Davout's republicanism had received many shocks. Like all other honourable men, he had hated and loathed the Terror. Moreover, he had seen on service how little the preachers of the equality of man carried out their doctrine in practice. As early as 1794 we find him writing to a friend: 'Ought we to be exposed to the tyranny of any chance revolutionary committee or club? . . . Why are not all Frenchmen witnesses of fraternity and of the republican virtues which reign in our camps; we have no brigands here, but have we not plenty at home?' Bonaparte knew well that Davout was not only his enthusiastic personal follower, but also thoroughly approved of the coup d'état of the 18th Brumaire, and in his desire for peace and stability at home would warmly back him up in his scheme of founding a tyranny under the guise of an Imperial Republic. Accordingly the First Consul published a most flattering account of him in the official *Moniteur*, and gave him command of the cavalry of the Army of Italy, under General Brune. In June, 1801, after the treaty of Luneville, in pursuance of his plan of congregating his friends at headquarters, he recalled him to Paris as inspector-general of cavalry.

It was while thus employed that Davout met his wife, Aimée Leclerc. Aimée, a sister of that Leclerc who married Pauline Bonaparte, had been educated at Madame Campan's school in Paris, along with the young Beauharnais and Bonapartes, and was the bosom friend of Caroline and Hortense. From many points of view the marriage was extremely appropriate; for although the Davouts belonged to the old nobility, and Aimée's father was only a corn merchant of Poitou, he had prospered in his business, and had been able to give his daughter an excellent education. The marriage brought Davout into close connection with the First Consul's family, and was successful from a worldly and a domestic point of view. The future Marshal was deeply attached to his wife, and spent every moment with her which he could snatch from his military duties. When absent on service scarcely a day passed on which he did not write to her, and his happiness was completely bound up in her welfare and that of his large family. The year following their marriage the Davouts bought the beautiful estate of Savigny-sur-Orge for the sum of seven hundred thousand francs. This was a great strain on their rather limited resources, and for some years they had to practise strict economy.

In September, 1803, the general was summoned to Bruges to command a corps of the Army of the Ocean, which later became the third corps of the Grand Army. There, in close communication with his great chief, he began to show those traits which made him respected as the most relentless and careful administrator of all the Marshals of France. His energy was indefatigable; everything had to undergo his personal scrutiny, be it the best means of securing the embarkation of a company in one of the new barges or the careful inspection of the boots of a battalion: for Davout, like Wellington, knew that a soldier's marching powers depended on two things, his feet and his stomach, and every man in the third corps had to have two pairs of good boots in his valise and one on his feet. Secrecy also, in his eyes, was of prime importance; he was quick to give a lesson to all spies, or would-be spies, in Belgium, and it was with stern exultation in his duty that he wrote to the First Consul, 'Your orders for the trial of the spy (Bülow) will be carried out, and within a week he will be executed.' Day by day, as he gained experience, the indefatigable soldier drew on him the approbation of the First Consul, and it was with no sense of favouritism that Napoleon, when he became Emperor, nominated him among his newly created Marshals, although in the eyes of the army at large he had not yet done enough to justify this choice.

The campaign of 1805 gave the Marshal his first opportunity of handling large bodies of troops of all arms in the field, and, though it did not bring him into such conspicuous notice as Murat, Lannes, Soult and Ney, it justified Napoleon in his selection of him as worthy of the Marshal's baton. In the operations round Ulm, Davout proved himself an excellent subordinate, whose corps was ever ready, at full strength, in the field, and at the hour at which it had been ordered, while the Marshal's stern checking of marauding was a new feature in French military discipline, and one which no other Marshal could successfully carry out without starving his troops. But it was Austerlitz which taught the students of war the true capabilities of this rising officer. There the Emperor, relying on his stubborn, methodical character, entrusted him with a duty which eminently suited his genius: he chose his corps as the screen to cover the trap which he set for the Russian left, and all day long it had to fight a stern rear-guard action against overwhelming odds, until it had tempted the enemy into dissipating his forces, and so weakening his centre that his left and right were defeated in detail. After Austerlitz, Davout was entrusted with the pursuit of the left wing of the Allies. Flushed with victory, the third corps pushed the disorganised enemy in hopeless rout, and it seemed as if the annihilation of the Russians was certain. Meanwhile, unknown to the Marshal, the Emperor had accepted the Czar's demands for an armistice. Davout first heard of the cessation of hostilities from the enemy, but, remembering Murat's mistake, he refused to halt his troops. 'You want to deceive me,' he said to the flag of truce; 'you want to make a fool of me . . . I am going to crush you, and that is the only order I have received.' So the third corps pushed on, and it was only the production of a despatch in the handwriting of the Czar himself that caused the victor at last to stay his hand.

Though Davout emerged from the Austrian campaign with the reputation in the army of having at last earned his Marshal's bâton to the general public he still appeared as 'a little smooth-pated, unpretending man, who was never tired of waltzing,' but the campaign of 1806 made him nearly the best known of all the Marshals. Auerstädt was a masterpiece of minor tactics. Napoleon, thinking that he had before him at Jena the whole of the Prussian army, summoned to his aid Bernadotte, and thus left Davout with a force of twenty-three thousand men isolated on his right wing, with orders to push forward and try to get astride of the enemy's line of retreat.

It was in pursuance of this order that early in the morning of October 14, 1806, the Marshal, at the head of the advance guard of his corps, crossed the river Saale at Kösen and proceeded to seize the defile beyond the bridge through which ran the road to Naumberg. True to his motto of never leaving to another anything which he could possibly do himself, he had personally, on the previous evening, carefully reconnoitred the line of advance, and knew the importance of the village of Hassenhausen at the further end of the defile. Hardly had his advance guard seized this position and the heights commanding the road, when through the fog they saw approaching the masses of the enemy's cavalry; the fiery Prussian commander, Blücher, at once hastened to the attack, and again and again led his horsemen to the charge. Meanwhile Brunswick counter-ordered the retreat of the infantry and artillery. Soon the whole of the Prussian army, forty-five thousand strong, was engaged in the attempt to crush the small French force. But the Marshal was in his element, carefully husbanding his resources only to hurl them into the fray at the critical moment; feinting at his enemy's flanks; utilising every feature of the ground to prolong his resistance;

galloping from square to square, his uniform black from powder, his cocked hat carried off by a bullet, encouraging his troops with short, sharp words, crying out, 'The great Frederick believed that God gave the victory to the big battalions, but he lied; it is the obstinate people that win, and that's you and your general.' From six in the morning the battle raged, but towards mid-day the Prussians, finding that they could make no impression on the enemy, began to slacken their attack. Davout seized the psychological moment to order his whole line to advance. Thereon the King of Prussia commanded his forces to retire, leaving a strong rear guard under Kalkreuth to prevent the French pursuit. But the French were in no condition to carry on an active pursuit, for out of twenty-three thousand men engaged they had lost almost eight thousand killed or wounded. It is quite true that man for man the French soldier in 1806 was superior in intelligence and patriotism to the Prussian, that the French staff was infinitely superior to the Prussian staff, and that there was no comparison between the morale of the two armies; but that alone does not explain how an army half the size of the enemy, caught as it was in the act of deploying from a defile, not only was not beaten absolutely, but actually defeated the superior force. The secret of the French success at Auerstädt lay in the character of their general. It was Davout's careful reconnaissance, his quickness to perceive in Hassenhausen the key of the position, his careful crowning of the heights covering the defile, the masterly way in which, while massing his men in the open to resist Blücher's fierce charges, he at the same time contrived so to expand his line as to threaten the flanks of his vastly superior foe, his indomitable courage in throwing his last reserve into the firing line, and his audacious counter-attack the moment he saw the Prussians wavering, which saved his force from what at the time looked like annihilation, and by sheer downright courage and self-confidence turned defeat into victory.

Pleased as the Emperor was at his lieutenant's victory, and much as he admired the way in which his subordinate had copied his own methods, showing that inflexibility of purpose, absolute disregard of the opinion of others, and unswerving belief in his own capacity which he knew were the factors of his own success, it did not suit his policy that a subordinate should attract the admiration of the army at large. Accordingly in his bulletins he glossed over the part played by Davout and belittled his success, but in his private letters he warmly praised the Marshal's courage and ability. Further, to reward him for lack of official praise, he gave the third corps the place of honour at the grand march past held at Berlin, when the inhabitants of the capital of Frederick the Great saw for the first time, with mingled hatred and surprise, 'the lively, impudent, mean-looking little fellows' who had thrashed their own magnificent troops. On the following day the Emperor inspected the third corps, and thanked the officers and men for the great services they had rendered him, and paid a tribute to 'the brave men I have lost, whom I regret as it were my own children, but who died on the field of honour.' Pleased as the Marshal was with this somewhat tardy acknowledgment of his achievement, he was in no way inflated with pride; as General Ségur says of him: 'Those who knew him best say that there was a sort of flavour of a bygone age in his inflexibility; stern towards himself and towards others, and above all in that stoical simplicity, high above all vanity, with which he ever strode forward, with shoulders square, and full intent to the accomplishment of his duty.' But though success brought no pride in its train, it brought its burdens: the jealousy of the other Marshals was barely concealed, and as Davout wrote to his wife, 'I am more than ever in need of the Emperor's goodwill... few of my colleagues pardon me the good fortune the third corps had in beating the King of Prussia.'

A winter spent in Poland amid these jealousies and far from his family was only endurable because of his attachment to the service and person of the Emperor. Immediately on entering the country which he was to govern for the next two years, the Marshal summed up the situation at a glance, and told the Emperor that the nobility would throw cold water on all schemes unless the French guaranteed them their independence.

With the spring of 1807 came the last phase of the war. At Heilsberg, Davout fought well, and two days later took his part in the great battle of Eylau, the most bloody of all Napoleon's battles. Bennigsen, the Russian commander, had turned at bay on his pursuers. On the morning of February 8th the French corps came hurrying up from all sides at the Emperor's commands. It was not, however, till mid-day that the third corps arrived on the scene, of the action. Heavy snow blizzards obscured the scene, but the struggle raged fiercely on all sides, the Russians fighting like bulls, as the French said. The Emperor, on Davout's arrival, placed his corps on the right and ordered him to advance, but the enemy's cavalry and artillery effectually barred his way. All day long the contest lasted, men fighting hand to hand in a confused mêlée. All day long Davout, with obstinate courage, clung to the village which he seized in the morning, whence he threatened the Russian line of retreat. When night came he still held his position; at last the Emperor, fearing a renewal of the fight on the next day, gave orders at eight o'clock for the third corps to fall back on Eylau. But the Marshal, hearing of the commencement of the Russian retreat, disobeyed the Emperor, and thus, by his bold front, in conjunction with Soult, he was mainly instrumental in causing the enemy to leave the field. If Davout had been less obstinate, the French would have had to fight another battle on the following day, but thanks to him they were spared this fate, and the twenty-five thousand dead and wounded Frenchmen had not spent their blood in vain. The third corps escaped the horrors of Friedland, as it had been detached to intercept the enemy's line of retreat in the direction of Königsberg, and Tilsit saw the end of Davout's second campaign against the Russians.

But peace did not bring the opportunity of returning to his beloved France and the joys of home life; the Emperor in peace, as in war, could not spare the great administrative capacity, the stern discipline, and the rigid probity of the Marshal. 'It is quite fair that I should give him enormous presents,' said the Emperor, 'for he takes no perquisites.' So Davout found himself established nominally as commander of the army of occupation, and really as special adviser to the Government of the newly constituted Grand Duchy of Warsaw. It was a situation that required infinite tact, patience, and a stern will. The Poles longed for a restored kingdom of Poland. The Emperor could not grant this without offending his new friend the Czar, who, with the Emperor of Austria, looked with suspicion on the experiment of creating a Grand Duchy. So on one side the Marshal had to try to inspire confidence in the Poles by pretending that the Grand Duchy was merely a temporary experiment in the larger policy of restoring the kingdom, while on the other hand he had to assure the Austrians and Russians that nothing was further from the Emperor's thoughts than creating a power at Warsaw dangerous to them. Meanwhile there was plenty of occupation in getting provisions for his troops in a land always poor and but lately devastated by war, and in attempting to maintain order in a country full of adventurers where police were unknown. It was useless to attempt to get assistance from the Government, for there was no organisation, no division of duties among the different ministers, and nobody knew what his own particular business was. The situation was well summed up in a caricature which showed the ministers nicely dressed in their various uniforms but without heads. It was well for the new Government that they had at their side such a stern, disinterested adviser as Davout, ready to take the initiative and accept the responsibility of any act which he thought good for the community. Under his supervision the ministers' spheres of action were duly arranged: the state was saved from bankruptcy by importing bullion from Prussia and deporting the adventurers who were filling their own coffers by draining the money from the country. The monks who preached against the Government and fanned popular discontent were three times given twenty-four hours' notice to put their houses in order, and then quietly escorted across the frontier. A strong Polish force was raised, armed and equipped by Prince Poniatowski under the Marshal's supervision. As a reward for his labours the Emperor granted Davout three hundred thousand francs to buy a town house in Paris, and followed this up, in May, 1808, by creating him Duke of Auerstädt. But what pleased the Marshal more than all was that the Emperor allowed the Duchess to join him at Warsaw. This was a politic move, for the Emperor, knowing well the secret intention of Austria, could not afford to withdraw the warden of the marches from his outpost at Warsaw; but by sending the Duchess of Auerstädt to Poland he kept his faithful lieutenant content. However, the Duchess's visit to Poland was not a long one. By September, 1808, it became certain that Austria was making immense efforts to recover her possessions, and accordingly Napoleon very wisely began to concentrate his troops in Central Europe, and the Duke of Auerstädt's corps was recalled to Silesia in

October, and was incorporated with the French troops in Prussia under the designation of the Army of the Rhine.

During the winter the Marshal was fully occupied in forcing Prussia to drain to the last dregs her cup of humiliation: extorting from her the immense ransom Napoleon had laid on her, and crushing her attempts at regeneration by hounding out of the country the patriotic Stein and his band of fellow-workers. From his cantonments round Berlin Davout was summoned in 1809 to take part in another struggle with Austria. The campaign opened disastrously for the French. The Archduke Charles commenced operations earlier than Napoleon had calculated, and accordingly the Grand Army found itself under the feeble command of the chief of the staff. Berthier, in blind obedience to the Emperor, who had misread the situation, was compelled to neglect the first principles of war and to attempt to block all possible lines of advance instead of concentrating in a strategic position. In consequence of this, the Duke of Auerstädt, in spite of his official protests, found himself at Ratisbon, isolated from the rest of the army, with no support within forty miles. From this dangerous position he was saved by the arrival of the Emperor at headquarters, who, recognising his own mistakes, immediately ordered a concentration, on Abensberg. The retreat, or rather the flank march, in the face of eighty thousand Austrians under the Archduke Charles, was successfully carried out, thanks to the stubborn fighting of the troops and the lucky intervention of a tremendous thunderstorm, which forced the enemy to give up their attack at the critical moment when the French were crossing a difficult defile. Two days later the Emperor once again tested Davout's stubborn qualities, entrusting him with the duty of containing the main Austrian force while he disposed of the rest of the enemy. The result was the three days' fighting at Eckmühl; during the first two, Davout, unaided, held his own till on the third the Emperor arrived with supports and gave the Austrians the coup-de-grâce, but rewarded the Marshal for his tenacity by bestowing on him the title of Prince of Eckmühl.

Though his corps was not actually engaged at the battle of Aspern-Essling the Marshal had a large share in preventing a complete catastrophe. As soon as he heard of the breaking of the bridge he set about to organise a flotilla of boats, and it was thanks to the supplies of ammunition thus ferried across that the French troops on the north bank were able to hold their own and cover the retreat to the Isle of Lobau. While both sides were concentrating every available man for the great battle of Wagram, Davout was entrusted with the task of watching the Archduke John, whose army at Pressburg was the rallying point for the Hungarians. The moment the French preparations were complete, the Marshal, leaving a strong screen in front of the Archduke, swiftly fell back on the Isle of Lobau, and by thus hoodwinking the Archduke gave the Emperor an advantage of fifty thousand troops over the enemy. The Prince of Eckmühl's duty at the battle of Wagram was to turn the left flank of the enemy and, while interposing his corps between the two Archdukes, at the same time to threaten the enemy's rear and give an opportunity to the French centre to drive home a successful attack. It was a most difficult and dangerous operation, for at any moment the Archduke John might appear on the exposed right flank. Whilst Davout was marching and fighting to achieve his purpose, the main battle went against the French. The left and centre were thrown back, and it seemed as if the Austrians were bound to capture the bridge at Enzerdorff. Amid cries of 'All is lost!' the French reserve artillery and baggage trains fled in confusion. But relief came at the critical moment, for the Prince of Eckmühl, hurling his steel-clad cuirassiers on the unbroken Austrian foot, losing nearly all his generals in the desperate hand-to-hand fighting on the slopes of the Neusiedel, at last gained the top of the plateau and forced the enemy to throw back his left flank and weaken his centre. The moment the Emperor saw the guns appear on the summit of the Neusiedel, he launched Macdonald's corps against the Austrian centre and sent his aide-de-camp to Masséna to tell him 'to commence the attack . . . the battle is gained.' But Davout was unable to pursue his advantage over the enemy's left, for at the moment he gained the top of the plateau news arrived that Prince John's advance guard was in touch with his scouts; accordingly he halted and drew up in battle formation, ready at any moment to face the Hungarian troops should they attempt to attack his rear. Fortunately for the French the Archduke John forgot that an enemy is never so weak as after a successful attack, and instead of hurling his fresh troops on the weakened and disorganised French, he halted, and withdrew after dark towards Pressburg. When, during the pursuit of the battle, the Archduke Charles sent in a flag of truce offering to discuss terms, the Emperor called a council of war. There was a certain amount of difference of opinion, but Davout was for continuing the fight, pointing out that 'once master of the road from Brünn, in two hours it would be possible to concentrate thirty thousand men across the Archduke's line of retreat.' The Marshal's arguments seemed about to prevail when news arrived that Bruyère, commanding the cavalry, was seriously wounded. Thereon the Emperor changed his mind, crying out, 'Look at it: death hovers over all my generals. Who knows but that within two hours I shall not hear that you are taken off? No; enough blood has been spilled; I accept the suspension of hostilities.'

After the evacuation of the conquered territories the Marshal was appointed to command the Army of Germany. His duties were to enforce the continental system and to keep a stern eye on Prussia. The marriage with Marie Louise for the time being relieved tension in Central Europe, and accordingly in 1810 Davout was able to enjoy long periods of leave. He was present as colonel-general of the Guard at the imperial wedding, and at the interment of Lannes's remains in the Pantheon, and he did his turn of duty as general in attendance on the imperial household. His letters to his wife throw an interesting light on the imperial ménage. The officers in attendance were supplied with good, comfortable rooms and food, but had to find their own linen, plates, wax candles, firewood, and kitchen utensils; in a postscript he adds, 'Not only must you send me all the above, but add towels, sheets, pillow-cases, &c.; until these arrive I have to sleep on the bare mattress.'

In 1811 the growing hostility of Russia required the attendance of the Prince of Eckmühl at the headquarters of his command. Napoleon knew well that nobody would be quicker to discern any secret movement hostile to his interests than the man who in 1808 had done so much to check the regeneration of Prussia by enforcing his orders, playing on the Prussian King's fears and exposing the cleverness of the proposals of the patriotic Stein. The Marshal reached his headquarters at Hamburg early in February, and soon found his hands full. It was no longer a question of so disposing the corps committed to his care that he might cripple the English, 'who since the time of Cromwell have played the game of ruining our commerce,' but of preparing a mixed force of French, Poles, and Saxons, amounting to one hundred and forty thousand, for the contingencies of a war with Russia, or for the absolute annihilation of Prussia. To no other of his Marshals did the Emperor entrust the command of one hundred and forty thousand troops, and consequently the old enmities and jealousies broke out with renewed force. It was whispered that the Marshal's income from his investments, pay, and perquisites was over two million francs a year; that nobody in the imperial family had anything like as much, and people said it was better to be a Davout than a Prince Royal. The Prince disregarded all the annoying scandal his wife sent him from Paris, and quietly busied himself with preparing transport and equipping magazines for the coming war, diversified by an occasional thundering declaration informing the King of Prussia that his secret schemes were well known to the French authorities. But the subterranean jealousies bore their fruit. Nobody had a good word to say for Davout, and there was nobody to take his part. Most disastrously for the Grand Army the misunderstanding which existed between Berthier and Davout prevented their co-operation; and thus during the Russian campaign the rash empty-headed Murat had greater weight with Napoleon than Davout, the cautious yet tenacious old fighter. Accordingly at the battle of Moskowa, when Napoleon had his last chance of annihilating the Russians, he refused to listen to the Marshal, who pleaded to be allowed to turn the Russian left during the night. 'No,' said the Emperor, 'it is too big a movement; it will take me too much off my objective and make me lose time.' Davout, sure of the wisdom of this advice, once again renewed his arguments, but the Emperor rudely interrupted him with 'You are always for turning the enemy; it is too dangerous a movement.' So the battle of Moskowa was a disastrous victory, opening as it did the gates of Moscow without the annihilation of the Russian armed forces in the field. But it was greatly due to the Marshal that it was a victory at all, for the Russians fought with the greatest stubbornness; nearly all the French generals were wounded or killed, and at one moment a panic seized the troops. Then it was that the Prince of Eckmühl himself rallied the broken battalions and led them to the charge. In spite of a wound in the pit of his stomach, with bare head and uniform encrusted with mud and blood, he forced his weary soldiers against the foe and, as at Auerstädt, by sheer indomitable courage, compelled his troops to beat the enemy. His corps bore its share in the horrors of the retreat from Moscow, forming for some time the rear guard.

When Napoleon deserted the relics of the Grand Army at Vilna the Marshal's difficulties naturally increased, for his enemy Murat was now in command, and, as he wrote to his wife earlier in the campaign, 'I am worth ten times as much when the Emperor is present, for he alone can put order into this great complicated machine.' But the King of Naples did not long retain his command: he had not Davout's confidence in Napoleon and was disgusted with the ill-success of the campaign and was afraid of losing his crown. The Marshal, ever loyal to the Emperor, would listen to none of the Gascon's diatribes, and told him plainly, 'You are only King by the grace of Napoleon and by the blood of brave Frenchmen. You can only remain King by Napoleon's aid, and by remaining united to France. It is black ingratitude which blinds you.' So Murat went off to Italy to plan treason, and Davout returned to Germany to place his life and reputation at the Emperor's service.

It fell to the Marshal's lot in 1813 to hold Northern Germany as part of the plan of campaign whereby the advance of the Allies was to be checked. The Emperor had determined to make an example of the town of Hamburg, to teach other German cities the fate to be expected by those who deserted him. His orders were that all those who had taken any share in the desertion were to be arrested and their goods sequestrated, and that a contribution of fifty million francs was to be paid by the towns of Lübeck and Hamburg. The Marshal carried out his orders. Hamburg writhed impotent at his feet and the 'heavy arm of justice fell on the canaille'. Only in the case of the contribution did he make any deviation from the Emperor's wishes, as it was inexpedient to drive all the wealthy people out of the state. In pursuance of the Emperor's plans, by the winter of 1813 Davout had made Hamburg impregnable. He had laid in huge supplies, and built a bridge of wood two leagues long joining Haarburg and Hamburg. With a garrison of thirty thousand men, danger threatened from within rather than from without, for Napoleon's bitter punishment of Hamburg, ending as it did with the seizure of eight million marks from the funds of the city bank, had made the name of France stink in the nostrils of the inhabitants. The Marshal was determined to hold the town to the last. In December, when provisions began to fail, the poor were banished from the city; those who refused to go were threatened with fifty blows of the cane. 'At the end of December people without distinction of sex or age were dragged from their beds and conveyed out of the town.' During the siege the Russian commander, Bennigsen, attempted by means of spies and proclamations to raise a rebellion in the fortress, but Davout's grip was too firm to be shaken, and a few executions cooled the ardour of the spies. It was not till April 15th that the Marshal was informed by a flag of truce of the fall of the Empire; not certain of the truth of the news, he refused to give up his command. At last, on April 28th, official news arrived from Paris, and on the following day the fifteen thousand men who remained of the original garrison of thirty thousand swore allegiance to the Bourbons and mounted the white cockade.

On May 11th General Gerard arrived to relieve Davout of his command. On his arrival in France the Prince of Eckmühl found himself charged with having fired on the white flag after being informed of Napoleon's abdication, of appropriating the funds of the Bank of Hamburg, and of committing arbitrary acts which caused the French name to become odious. His reply was first that until he had received official information of the fall of the Empire it was his duty to take measures to prevent Hamburg being surprised; that the appropriation of the funds of the bank was the only means of finding money to hold Hamburg; that he was not responsible for the continental system, and as a soldier he had only obeyed commands; that as a matter of fact he had contrived to have the heavy contribution lightened, and lastly, that during the siege he had only had two spies shot and one French soldier executed for purloining hospital stores. But in spite of his defence and the prayers of his fellow Marshals Louis refused to allow Davout to take the oath of allegiance, and accordingly when, in 1815, Napoleon returned from Elba, the Prince of Eckmühl alone of all the Marshals could hasten to the Emperor without a stain on his honour.

Immediately on his return the Emperor made a great call on the faithfulness of his friend, and told him he had chosen him as Minister of War. The Marshal begged for service in the field, but the Emperor was firm; Davout alone had held to him and all others had the Bourbon taint. Still the Marshal refused, pleading his brusque manners and well-known harshness; but at last the Emperor appealed to his pity, pointing out that all Europe was against him, and asking him if he also was going to abandon his sovereign. Thereon the Marshal accepted the post. It was no light burden that he had undertaken, prince of martinets though he was, to regenerate an army scattered to the winds. Everything was lacking - men, horses, guns, transports, stores, and ammunition. Yet he worked wonders, and by the beginning of June the Emperor had a field army of one hundred and twenty thousand men, with another quarter of a million troops in formation in France. On the return of the Emperor to Paris after the disaster at Waterloo the Marshal in vain besought him to dissolve the assemblies and proclaim a dictatorship, but Napoleon's spirit was broken and the favourable moment passed by. Meanwhile, the Emperor remained in idleness at Malmaison, and by the 28th of June the Prussians arrived near Paris with the intention of capturing him; but the Prince of Eckmühl warded off the danger by barricading or burning the bridges across the Seine and manoeuvring sixty thousand troops in front of Blücher. Thanks to this Napoleon escaped to Rochfort, and owed his safety to Davout, for Blücher had sworn to catch him, dead or alive.

On the evacuation of Paris the Marshal withdrew westwards with the remnant of the imperial army, now called the Army of the Loire. But as soon as Louis had once again ascended the throne he relieved Davout, making Gouvion St. Cyr Minister of War and Macdonald commander of the Army of the Loire. The Marshal spent some months in exile, but was allowed to return to France in 1816. However, the mutual distrust between him and the Bourbons could not be overcome, and, although he took the oath of allegiance and received the cross of St. Louis, he never attempted to return to public life, and died of an attack of pleurisy on June 1, 1823.

The causes of the success of the Prince of Eckmühl are easy to ascertain: acute perception, doggedness of purpose, and a devotion which never faltered or failed, are gifts which are bound to bring success when added to an exceptional run of good fortune. Among the Marshals there were many, no doubt, who had as quick a perception and as vivid an imagination as Davout, but there was no one who had his massive doggedness and determination, and Bessières alone perhaps surpassed him in personal devotion to the Emperor. Much as we may see to blame in his untiring hounding down of the patriot Stein in Prussia, in his cruel exactions in Hamburg, and in the remorseless way he treated spies and deserters, we must remember that he did it all from motives of patriotism. Moreover, we cannot fail to admire a man who made it a principle, when he had received rigorous orders, to accept all the odium arising from their performance because he considered that, since the sovereign is permanent and the officials are changeable, it is important that officials should brave the temporary odium of measures which are but temporary. In his opinion the phrase, 'If the King only knew,' was a precious illusion which was one of the foundation-stones of all government: thus it was that in carrying out severe orders the Marshal never attempted to shield himself behind the name of the Emperor.

It was therefore from a spirit of patriotism, as the servant of the French Emperor, that Davout pressed relentlessly on those who tried to shake off the yoke of France. Stern as his nature was, he did not disguise from himself that his policy bore hardly on the conquered, for when Napoleon asked him, 'How would you behave if I made you King of Poland?' he replied, 'When a man has the honour to be a Frenchman, he must always be a Frenchman,' but he added, 'from the day on which I accepted the crown of Poland I would become entirely and solely a Pole, and I would act in complete contradiction to your Majesty if the interests of the people whose chief I was demanded that I should do so.' As a soldier and an administrator, though he is rightly called the prince of martinets, yet nothing was more abhorrent to his eyes than red tape. Efficiency was everything, and efficiency he considered was only to be gained by personal inspection of detail considered in relation to existing conditions, and not by blind obedience to hard and fast rules. It was this habit of mind and readiness for all contingencies which won for him his titles of Duke of Auerstädt and Prince of Eckmühl, and made him the right-hand man of the great Emperor, who confessed that, 'If I am always prepared, it is because before entering on an undertaking, I have meditated for long and foreseen what may occur. It is not genius which reveals to me suddenly and secretly what I should do in circumstances unforeseen by others: it is thought and meditation.'

9

JACQUES ÉTIENNE JOSEPH ALEXANDRE MACDONALD, MARSHAL, DUKE OF TARENTUM

JACQUES ÉTIENNE JOSEPH ALEXANDRE MACDONALD, Duke of Tarentum, was the son of a Uist crofter, Macachaim. The Macachaims of Uist were a far-off sect of the Macdonalds of Clanranald. The future Marshal's father was educated at the Scots College in Paris, and was for some time a tutor in Clanranald's household. Owing to his knowledge of French he was entrusted with the duty of helping Flora Macdonald to arrange the escape of Prince Charles. He accompanied the Prince to France, and obtained a commission in Ogilvie's regiment of foot. In 1768 Vall Macachaim, or Neil Macdonald, as he was called in France, retired on a pension of thirty pounds a year. On this pittance he brought up his family at Sancerre. The future Marshal was born at Sedan on November 17, 1765. He was educated for the army at a military academy in Paris, kept by a Scotchman, Paulet, but, owing to bad mathematics, he was unable to enter the Artillery and Engineering School. This failure came as a bitter blow to the keen young soldier, who, after reading Homer, already imagined himself an Achilles. But in 1784 his chance came; the Dutch, threatened by the Emperor Joseph II, had to improvise an army, and Macdonald accepted a pair of colours in a regiment raised by a Frenchman, the Count de Maillebois. A few months later the regiment was disbanded, as the Dutch bought the peace they could not gain by arms. The young officer, thus thrown on his own resources, was glad to accept a cadetship in Dillon's Irish regiment in the French King's service, and at the moment the Revolution broke out he was a sub-lieutenant in that corps. Owing to emigration and the fortune of war, promotion came quickly. Macdonald also was lucky in having a friend in General Beurnonville, on whose staff he served till he was transferred to that of Dumouriez, the commander-in-chief. As a reward for his services at Jemmappes and elsewhere he was made lieutenant-colonel, and early in 1793 his friend Beurnonville, who had become War Minister, gave him his colonelcy and the command of the Picardy regiment, one of the four senior corps of the old French infantry. The young colonel of twenty-eight could not expect to be always so favoured by fortune. Dumouriez's failure at Neerwinden and subsequent desertion to the Allies cast a cloud of suspicion on his protégé at a moment when to be suspected was to be condemned. Luckily, some of the Commissioners from the Convention could recognise merit, but Macdonald spent many anxious months amid denunciations and accusations from those who grudged him his colonelcy. To his intense surprise he was at last summoned before the dread Commissioners and told that, for his zeal, he was to be promoted general of brigade. Overcome by this unexpected turn of fortune, he wished to refuse the honour, and pleaded his youth and inexperience, and was promptly given the choice of accepting or becoming a 'suspect' and being arrested. Safe for the moment, Macdonald threw himself heart and soul into his new duties, but still denunciations and accusations were hurled against him. Fresh Commissioners came from the Assembly, and it was only their fortunate recall to Paris that saved the general from arrest. Then came the decree banishing all 'ci-devant' nobles. Macdonald, fearing after this order that if he met with the slightest check he would be greeted with cries of treachery, demanded written orders from the new Commissioners confirming him in his employment. These were refused, as also his resignation, with the curt reply, 'If you leave the army we will have you arrested and brought to trial.' In this dilemma he found a friend in the representative Isore, who, struck by his ability and industry, took up his cause, and from that moment Macdonald had nothing to fear from the revolutionary tribunal.

In November, 1794, he was quite unexpectedly gazetted general of division in the army of Pichegru, and took part in the winter campaign against Holland, where he proved his capacity by seizing the occasion of a hard frost to cross the Vaal on the ice and surprise the Anglo-Hanoverian force at Nimeguen. A few days later, during the general advance, he captured Naarden, the masterpiece of the great engineer Cohorn. Proud of his success, he hastened to inform the commander-in-chief, Pichegru, and was greeted by a laugh, and, 'Bah! I pay no attention now to anything less than the surrender of provinces.' The blasé commander-in-chief a week or two later himself performed the exploit of capturing the ice-bound Dutch fleet with a cavalry brigade and a battery of horse artillery.

After serving on the Rhine in 1796 Macdonald was transferred in 1798 to the Army of Italy, and sent to Rome to relieve Gouvion St. Cyr. When war broke out between France and Naples, the troops in Southern Italy were formed into the Army of Naples under Championnet. The commander-in-chief overrated the fighting qualities of the Neapolitan troops and thought it prudent to evacuate Rome. Macdonald was entrusted with this duty, and was further required to cover the concentration of Championnet's army. The hard-headed Scotchman had, however, gauged to a nicety the morale of the Neapolitan army, and, although he had but five thousand troops against forty thousand Neapolitans, under the celebrated Austrian general Mack, he engaged the enemy at Cività Castellana, defeated them, followed them up, drove them out of Rome and over the frontier, and practically annihilated the whole force. Unfortunately he wrote a comical account of the operations to his chief, who, having no sense of humour, felt that his evacuation of Rome had, to say the least of it, been hurried and undignified. Championnet therefore greeted his victorious lieutenant with the words, 'You want to make me pass for a damned fool,' and no explanations could appease his rage. So bitter became the quarrel that Macdonald had to resign his command.

By February, 1799, Championnet had fallen into disgrace with the Directory, and Macdonald was gazetted in his place commander-in-chief. When he arrived in Naples and took up his command the situation seemed quiet. But the farseeing soldier read the signs of the times. The élite of the French army was locked up in Egypt. Austria and Russia were bent on extinguishing France and her revolutionary ideas. Accordingly the general at once set about quietly concentrating his troops to meet an invasion of Northern Italy by the Allies. With his keen military insight he desired to evacuate all Southern Italy, retaining only such fortresses as could be well supplied. But the principle of keeping everything gained the day. Still, on the news of Schérer's defeat at Magnano by the impetuous Suvaroff, the Army of Naples was ready at once to start for the north, and set off to try and pick up communication with General Moreau, who was re-forming the Army of Italy at Genoa. The idea was that a concentrated movement should be made against the Allies through the Apennines. Unfortunately there existed a bitter rivalry between the Army of Italy and the Army of Naples. Consequently on June 17th Macdonald found himself with twenty-five thousand men near Piacenza, in the presence of the enemy, with no support save two divisions of the Army of Italy, which had come in from Bologna, and whose commanders were jealous of his orders. Still there was always the hope that Moreau might after all be coming to his assistance, and accordingly he determined to stand and fight. In the action of June 17th, owing to the lack of co-operation from one of the attached divisions, the general was ridden over by a division of the enemy's cavalry. Carried about in a litter, he directed all movements during the 18th, and held the enemy at bay along the mountain torrent of the Trebbia. On the 19th he determined to take the initiative, but, owing to the collapse of the attached division which formed his centre, he had to fall back on his old position, which he held throughout the whole day. During the three days' fighting on the Trebbia the French had lost a third of their men and nearly all their officers. Still, early on the morning of the 20th the retreat was effected in good order, save that one of the attached divisions under Victor started so late that it was overtaken by the enemy and abandoned all its guns. But Macdonald at once returned to its aid and saved the artillery, for, as he sarcastically wrote to Victor, 'he found neither friends nor foes.' Both sides had run away.

The battle of the Trebbia brought into notice the sterling qualities of the French commander, and when he was recalled to Paris he found that military opinion was on his side and that Bonaparte himself highly approved of his conduct. 'Thenceforward the opinion of my amphitryon was settled in my favour!' Macdonald's next employment was in command of the Army of the Grisons, whose duty was to cover Moreau's right rear in his advance down the Danube, and to keep up communication with the Army of Italy in the valley of the Po. It was in the performance of this duty that the Army of the Grisons crossed the Splügen Pass in winter in spite of glaciers and avalanches, a feat immeasurably superior to Bonaparte's task in crossing the much easier Great St. Bernard Pass, after the snows had melted. Unfortunately for Macdonald, Bonaparte believed him to belong to Moreau's faction. After Hohenlinden the future Emperor, who was afraid that Moreau's glory would outshine his own, placed all that general's friends on the black book. Further, owing to his outspokenness, Talleyrand had conceived a hatred of the hero of the Splügen. Accordingly, he found himself in deep disgrace. First he was exiled as ambassador at Copenhagen, then his enemies tried to get him sent to Russia in the same capacity, but he refused to go, and for the next few years lived the life of a quiet country gentleman on his estate of Courcelles le Roi. Like most of the generals, Macdonald was by now comparatively well off, for the French Government, on the conquest of a country, had allowed its generals to take what works of art they chose, after the Commissioners had selected the best for the national collection at the Louvre. The general's share as commander-in-chief at Naples had been valued by experts at thirty-four thousand pounds. Unfortunately, however, this booty and many masterpieces which he had bought himself were all lost in the hurried march north that ended in the battle of the Trebbia.

It was not till 1809 that Macdonald was summoned from his retreat. In that year the Emperor needed every soldier of ability, with the Spanish ulcer eating at his vitals and the war with Austria on his hands. Accordingly, at a day's notice, he was ordered to hurry off to Italy to help Napoleon's stepson, Prince Eugène, who was opposed by an Austrian army under the Archduke John.

On arriving in Italy the old soldier found that Prince Eugène, unaccustomed to an independent command, had opened the gate of Italy to the Austrians by his impetuous action at Sacile. The French troops were in complete disorganisation, and the slightest activity on the part of the Austrians would have turned the retreat into a rout.

Prince Eugène, who was without a spark of jealousy, and in reality a man of considerable character, greeted his mentor with delight. Macdonald at once pointed out that it was unnecessary to retire as far as Mantua, because the Archduke would not venture to penetrate far into Italy until a decision had been arrived at between the main armies on the Danube. Under his careful supervision, order and discipline were restored among the French troops on the line of the Adige. The news of the French success at Eckmühl and Ratisbon automatically cleared the Austrians out of Northern Italy. During the pursuit the general had to impose on himself the severest self-control, because, though Prince Eugène invariably accepted his advice, the disaster at Sacile had for the time broken his nerve, and, again and again, he spoiled his mentor's best combinations by ordering a halt whenever the enemy appeared to be going to offer any resistance. It was hard indeed to accept subsequent apologies with a courteous smile, when it was success alone that would win back the Emperor's favour. But at last patience had its reward: while the viceroy himself pursued the main force of the enemy, he detached his lieutenant with a strong corps to take Trieste and to pick up communication with Marmont, who was bringing up the army of Dalmatia. Macdonald was given carte blanche. Trieste and Görz were taken; the junction with Marmont was speedily effected, and the combined forces hurried on towards Vienna. The great entrenched camp at Laybach blocked the way. Macdonald had not the necessary heavy artillery with which to capture it. He determined therefore to make a threatening demonstration by day and slip past it by night. But at ten o'clock in the evening a flag of truce arrived offering a capitulation. 'You are doing wisely,' said the imperturbable Scotchman; 'I was just going to sound the attack.'

At Gratz he overtook Prince Eugène's army at the moment that the ill news of the battle of Aspern-Essling arrived. Then came the summons to hurry to the assistance of the Emperor. After marching sixty leagues in three days the Army of Italy arrived at nine o'clock at night on July 4th at the imperial headquarters at Ebersdorf. During that night it crossed the Danube, under cover of the terrific thunderstorm which hid the French advance from the Austrians. On the afternoon Of July 5th it fell to the lot of Macdonald to attempt to seize the plateau which formed the Austrian centre. As the general well knew, the Emperor had been mistaken in thinking that the enemy were evacuating their position; still, he had to obey orders, and night alone saved his cruelly shaken battalions. Next day was fought the terrible battle of Wagram. At the critical moment of the fight, when the Emperor heard that Masséna, on his left wing, was being driven in on the bridge-head, amid the confusion and rout he ordered Macdonald to attempt by a bold counter-stroke to break the enemy's centre. The Austrians were advancing in masses, with nothing in front of them, and the bridge, the only line of retreat, was threatened. To meet this situation Macdonald deployed four battalions in line, at the double; behind them he formed up the rest of his corps in two solid columns, and closed the rear of this immense rectangle of troops by Nansouty's cavalry. Covered by the fire of a massed battery of a hundred guns, he discharged this huge body of thirty thousand troops against the Austrians, and in spite of vast losses from the enemy's artillery, by sheer weight of human beings he completely checked the Austrian advance and broke their centre. If the cavalry of the Guard had only charged home the enemy would have been driven off the field in complete rout. Still unsupported, the column continued its victorious career, taking six thousand prisoners and ten guns, the only trophies of the day. Next morning the hero of Wagram, lame from the effect of a kick from his horse, was summoned before the Emperor.

Napoleon embraced him with the words, 'Let us be friends.' 'Till death,' replied his staunch lieutenant. Then came his reward. 'You have behaved valiantly,' continued the Emperor, 'and have rendered me the greatest services, as, indeed, throughout the entire campaign. On the battlefield of your glory, where I owe you so large a share of yesterday's success, I make you a Marshal of France. You have long deserved it.'

After the ratification of peace, the Emperor created his new Marshal Duke of Tarentum, granted him a present of sixty thousand francs, and presented him with the Grand Cordon of the Legion of Honour. Having at last regained the Emperor's favour, the Marshal had never again to complain of lack of employment. From Wagram he was sent to watch the army of the Archduke John; thereafter he was appointed commander-in-chief of the Army of Italy. In 1810 he was despatched to Spain to take command in Catalonia. Like his fellow Marshals, Macdonald hated the Spanish war, which was a war of posts, and devoid of glory. But he showed his versatility by capturing, without artillery, the stronghold of Figueras.

It was while suffering from a bad attack of gout after this success that he was summoned from Spain to Tilsit, to command the corps comprised of Prussian troops which was to join the Grand Army in its advance into Russia. As he graphically put it, 'I had left my armchair in the fortress of Figueras, I left one crutch in Paris and the other in Berlin.' The Duke of Tarentum's duty was to guard the tête-du-pont at Dunaberg, near the mouth of the Dwina; consequently he was spared a great many of the horrors of the terrible retreat. Still, he had his full share of troubles, for the Prussians deserted him and went over to the enemy. So confident was he of the loyalty of his subordinates that this desertion took him quite unawares, and, in spite of warnings, he waited for the divisions to rejoin him, declaring that, 'My life, my career, shall never be stained with the reproach that I have committed the cowardly action of deserting troops committed to my care.' Fortunately his eyes were opened by letters which he intercepted. With a handful of troops he escaped to Dantzig. On returning to Paris Macdonald was greeted with a cold reception by the Emperor, who thought that the desertion of the Prussians was due to his negligence. But the Marshal's character was soon cleared and a reconciliation followed. In the campaign of 1813 it fell to the lot of the Duke of Tarentum to watch the Prussian army under Blücher in Silesia while the Emperor operated against the Austrians round Dresden. Whilst thus employed he was defeated on August 26th at the Katzbach. The Prussians had established themselves on the heights at Jauer. Macdonald attempted, by a combined frontal attack and a turning movement, to dislodge them. Unfortunately the rain came down in torrents, the French artillery became embedded in the mud, the infantry could not fire, the cavalry could not charge, and a hurried retreat alone saved the Army from absolute annihilation, for, as Macdonald wrote in his despatch, 'The generals cannot prevent the men from seeking shelter, as their muskets are useless to them.'

The repulse at the Katzbach did not weaken the Emperor's esteem for the Marshal, and a few days later he sent to inquire his views of the general situation. With absolute courage he told the truth. The situation was hopeless; the only wise course was to evacuate all garrisons in Germany and retire on the Saale. Unfortunately, such a retirement would have meant the loss of Napoleon's throne.

On the third day of the battle of Leipzig, in the midst of the action, Macdonald was deserted by all the Hessian troops under his command, and, at the same time, Marshal Augereau, who was supposed to cover his right, withdrew from the combat. Accordingly, the Marshal retired with the remnants of his corps to the Elster, only to find the bridge blown up. Dragged along by the crowd of fugitives, he determined not to fall alive into the hands of the enemy, but either to drown or shoot himself. More fortunate, however, than Prince Poniatowski, he managed to cross the river on his horse. Once safely across, he was greeted by cries from the other bank, 'Monsieur le Maréchal, save your soldiers, save your children!' But there was nothing to be done; no advice could he give them save to surrender.

The Duke of Tarentum was mainly instrumental in saving the remnants of the army which had managed to cross the Elster. Going straight to the Emperor, he laid the situation before him, ruthlessly tore aside the tissue of lies with which the staff were trying to cajole him, and, by his force of will, compelled Napoleon, who for the time was quite unnerved and mazed, to hurry on the retreat to the Rhine. It was entirely owing to the Marshal that the Bavarians were brushed aside at Hanau, and that some few remnants of the great army regained France.

In the famous campaign of 1814 Macdonald fought fiercely to drive the enemy out of France. His corps was one of those which the Emperor summoned to Arcis sur Aube. There again he had to tell Napoleon the truth and convince him that the enemy were not retreating, but were in full advance on Paris. When the Emperor tried to retrieve his mistake by following in the rear, the Marshal was in favour of the bolder course of advancing into Alsace and Lorraine, and of raising the nation in arms, and thus starving out the Allies by cutting off their supplies and reinforcements; and no doubt he was right, for the Czar himself said that the Allies lost more than three thousand troops in the Vosges without seeing a single French soldier.

When Napoleon reached Fontainebleau he found that he had shot his bolt. So tired were his officers and men of continual fighting that, when ordered to charge, a general officer in front of his men had called out, 'Damn it, let us have peace!' Consequently when Macdonald and the other Marshals and generals were informed that the Allies would no longer treat with Napoleon, they determined to make him abdicate. The Emperor, on summoning his council, found that they no longer feared him, and refused to listen to his arguments. Hoping to save the throne for his son, he despatched Caulaincourt, Ney, Marmont, and Macdonald to the Czar, offering to abdicate. The best terms the Commissioners could get from the Czar were that Napoleon must give up all hope of seeing his son succeed him, but that he should retain his imperial title and should be allowed to rule the island of Elba. The Czar magnanimously added, 'If he will not accept this sovereignty, and if he can find no shelter elsewhere, tell him, I say, to come to my dominions. There he shall be received as a sovereign: he can trust the word of Alexander.'

Ney and Marmont did not accompany the other Commissioners with their sorrowful terms; like rats they left the sinking ship. But Macdonald was of a strain which had stood the test of the '45, and his proud Scotch blood boiled up when the insidious Talleyrand suggested that he should desert his master, telling him that he had now fulfilled all his engagements and was free. 'No, I am not,' was the stern reply, 'and nobody knows better than you that, as long as a treaty has not been ratified, it may be annulled. After that formality is ended, I shall know what to do.' The stricken Emperor met his two faithful Commissioners, his face haggard, his complexion yellow and sickly, but for once at least he felt gratitude. 'I have loaded with favours,' he said, 'many others who have now deserted and abandoned me. You, who owe me nothing, have remained faithful. I appreciate your loyalty too late, and I sincerely regret that I am now in a position in which I can only prove my gratitude by words.'

After Napoleon started for Elba, Macdonald never saw him again. Like all his fellow Marshals, except Davout, he swore allegiance to Louis XVIII, looking on him as the only hope of France, but, unlike the most of them, he served him loyally, though, as he truly said, 'The Government behaved like a sick man who is utterly indifferent to all around him.' As a soldier and a liberal he could not disguise his repugnance for many of its measures. As secretary to the Chamber of Peers, he fought tooth and nail against the Government's first measure, a Bill attempting to restrict the liberties of the peers. The King summoned the Marshal and rebuked him for both speaking and voting against the Government, adding, 'When I take the trouble to draw up a Bill, I have good reasons for wishing it to pass.' But the old soldier, who had never feared to speak the truth to Napoleon himself, was not to be overawed by the attempted sternness of the feeble Bourbon. He pointed out that if all Bills presented by the King were bound to pass, 'registration would serve equally well, since to you belongs the initiative,' adding with quiet sarcasm, 'and we must remain as mute as the late Corps Legislatif.' The Chancellor stopped him as he left the King's presence, telling him he should show more reserve and pick his words. 'Sir Chancellor,' said the Marshal, 'I have never learned to twist myself, and I pity the King if what he ought to know is concealed from him. For my part, I shall always speak to him honestly and serve him in the same manner.'

When neglect of the army, the partiality shown to favourites, and the general spirit of discontent throughout France tempted Napoleon once again to seize the reins of government, Macdonald was commanding the twenty-first military division at Bourges. As he says, 'The news of the Emperor's return took away my breath, and I at once foresaw the misfortunes that have since settled upon France.' Placing his duty to his country and his plighted faith before the longings of his heart, he remained faithful to the Bourbons. It was the Marshal who at Lyons vainly endeavoured to aid the Count of Artois to organise resistance to Napoleon's advance. It was he who showed the King the vanity of Ney's boast that he would bring back the Emperor in an iron cage, who impressed on him Napoleon's activity, and who persuaded him to retire northwards to Lille and there attempt to rally his friends to his aid. Ministers and King were only too thankful to leave all arrangements to this cautious, indefatigable soldier, who supervised everything. Through every town the monarch passed he found the same feeling of apathy, the same tendency among the troops to cry 'Vive l'Empereur,' the same lack of enterprise among the officials. Typical of the situation was the sub-prefect of Bethune, who stood at the door of the royal carriage, one leg half-naked, his feet in slippers, his coat under his arm, his waistcoat unbuttoned, his hat on his head, one hand struggling with his sword, the other trying to fasten his necktie. The Marshal, ever mindful of Napoleon's activity, had to hurry the poor King, and Louis' portmanteau, with his six clean shirts and his old pair of slippers, got lost on the road. This loss, more than anything else, brought home to the monarch his pitiable condition. 'They have taken my shirts,' said he to Macdonald. 'I had not too many in the first place; but what I regret still more is the loss of my slippers. Some day, my dear Marshal, you will appreciate the value of slippers that have taken the shape of your feet.' With Napoleon at Paris, Lille seemed to offer but little security, and accordingly the King determined to seek safety in Belgium. The Marshal escorted him to the frontier and saw him put in charge of the Belgian troops. Then, promising to be faithful to his oath, he took an affectionate farewell of the old monarch with the words, 'Farewell, sir; au revoir, in three months!'

Macdonald returned to Paris and lived quietly in his own house, refusing to have any intercourse with Napoleon or his ministers. Within three months came the news of Waterloo. Thereafter, against his will, but in accordance with orders, he joined Fouché, who had established a provisional government. Fouché, who knew the importance of outward signs, sent him off to try and persuade the returning monarch to win over the army by mounting the tricolour instead of the white cockade. But the King was obstinate; the Marshal quoted Henry IV's famous saying, 'Paris is worth a mass.' The King countered with, 'Yes; but it was not a very Catholic one.' But though the King would not listen to his advice he called on him to show his devotion. The imperial army had to be disbanded - a most unpopular and thankless task, requiring both tact and firmness. At his sovereign's earnest request, Macdonald undertook the duty, but with two stipulations: first, that he should have complete freedom of action; secondly, that he should be in no way an instrument for inflicting punishment on individuals. Immediately on taking up his appointment at Bourges, the Marshal summoned all the generals and officers to his presence, and informed them that, under Fouché's supervision, a list of proscribed had been drawn up. His advice was that all on this list should fly at once. That same evening police officials arrived in the camp to arrest the proscribed; playing on the fears of the mouchards, he locked them up all night, alleging that it was to save them from the infuriated soldiery. Thus all the proscribed escaped; but neither Fouché nor the Duc de Berri cared to bring the old soldier to task for this action. So the Marshal was left to work in his own way, and by October 21, 1815, thanks to his firmness and tact, 'the bold and unhappy army, which had for so long been triumphant,' was quietly dissolved without the slightest attempt at challenging the royal decision.

The Marshal did not mix much in politics. The King, at the second Restoration, created him arch-chancellor of the Legion of Honour. This post gave him considerable occupation, as it entailed the supervision of the schools for the children of those who had received the Cross, and he was for long happily employed in looking after the welfare of the descendants of his late comrades-in-arms. In November, 1830, the plea of the gout came opportunely at the moment of the commencement of the July monarchy, and the Marshal resigned the arch-chancellorship and returned to his estate of Courcelles, where he lived in retirement till his death, on September 25, 1840, at the age of seventy-five.

It was a maxim of Napoleon that success covers everything, that it is only failure which cannot be forgiven. Against the Duke of Tarentum's name stood the defeats of Trebbia and the Katzbach. But in spite of this, Napoleon never treated him as he treated Dupont and the other unfortunate generals. For Macdonald possessed qualities which were too important to be overlooked. With all the fiery enthusiasm of the Gael, he possessed to an unusual degree the caution of the Lowland Scot. Possessed of great reasoning powers and of the gift of seeing clearly both sides of a question, he had the necessary force of character to make up his mind which course to pursue, and to persevere in it to the logical issue. In the crossing of the Vaal, in the fighting round Rome, in the campaign with Prince Eugène in Italy, before and after Leipzig, and in his final campaign in France, he proved the correctness of his judgment and his capacity to work out his carefully prepared combinations. His defeat at the Trebbia was due to the treachery of the general commanding one of the attached divisions; the rout at the Katzbach was primarily due to climatic conditions and to the want of cohesion among the recently drafted recruits which formed the bulk of his army. On the stricken field of Wagram, and in the running fight at Hanau, his inflexible will and the quickness with which he grasped the vital points of the problem saved the Emperor and his army.

The only black spot in his otherwise glorious career is the battle of Leipzig. Long must the cry of 'Monsieur le Maréchal, save your soldiers, save your children!' have rung in his ear. For once he had forgotten his proud boast that he never deserted troops entrusted to his command. Like the Emperor and his fellow Marshals and most of the generals, for the moment he lost his nerve; but he could still, though humbly, boast that he was the first to remember his duties and to try and save the remnant of the troops who had crossed the Elster.

Duty and truth were his watchwords. Once only he failed in his duty; never did he shirk telling the truth. It was this fearless utterance of the truth more than any connection with Moreau which was the cause of his long years of disgrace; it was this fearlessness, strange to say, which, in the end, conquered the Emperor, and which so charmed King Louis that he nicknamed him 'His Outspokenness'.

10

AUGUSTE FRÉDÉRIC LOUIS VIESSE DE MARMONT, MARSHAL, DUKE OF RAGUSA

AUGUSTE FRÉDÉRIC LOUIS VIESSE DE MARMONT, the youngest of Napoleon's Marshals, was born at Châtillon-sur-Seine on July 25, 1774. The family of Viesse belonged to the smaller nobility, who from the days of Richelieu had supplied the officers of the line for the old royal army. Marmont's father had destined him from the cradle for the military career, and had devoted his life to training him, both in body and mind, for the profession of arms. His hours of patience and self-denial were not thrown away, for, thanks to his early Spartan training, the Duke of Ragusa seldom knew fatigue or sickness, and owing to this physical strength was able, without neglecting his professional duties, to spend hours on scientific and literary work. In 1792 young Marmont, at the age of eighteen, passed the entrance examination for the Artillery School at Chilons, and started his military career with his father's oft-repeated words ringing in his ears, 'Merit without success is infinitely better than success without merit, but determination and merit always command success.' The young artillery cadet had both determination and capacity and his early career foreshadowed his future success. Aristocratic to the bone, Marmont detested the excesses of the Revolution; but politics, during his early years, had little effect on his thoughts, which were solely fixed on military glory. The exigencies of the revolutionary wars cut short his student days at Châlons, and before the end of 1792 he was gazetted to the first artillery regiment. In February, 1793, he saw his first active service with the Army of the Alps, under General Kellermann. Owing to the dearth of trained officers, though only newly gazetted, he performed all the duties of a senior colonel, laying out entrenched camps and commanding the artillery of the division to which he was attached. It was with this promising record already behind him that he attracted Bonaparte's attention at the siege of Toulon by his admirable handling of the guns under his command, and by his inventive powers, which overcame all obstacles. From that day the Corsican destined him for his service, and during the campaign in the Maritime Alps used him as an unofficial aide-de-camp. So devoted did Marmont become to the future Emperor, that when Bonaparte was arrested at the time of Robespierre's fall, he and Junot formed a plan of rescuing their idol by killing the sentries and carrying him off by sea.

When Bonaparte returned to Paris Marmont accompanied him, and was offered the post of superintendent of the gun factory at Moulins. He contemptuously refused this position, telling the inspector of ordnance that he would not mind such a post in peace time, but that he was going to see as much active service as he could while the war lasted, so at his own request he was posted to the army of Pichegru, which was besieging Maintz.

A temporary suspension of hostilities on the Rhine gave him the opportunity of once again joining his chosen leader, and early in 1796 he started for Italy on Bonaparte's staff. Lodi was one of the great days of his life. Early in the action he captured one of the enemy's batteries, but a moment later he was thrown from his horse and ridden over by the whole of the cavalry, without, however, receiving a single scratch. Scarcely had he mounted when he was despatched along the river, under fire of the whole Austrian force on the other bank, to carry orders to the commander of the cavalry, who was engaged in fording the river higher up. Of his escort of five, two were killed, while his horse was severely wounded, yet he managed to return in time to take his place among the band of heroes who forced the long bridge in the face of a storm of bullets and grape. Castiglione added to his laurels, for it was his handling of the artillery that enabled Augereau to win his great victory. The Marshal, in his Memoirs, asserts that this short campaign was the severest strain he ever underwent. 'I never at any other time endured such fatigue as during the eight days of that campaign. Always on horseback, on reconnaissance, or fighting, I was, I believe, five days without sleep, save for a few stolen minutes. After the final battle the general-in-chief gave me leave to rest and I took full advantage of it.

I ate, I lay down, and I slept twenty-four hours at a stretch, and, thanks to youth, hardiness, a good constitution, and the restorative powers of sleep, I was as fresh again as at the beginning of the campaign.'

Though Castiglione thus brought him fresh honours, it nearly caused an estrangement between him and his chief. For Bonaparte, ever with an eye to the future, desiring to gain as many friends as possible, chose one of Berthier's staff officers to take the news of the victory to Paris. This was a bitter blow to his ambitious aide-de-camp, whose pride was further piqued because his hero, forgetting that he had not to deal with one of the ordinary adventurers who formed so large a number of the officers of the Army of Italy, with great want of tact, had offered him opportunities of adding to his wealth by perquisites and commissions abhorrent to the eyes of a descendant of an honourable family. But the exigencies of war and the thirst for glory left little time for brooding, and Bonaparte, recognising with whom he had to deal, took the opportunity of the successful fighting which penned Würmser into Mantua to send Marmont with despatches to Paris. As his reward the Minister of War promoted him colonel and commandant of the second regiment of horse artillery. A curious state of affairs arose from this appointment, for promotion in the artillery ran quite independent of ordinary army rank. Accordingly, the army list ran as follows: Bonaparte, lieutenant-colonel of a battalion of artillery, seconded as general-in-chief of the Army of Italy. Marmont, colonel of the second regiment horse artillery, seconded as aide-de-camp to Lieutenant-Colonel Bonaparte, the commander-in-chief of the Army of Italy.

Marmont hurried back to Italy in time to join Bonaparte's staff an hour before the battle of Arcola. The Austrians were making their last effort to relieve the fortress of Mantua, and it seemed as if they would be successful, as Alvinzi had concentrated forty thousand troops against twenty-six thousand. The French attempted a surprise, but were discovered, and for three days the fate of the campaign hung on the stubborn fight in the marshes of Arcola. It was Marmont who helped to extricate Bonaparte when he was flung off the embankment into the ditch, a service which Bonaparte never forgot. Diplomatic missions to Venice and the Vatican slightly turned the young soldier's head, and his chief had soon to give him a severe reprimand for loitering among Josephine's beauties at Milan instead of hastening back to headquarters. But to a man of Marmont's character one word of warning was enough; his head governed his heart; glory was his loadstar. Ambitious though he was, he was essentially a man of honour and fine feelings, and refused the hand of Pauline Bonaparte - for the simple reason that he did not truly love her.

A year later he made a love match with Mademoiselle Perrégaux, but differences of temperament and the long separation which his military career imposed caused the marriage to turn out unhappily, and this lack of domestic felicity spoiled the Marshal's life and nearly embittered his whole character, turning him for the time into a self-centred man with an eye solely to his own glory and a sharp tongue which did not spare even his own friends. Yet in his early days Marmont was a bright and cheerful companion and no one enjoyed more a practical joke, getting up sham duels between cowards or sending bogus instructions to officious commanders. But fond as he was of amusement, even during his early career he could find delight in the society of men of science and learning like Monge and Berthollet.

After the peace of Campo Formio he accompanied his chief to Paris, where an incident occurred which illustrates well the character of the two men. The Minister of War wanted detailed information regarding the English preparations against invasion, and Bonaparte offered to send his aide-de-camp as a spy. Marmont indignantly refused to go in such a capacity, and a permanent estrangement nearly took place. Their standards had nothing in common; in the one honour could conquer ambition, in the other ambition knew no rules of honour.

However, their lust for glory brought them together again, and Marmont sailed with the Egyptian expedition. He was despatched north to command Alexandria after the battle of the Pyramids, where his guns had played so important a part in shattering the Mamelukes. Later he was entrusted with the control of the whole of the Mediterranean littoral. His task was a difficult one, but a most useful training for a young commander. With a tiny garrison he had to hold the important town of Alexandria and to keep in order a large province; to organise small columns to repress local risings; to make his own arrangements for raising money to pay his troops, and consequently to reorganise the fiscal system of the country; to reconstruct canals and to improvise flotillas of barges to supply Alexandria with provisions; to keep in touch with the remnant of the French fleet and thus to try to establish communications with Europe. He was responsible for resisting any attempt at invasion by the Turks or the English, and it was mainly owing to his measures that when the former landed at Aboukir they were destroyed before they could march inland. While his comrades were gaining military glory in Syria, he was fighting the plague at Alexandria, learning that patient attention to detail and careful supervision of the health of his troops were as important attributes of a commander as dash and courage in the field.

Marmont quitted Egypt with joy; he had learned many useful lessons, but, like the rest of the army, he hated the country and the half Oriental life, and above all, as he said, 'seeing a campaign and not taking part in it was a horrible punishment.' On returning to Paris his time was fully occupied in winning over the artillery to Bonaparte. He had no false ideas on the subject, for, as he said to Junot before the Egyptian expedition, 'You will see, my friend, that on his return Bonaparte will seize the crown.' As his reward the First Consul gave him the choice of the command of the artillery of the Guard or a seat as Councillor of State. Jealous of Lannes, and flattered by the title, he chose the councillorship, in which capacity he was employed on the War Committee and entrusted with the reorganisation of the artillery. His first business was to provide a proper train to ensure the quick and easy mobilisation of the artillery. After the Marengo campaign he took in hand the reform of the matériel. Too many different types of guns existed. Marmont reorganised both the field and the fortress artillery, replacing the seven old types of guns by three - namely, six-pounders, twelve-pounders and twenty-four pounders; he also reduced the different types of wheels for gun carriages, limbers and wagons from twenty-four to eight, thus greatly simplifying the provision of ammunition and the work of repair in the field.

The Marengo campaign added to his prestige as an artillery officer.

It was owing to his ingenuity that the guns were unmounted and pulled by hand in cradles up the steep side of the mountain and thus safely taken over the St. Bernard Pass. It was his ingenious brain which suggested the paving of the road with straw, whereby the much-needed artillery was forwarded to Lannes by night, without any casualties, right under the batteries of the fortress of Bard. It was owing to his foresight that the reserve battery of guns, captured from the enemy, saved the day at Marengo by containing the Austrians while Desaix's fresh troops were being deployed, and it was the tremendous effect of his massed battery which gave Kellermann the opportunity for his celebrated charge. The First Consul marked his approval by promoting Marmont a general of division, and thus at the age of twenty-six the young artillery officer had nearly reached the head of his profession. After Marengo he continued his work of reorganisation, but before the end of the year he was once again in Italy, this time as a divisional commander under Brune, who, being no great strategist, was glad to avail himself of the brains of the First Consul's favourite: it was thanks to Marmont's plans that the French army successfully crossed the Mincio in the face of the enemy and forced on him the armistice of Treviso. When Moreau's victory of Hohenlinden induced Austria to make peace, the general was sent to reorganise the Italian artillery on the same principles he had laid down for the French. He established an immense foundry and arsenal at Pavia, and the excellence of his plans was clearly proved in many a later campaign. From Italy he was recalled to Paris in September, 1802, as inspector-general of artillery. He threw himself heart and soul into his new duties, but found time to increase his scientific knowledge and to keep himself up to date with everything in the political and scientific world. He keenly supported Fulton's invention of the steamboat, and pressed it on the First Consul, and to the day of his death he was convinced that, if the Emperor had adopted the invention, the invasion of England would have been successful.

The year 1804 brought him the delight of his first important command. In February he was appointed chief of the corps of the Army of the Ocean which was stationed in Holland. He entered on his task with his usual fervour. His first step was to make friends with all the Dutch officials, and thus to secure the smooth working of his commissariat and supply departments; then he turned to the actual training of his troops. For this purpose he obtained permission to hold a big camp of instruction, where all the divisions of his corps were massed. So successful was this experiment that it became an annual institution. But amid all the pleasure of this congenial work came the bitter moment when he found the name of so mediocre a soldier as Bessières included in the list of the new Marshals and his own omitted. It was a sore blow, and his appointment as colonel-general of the horse chasseurs and Grand Eagle of the Legion of Honour did little to mitigate it. The Emperor, careful as ever to stimulate devotion, later explained to him that a dashing officer like himself would have plenty of opportunities of gaining distinction, while this was Bessières's only chance. But in spite of this the neglect rankled, and from that day he was no longer the blindly devoted follower of Napoleon.

On the outbreak of the Austrian War Marmont's corps became the second corps of the Grand Army. In the operations ending in Ulm the second corps formed part of the left wing. After the capitulation it was detached to cover the French communications from an attack from the direction of Styria. In the summer of the following year Marmont was despatched as commander-in-chief to Dalmatia, where he spent the next five years of his life. Dalmatia had been ceded to France by the treaty of Pressburg. In Napoleon's eyes the importance of the province lay in the harbour of Cattaro, which he regarded as an outlet to the Balkan Peninsula. His intention was to get possession of Montenegro, to come to an understanding with Ali Pacha of Janina and the Sultan, and oppose the policy of Russia. But the Russians and Montenegrins had seized Cattaro, and were threatening to besiege Ragusa. It was to meet this situation that the Emperor in July, 1806, hastily sent his former favourite to Dalmatia. The new commander-in-chief found himself, as in Egypt, faced with the difficulty of supply. Half the army was in hospital from want of proper nourishment and common-sense sanitation. Having, by his care of his men, refilled his battalions, he advanced boldly on the enemy, and drove them out of their positions. This punishment kept the Montenegrins quiet for the future, and the Russians fell back on

Cattaro. From there he was unable to drive them owing to the guns of their fleet, and it was not till the treaty of Tilsit that the French got possession of the coveted port. The French commander's chief difficulty in administering his province was that which is felt in all uncivilised countries, the difficulty of holding down a hostile population where roads do not exist. Otherwise his just but stern rule admirably suited the townsmen of the little cities on the coast, while order was kept among the hill tribes by making their headmen responsible for their behaviour, and by aiding them in attacking the Turks, who had seized certain tracts of territory and maltreated the inhabitants. But it was not gratitude which kept the hill-men quiet, so much as the miles of new roads on which the French commander employed his army when not engaged on expeditions against restless marauders. During his years in the Dalmatian provinces Marmont constructed more than two hundred miles of roads, with the result that his small force was able with ease to hold down the long narrow mountainous province by the speed with which he could mobilise his punitive expeditions. Moreover, owing to the increased means of traffic the peasants were able to find a market for their goods, and the prosperity of the country increased beyond belief. With prosperity came contentment: manufactures were established, and the mines and the other natural resources of the country were exploited to advantage. As the Emperor of Austria said to Metternich in 1817, when visiting the province, 'It is a great pity that Marshal Marmont was not two or three years longer in Dalmatia.'

The years spent at Ragusa were probably the happiest of Marmont's life. His successful work was recognised in 1808, when the Emperor created him Duke of Ragusa. Each day was full of interest. He was head of the civil administration and of the judicial and fiscal departments. As commander-in-chief he was responsible for the health, welfare, and discipline of the troops, and for the military works which were being erected to protect the province from Austrian aggression. He had his special hobby - the roads. Yet in spite of all this business he found time to put himself in the hands of a tutor and to work ten hours a day at history, chemistry, and anatomy. To aid him in his studies he collected a travelling library of six hundred volumes which accompanied him in all his later campaigns.

The Austrian campaign of 1809 called him from these congenial labours to the even more congenial operations of war. The duty of the Army of Dalmatia was to attempt to cut off the Archduke John on his retirement from Italy; but the Duke of Ragusa had not sufficient troops to carry out this operation successfully, although he effected a junction with the Army of Italy. After a succession of small engagements the united armies found themselves on the Danube in time to take part in the battle of Wagram. In reserve during the greater part of the battle, Marmont's corps was entrusted with the pursuit of the enemy. Unfortunately, either from lack of appreciation of the situation or from jealousy, their commander refused to allow Davout to co-operate with him, and consequently, although he overtook the Austrians, he was not strong enough to hold them till other divisions of the army came up. However, at the end of the operations Napoleon created him Marshal. But the Duke of Ragusa's joy at receiving this gift was tempered by the way it was given. For the Emperor, angry doubtless at the escape of the Austrians, told him, 'I have given you your nomination and I have great pleasure in bestowing on you this proof of my affection, but I am afraid I have incurred the reproach of listening rather to my affection than to your right to this distinction. You have plenty of intelligence, but there are needed for war qualities in which you are still lacking, and which you must work to acquire. Between ourselves, you have not yet done enough to justify entirely my choice. At the same time, I am confident that I shall have reason to congratulate myself on having nominated you, and that you will justify me in the eyes of the army.' Unkind critics of the three new Marshals created after Wagram said that Napoleon, having lost Lannes, wanted to get the small change for him, but it is only fair to remember that though Macdonald, Marmont, and Oudinot were all inferior to Lannes, they were quite as good soldiers as some of the original Marshals.

After peace was declared the new Marshal returned to Dalmatia and took up the threads of his old life. He had won the respect of the inhabitants and the fear of their foes, the Turks, and save for an occasional expedition against the brigands or friction with the fiscal officials, his time passed peaceably and pleasantly. But in 1811 he was recalled to Paris to receive orders before starting on a new sphere of duty. Masséna, 'the spoiled child of victory', had met his match at Torres Vedras, and Napoleon, blaming the man instead of the system, had determined to try a fresh leader for the army opposing Sir Arthur Wellesley. The Emperor did not hide from himself the fact that in selecting Marmont he was making an experiment, for he told St. Cyr that he had sent Marmont to Spain because he had plenty of talent, but that he had not yet tested to the full his force of character, and he added, 'I shall soon be able to judge of that, for now he is left to his own resources.' The new commander of the Army of Portugal set out with the full confidence that the task was not beyond his powers, and with the promise of the vice-royalty of one of the five provinces into which Spain was to be divided. He arrived at the front two days after the battle of Fuentes d'Onoro, and found a very different state of affairs from what he had expected. The country was a howling waste covered with fierce guerrillas. The French army, so long accustomed to success, was absolutely demoralised by repeated disappointments and defeats. It was necessary to take stringent measures to restore the morale of the troops before he could call on them to face once more 'the infantry whose fire was the most murderous of all the armies of Europe.'

Accordingly he withdrew from the Portuguese frontier, put his army into cantonments round Salamanca, and set to work on the difficult task of collecting supplies from a country which was already swept bare. Meanwhile he split up his army into six divisions, established direct communications between himself and the divisional officers, and, to get rid of the grumblers, gave leave to all officers, who so desired, to return to France. At the same time he distributed his weak battalions among the other corps so that each battalion had a complement of seven hundred muskets. He also broke up the weak squadrons and batteries and brought up the remainder to service strength. Scarcely was this reorganisation completed when Soult, who had been defeated at Albuera, called on Marmont to aid him in saving Badajoz. In spite of his personal dislike for the Duke of Dalmatia, the Marshal hurried to his aid and for the time the important fortress was saved. During the rest of the summer the Army of Portugal lay in the valley of the Tagus, holding the bridge of Almaraz, and thus ready at any moment to go to the relief of Badajoz or Ciudad Rodrigo, the two keys of Portugal. When, in the autumn, Wellington threatened Ciudad Rodrigo, the Marshal, calling to his aid Dorsenne, who commanded in Northern Spain, at the successful engagement of El Bodin drove back the advance guard of the Anglo-Portuguese and threw a large quantity of provisions into the fortress.

The year 1812 was a disastrous one for the French arms all over Europe. The Emperor attempted to direct the Spanish War from Paris. In his desire to secure all Southern Spain, he stripped Marmont's army to reinforce Suchet in his conquest of Valencia. Accordingly in January the Marshal was powerless to stop Wellington's dash at Ciudad Rodrigo, and was unable later to make a sufficient demonstration in Portugal to relieve the pressure on Badajoz; so both the fortresses fell, and the Duke of Ragusa was blamed for the Emperor's mistake. He was thereafter called upon to try to stem the victorious advance of the English into Spain. Short of men, of horses, and of supplies, he did wonders. Thanks to his strenuous efforts, supplies were massed at Salamanca, good food and careful nursing emptied the hospitals and filled the ranks, and the cavalry was supplied with remounts by dismounting the 'field officers' of the infantry. The month of July saw an interesting duel round Salamanca between Marmont and Wellington. The two armies were very nearly equal in numbers, the French having forty-seven thousand men and the English forty-four thousand. The French had the advantage of a broad base with lines of retreat either on Burgos or Madrid. The English had to cover their single line of communication, which ran through Ciudad Rodrigo. The French had the further advantage that their infantry marched better than the English. Owing to these causes their commander was so far able to outgeneral his adversary that by July 22nd he was actually threatening the English line of retreat. But a tactical mistake threw away all these strategic advantages. In his eagerness he allowed his leading division to get too extended, forgetting that he was performing the dangerous operation of a flank march. Wellington waited till he saw his opportunity and then threw himself on the weak French centre and cut the French army in half, thus proving his famous dictum that the great general is not he who makes fewest mistakes, but he who can best take advantage of the mistakes of his enemy. Marmont saw his error as soon as the English attack began, but a wound from a cannon ball disabled him at the very commencement of the action. This injury to his arm was so serious that he had to throw up his command and return to France, and for the whole of the next year he had to wear his arm in a sling.

Napoleon, furious with the Marshal for his ill-success, most unjustly blamed him for not waiting for reinforcements: these actually arrived two days after the battle. Joseph, however, had told him distinctly that he was not going to send him any help, and if it had not been for his tactical blunders, Marmont would undoubtedly have caused Wellington to fall back on Portugal. But in 1813 the exigencies of war demanded that France should send forth every soldier, and accordingly in March the Duke of Ragusa was gazetted to the command of the sixth corps, which was forming in the valley of the Maine. On taking up this command he found that his corps was mainly composed of sailors drafted from the useless ships, and of recruits, while his artillery had no horses and his cavalry did not exist. With these raw troops he had to undergo some difficult experiences at Lützen and Bautzen, but, as the campaign progressed, he moulded them into shape, and his divisions did good service in the fighting in Silesia and round Dresden. At the rout after the battle of Leipzig, Marmont, like most of the higher officers of the army, thought more of his personal safety than of his honour, and allowed himself to be escorted from the field by his staff officers.

But in the campaign of 1814 he made amends for all his former blunders, and his fighting record stands high indeed. At Saint-Dizier, La Rothière, Arcis-sur-Aube, Nogent, Sézanne, and Champaubert, he held his own or defeated the enemy with inferior numbers in every case. Once only at Laon did he allow himself to be surprised. When the end came it was Marmont who, at Joseph's command, had to hand over Paris to the Allies. Thereafter he was faced with a terrible problem. His army was sick of fighting, officers and men demanded peace. He had to decide whether his duty to Napoleon was the same as his duty to France. Unfortunately he acted hurriedly, and, without informing the Emperor, entered into negotiations with the enemy. The result was far-reaching, for his conduct showed Alexander that the army was sick of war and would no longer fight for Napoleon. It thus cut away the ground of the Commissioners who were trying, by trading on the prestige of the Emperor and the fear of his name, to persuade the Czar to accept Napoleon's abdication on behalf of his son, the King of Rome. The Marshal's enemies put down his action to illwill against the Emperor for withholding for so long the marshalate and for his treatment after Salamanca. But Marmont asserted that it was patriotism which dictated his action, and further maintained that Napoleon himself ought to have approved of his action, quoting a conversation held in 1813. 'If the enemy invaded France,' said the Emperor, 'and seized the heights of Montmartre, you would naturally believe that the safety of your country would command you to leave me, and if you did so you would be a good Frenchman, a brave man, a conscientious man, but not a man of honour.'

The defection of the Duke of Ragusa came as a bitter blow to Napoleon. 'That Marmont should do such a thing,' cried the fallen Emperor, 'a man with whom I have shared my bread, whom I drew out of obscurity! Ungrateful villain, he will be more unhappy than I.' The prophecy was true. The Duke of Ragusa stuck to the Bourbons and refused to join Napoleon during the Hundred Days, going to Ghent as chief of the military household of the exiled King. He returned with Louis to Paris, and was made major-general of the Royal Guard and a peer of France, in which capacity he sat as one of the judges who condemned Ney to death. But men looked askance at him, and from 1817 he lived in retirement, occupying his leisure in experimental farming, with great injury to his purse, for his elaborate scheme of housing his sheep in three-storeyed barns and clothing them in coats made of skin was most unprofitable. Retirement was a bitter blow to the keen soldier, but the Bourbon monarchs clearly understood that the deserter of Napoleon and the judge of Marshal Ney could never be popular with the army.

Still, when in July, 1830, discontent was seething, Charles X remembered his sterling qualities and summoned him to Paris as governor of the city. It was an unfortunate nomination, for the Marshal's unpopularity weakened the bonds of discipline, whilst his eagerness to show his loyalty caused him to adopt such measures as the King ordered, irrespective of their military worth. In vain he warned the King that this was not a revolt but a revolution; the counsels of Polignac were all powerful. The Marshal's political suggestions were unheeded and his military plans overridden. The mass of the troops of the line, kept for long hours without food in the streets, mutinied and went over to the populace, while those who remained loyal, and the royal guards, instead of being concentrated and protected by batteries of artillery, were frittered away in useless expeditions into outlying parts of the city. After two days' fighting the royalists had to evacuate the city. Thus it fell to the lot of the Marshal once more to hand over Paris to the foes of those to whom his allegiance was due.

The Duke of Ragusa accompanied Charles to Cherbourg and quitted France in August, 1830, never to return. The remainder of his life was spent in foreign countries. He made Vienna his headquarters, and from there took journeys to Russia, Turkey, Egypt, and Italy. Deeply interested in science and history, he devoted his leisure to writing his Memoirs, to works on military science, philanthropy, and travel. Thus occupied, though an exile from his country, he lived a busy, active, and on the whole useful life till death overtook him at Vienna in 1852.

Marshal Marmont has been called one of Napoleon's failures, but this criticism is one-sided and unjust. True it is that his name is intimately connected with the failure in Spain and with the fall of the Empire, but to judge his career by these two instances and to neglect his other work, is to generalise from an insufficient and casual basis. The Duke of Ragusa owed his marshalate, like many others, to his intimacy with Napoleon, but unlike several of the Marshals he really earned his baton. His great powers of organisation, so unstintedly given to the rearmament of France and Italy, and his work of regeneration in Dalmatia, together with his military operations in Styria, Spain, and during the campaign of 1814, mark him out as a soldier of great capabilities. Organisation was his strong point, but he also possessed great physical bravery and many of the qualities of a commander. His love for his profession was great, and not only had he graduated under Napoleon's eye, but much of his time was spent in studying his calling from a scientific and historical point of view. As a strategist he probably stood as high as any of his fellow Marshals, and his operations in Dalmatia, Spain, and France deserve the careful study of all students of military history. But he failed as a tactician. Salamanca and Laon prove not only that he made mistakes and had not the faculty of retrieving his errors, but above all he lacked the capacity of seizing on the mistakes of his enemy. In 1811 at El Bodin he had Wellington at his mercy, but he hesitated to strike, for he could not believe his great opponent could make the glaring error of leaving his divisions unsupported. Again and again during his career he showed that lack of resolution which was responsible for his last catastrophe in Paris, where he allowed his own judgment to be overruled by King Charles's personal desires. In a word, he had the gift of a great quartermaster-general rather than of a commander-in-chief. As a man the Marshal's character is an interesting study. In youth the thirst for personal glory and ambition were the dominant traits, and what stability he had he drew from his proud sense of honour, which refused to allow him to take plunder or bribes. But responsibility developed many latent qualities. The desire to keep his troops efficient led him to pay especial care to their physical well-being, and from doing this as a duty he learned to do it as a labour of love. As time went on, desire for personal glory became merged in keen delight in the glory of France, and hence grew up a patriotism which rightly or wrongly led to the scenes of 1814 and 1830. Misfortune also had its share in the enlarging of his character. His unhappy marriage, his bitterness at the withholding of the marshalate, his unpopularity after 1814, led him to remember his father's warning that success is not everything, and turned his attention to the development of those scientific and literary abilities to which he had always shown strong leanings. Hence, though the blight of his marriage and his unpopularity, arising from his desertion of Napoleon, embittered him and caused his Memoirs to teem with cutting descriptions of his contemporaries and former friends, his old age, though spent in exile, was soothed by congenial work which proved 'that to the eye of a general he united the accomplishments of a scholar and the heart of a philanthropist.'

11

LOUIS GABRIEL SUCHET, MARSHAL, DUKE OF ALBUFERA

LOUIS GABRIEL SUCHET, the son of a silk manufacturer, was born at Lyons on March 2, 1770. His father had acquired a certain eminence by his discoveries in his profession, and had occupied a prominent place in the municipality of Lyons. Louis Gabriel, who received a sound education at the College of Isle Barbe, early showed that he inherited his father's gifts of organisation and research. In 1792 he entered a corps of volunteer cavalry. His education and ability soon brought him to the front, and after two years' service he became lieutenant-colonel of the eighteenth demi-brigade, in which capacity he took part in the siege of Toulon. There he had the double good fortune to make prisoner General O'Hara, the English governor of the fortress, and to gain the friendship of Bonaparte. Suchet and his brother accompanied the future Emperor on many a pleasant picnic, and the three were well known among a certain class of Marseilles society. But this was but a passing phase, and soon the thirst for glory called the young soldier to sterner things. The campaigns of 1794-5 in the Maritime Alps, the battle of Loano, and the fierce fights in 1796 at Lodi, Rivoli, Arcola, and Castiglione proved Colonel Suchet's undaunted courage and ability as a regimental commander. In 1797, for his brilliant conduct at Neumarkt, in Styria, Bonaparte, gazetted him general of brigade. In his new capacity Suchet proved that he could not only carry out orders but act in semi-independence as a column commander, and as a reward for his success in Switzerland under General Brune he had the honour of carrying twenty-three captured stands of colours to the Directory. At Brune's request he was sent back to Switzerland to act as chief of his staff. Suchet had to a great extent those qualities which go to make an ideal staff officer. He had a cheery smile and word for everybody, and his tall upright figure and genial face inspired confidence in officers and men alike; as a regimental commander and a general of brigade he had a sound knowledge of the working of small and large corps, and his early experience as a cavalry officer and his intimate acquaintance with the officers of the artillery stood him in good stead. He had a natural aptitude for drafting orders, and his tact and energy commended him to all with whom he served, but above all he had the secret of inspiring those around him with his own vehemence and enthusiasm. Brune, Joubert, Masséna, and Moreau all proved his worth, and Moreau only expressed the opinion of the others when he said to a friend, 'Your general is one of the best staff officers in all the armies of France.' As general of division Suchet acted as chief of the staff to Joubert in Italy in 1799. Later in the year he commanded one of the divisions of the Army of the Alps under Masséna, and fought against the celebrated Suvaroff. But when Joubert was hurriedly despatched to Italy he at once demanded to have Suchet as chief of the staff. On Joubert's death at the battle of Novi, Suchet served Masséna in a similar capacity; the latter was so delighted with him that he wanted to carry him off to the Army of the Rhine. But in that disastrous year men of ability could not be spared, and Bernadotte, as Minister of War, retained him in Italy to aid the new commander-in-chief 'with his clear insight as the public weal demands'. When Masséna took command of the Army Italy in March, he detached Suchet to cover France on the line of the Var, while he, with the rest of the army, threw himself into Genoa. The commander-in-chief had absolute confidence in his lieutenant; he had tried him again and again in the Swiss campaign, and when Suchet had by a marvellous march escaped the tangles of the Russians, his only comment had been 'I was quite sure he would bring me back his brigade.' The young general acted once again up to his reputation, and evinced those resources in difficulty, and that resolution in adversity, which so marked his career. With a mere handful of troops, by his energy and tactical ability he stemmed the flood of the Austrian invasion on the Var, and when Napoleon debouched through the St. Bernard Pass on the enemy's rear, by a masterly return to the initiative he drove the Austrians before him, and by capturing seven thousand prisoners he materially lightened the First Consul's difficulties in the Marengo campaign. Carnot, the War Minister, wrote to him in eulogistic terms: 'The whole Republic had its eyes fixed on the new Thermopylae. Your bravery was as great and more successful than that of the Spartans.' But in spite of this feat of arms and the unselfish way he disengaged Dupont from his difficulties at the crossing of the Mincio, in the campaign which followed Marengo, Suchet found himself neglected and passed over when the Emperor distributed his new honours and rewards. In spite of his former friendship and the remembrance of many a pleasant day spent together in earlier years, Napoleon could not forgive his stern unbending republicanism. He knew his force of character too well to think he could influence his opinions by mere honours, and he determined to see if he could conquer him by neglect. After holding the office of inspector-general of infantry, Suchet found himself in 1803, sent to the camp of Boulogne as a mere divisional commander in Soult's army corps. In the same capacity he loyally served under Lannes in the Austrian campaign of 1805, and distinguished himself at Ulm and Austerlitz, where his division had the good fortune to break the Russian centre. In the following year at Saalfeld and Jena he added to his reputation, and the Emperor did him the honour of bivouacking in the middle of his division on the eve of the battle of Jena. Pultusk and Eylau bore witness to his bravery and address on the battlefield, and Napoleon began to relent. For his share of the victory of Austerlitz the Emperor had created him Grand Eagle of the Legion of Honour and presented him with twenty thousand francs; in August, 1807, he gave him the temporary command of the fifth corps; a few months later he gazetted him Chevalier of the Iron Crown, and in March, 1808, made him a Count of the Empire. In 1807 Suchet married one of the Clarys, a relative of Joseph Bonaparte's wife, and thus to a certain extent bound himself to the Napoleonic dynasty. Still it was only as a divisional commander of the fifth corps under Lannes that in 1808 he entered Spain, the scene of his glory. But when the war brought to light the poor quality of many of the Marshals, and the approaching conflict with Austria caused him to withdraw his best lieutenants to the Danube, Napoleon bethought him of his new relative and former comrade. After the siege of Saragossa he gave him the command of the third corps, now known as the Army of Aragon. Suchet's hour of probation had at last arrived. He had so far shown himself an excellent interpreter of the ideas of others, a man of energy and resource in carrying out orders; it remained to be seen whether he could rise to the height of thinking and acting for himself in the plain of higher strategy.

The situation the new general was called on to meet might have depressed a weaker man. The third corps or Army of Aragon had been severely shaken by the long, stubborn siege of Saragossa. Many of its best officers and men were dead or invalided to France; the ranks were full of raw recruits who had not yet felt the bit of discipline. There were no magazines, the men's pay was months in arrears, the morale of the troops was bad; but the General was told that he must expect no reinforcements and that his army must live off the province of Aragon. To increase his difficulties further he was informed that, while lending an obedient ear to all commands from Madrid, he was really to obey orders which came from the major-general in Paris. Meanwhile, all around him Aragon and even Saragossa were seething with discontent, and Spanish forces, elated by partial success, were springing up on all sides. It was thus situated that Suchet had his first experience of commanding in war, and of showing that success depends on achieving the object desired with the means at hand. Luckily for his reputation he fulfilled Napoleon's dictum that 'a general should above all be cool-headed in order to estimate things at their value: he must not be moved by good or bad news. The sensations which he daily receives must be so classed in his mind that each should occupy its appropriate place.' Accordingly he at once grasped the vital points of the problem, and strove to restore the morale of the troops so that he might be in a position to meet and overcome the organised forces which were moving against him. His first step was to hold a review of his new command, and then he proceeded to visit his troops in their quarters and to get into personal touch with the officers and men by watching them at their company and battalion drills, encouraging them and supervising the interior economy of the various regiments and brigades. His reputation and his personal magnetism soon began to effect a complete change in his army. But unfortunately the enemy, fighting in their own country, where every inhabitant was a spy on their side, knew as well as the general himself the exact state of the French morale, the position of every unit, and the strength of each company and squadron. So accurate was their information that on one occasion, when a battalion was despatched on a reconnaissance to occupy a small town, and the officer commanding demanded a thousand rations for his men and a hundred for his horse, the Alcalde at once replied, 'I know that I must furnish rations for your troops, but I will only supply seven hundred and eighty for the men and sixty for the horses,' as he knew beforehand the exact number of men and horses in the column.

The Spanish General Blake, with this wonderful intelligence organisation at his command, called together his troops, and took the initiative against the new French commander by advancing towards Saragossa. Suchet, recognising the importance of utilising to the full the élan which the French soldier always derives from the sense of attacking, advanced to meet him near Alcaniz, but Blake easily beat off the French attack. So demoralised was the Army of Aragon that on the following night, when a drummer cried out that he saw the Spanish cavalry advancing, an entire infantry regiment threw down their arms before this phantom charge. The offender was brought at once before a drumhead court martial and shot, but with troops in such a condition the French commander very wisely slowly fell back the next day towards Saragossa. The situation was extremely critical: a hurried retreat would have roused all Aragon to the attack. Fortunately the morale of the Spanish troops was also none too good, and Blake waited for reinforcements before advancing. Meanwhile Suchet spent every hour reorganising his army, visiting with speedy punishment all slackness, encouraging where possible by praise, everywhere showing a cheerfulness and confidence he was far from feeling. Every day the troops were drilled or attended musketry practice; the ordinary routine of peace was carried out in every detail, and the civil and military life of Saragossa showed no signs of the greatness of this crisis. Meanwhile care and attention soon showed their effect, and when three weeks later the enemy appeared at Maria before Saragossa, Suchet had under his command a force full of zealous desire to wipe out its late disgrace and absolutely confident in its general. Fortunately the Spanish commander, by attempting a wide encircling movement, weakened his numerical superiority, and Suchet, as usual assuming the offensive, broke the Spanish centre with his cavalry, hurled his infantry into the gap, and amid a terrific thunder-shower drove the Spanish from the field. The battle before Saragossa saved Aragon for the French, but it did not satisfy their commander, who knew that 'to move swiftly, strike vigorously, and secure all the fruits of victory is the secret of successful war'; accordingly with his now elated troops he pursued the enemy and attacked them at Belchite. The Spanish morale was completely broken; a chance shot at the commencement of the engagement blew up an ammunition wagon, and thereon the whole army turned and bolted; for the rest of the war, no regular resistance existed in Aragon.

The battles of Saragossa and Belchite marked the commencement of a fresh stage in the conquest of Eastern Spain. From this time onwards Aragon became the base from which was organised the conquest of Catalonia and Valencia. It was in pursuance of this scheme that Suchet's next task was the organisation of the civil government of the ancient kingdom of Aragon. Fortunately for the commander-in-chief the old local patriotism burnt strong in the hearts of the Aragonese; jealous of the Castilians, they placed their love of Aragon far above their love of Spain. Suchet, an ardent student of human nature, was quick to appreciate how to turn to his use this provincialism. Loud in his praises of their stubborn resistance to the French arms, he approached the nobles and former civil servants and prayed them to lend him their help in restoring the former glories of the ancient kingdom of Aragon. Meanwhile the people of the towns and villages were propitiated by a stern justice and a new fiscal system, which, while it drew more from their pockets, was less aggravating and inquisitorial than the former method, which exacted a tax on the sale and purchase of every individual article. Meanwhile the needs of the French army created a market for both agricultural produce and for manufactured articles, and hence both the urban and rural populations, while paying heavier taxes, made greater profits than formerly. Such was the ability with which Aragon was administered that a province, which even in its most prosperous days had never contributed more than four million francs to the Spanish treasury, was able to produce an income of eight million francs for the pay of the troops alone, without counting the cost of military operations, and at the same time to maintain its own civil servants, while works of public utility were commenced in Saragossa and elsewhere.

But it was not only from the point of finance that Suchet proved to the full the maxim that the art of war is nothing but the art of feeding your troops: his military operations were no whit less remarkable than his success as a civil administrator. Immediately after Belchite he swept all the guerrillas out of Aragon, and by a carefully thought out plan of garrisons gave the country that peace and certainty which is requisite for commerce and agriculture alike. He then proceeded to wrest from the enemy the important fortresses of Lerida and Mequinenza, which command the approaches to Catalonia. Suchet's conquest of Aragon, Catalonia, and Valencia was marked by succession of brilliant sieges. Lerida, Mequinenza, Tortosa, the fort of San Felipe, the Col of Balanquer, Tarragon, Sagunto, and Valencia all fell before his conquering arm, for Spain had to be won piece by piece. Each forward step was marked by a siege, a battle to defeat the relieving force, the fall of the fortress, and its careful restoration as base for the next advance. It was not owing to any weakness or want of precaution on the part of the enemy that Suchet thus captured all the noted fortresses of central Spain: in every case the Spaniards fought with grim determination, and the regular Spanish armies, aided by swarms of guerrillas, made desperate efforts to relieve their beleaguered countrymen. But the French success was due to the qualities of their general. With a patience equal to that of Marlborough, with a power of supervision over detail like that of his great chief, Suchet knew exactly how to pick his staff and how far to trust his subordinates. Above all, he had absolute self-control. In the blackest hour he never gave way, under the most extreme provocation he never lost his temper; hence his own troops idolised him, while his perfect justice impressed itself on the enemy. Though the Spanish priests were teaching the catechism in every village that it was one's duty to love all men except the French, that it was not only lawful but one's sacred duty to kill all Frenchmen, though a letter was captured in which a guerrilla chief ordered his subordinates to make every effort to capture Madame Suchet and to cut her throat, especially because she was pregnant, the commander-in-chief kept his men in absolute control, and punished with the greatest severity every outrage committed by his troops. The battle and siege of Valencia in 1811 were the crowning success of his career, and brought as their reward the long-coveted Marshal's bâton and the title of Duke of Albufera: to support his title the Emperor granted him half a million francs, a greater sum than he gave to any other of his Paladins. The year 1812 saw the Marshal busily engaged in reorganising the province of Valencia on the lines he had found so successful in Aragon. But his work there had never time to take root. The necessities of the Russian campaign had forced Napoleon to recall from Spain many of his best troops, while the successful advance of Wellington on Madrid showed how unstable was the French rule. It was the province of Valencia alone which supplied the money and provisions for the armies which the Spanish capital for King Joseph. In 1813 the victorious advance of Wellington and the battle of Vittoria compelled Suchet to evacuate Valencia. The fall of Pampeluna caused him to evacuate Aragon. Deprived of all his trustworthy troops, he still, by his bold counter-attacks, delayed the advance of the English and Spaniards under Bentinck, but by the time Napoleon abdicated he had been compelled with his handful of men to fall back on French territory.

Under the Restoration the Marshal was retained in command of the tenth division, but on Napoleon's return from Elba he once again rejoined his old leader, whom he had not seen since 1808. The Emperor greeted him most cordially. 'Marshal Suchet,' he said, 'you have grown greatly in reputation since last we met. You are welcome; you bring with you glory and all the glamour that heroes give to their contemporaries on earth.' The Marshal was at once sent off to his old home of Lyons to organise there out of nothing an army which was to cover the Alps. Men there were in plenty, but the arsenals were empty; still, the Marshal with ten thousand troops beat the Piedmontese on June 15th and a few days afterwards defeated the Austrians. But the occupation of Geneva by the Allies forced him to evacuate Savoy and fall back on Lyons, where he was greeted with the news of Waterloo. Under the second Restoration the Marshal never appeared in public life, and died at the chateau of Saint Joseph at Marseilles on January 3, 1826.

Talking to O'Meara at St. Helena, Napoleon said, 'Of the generals of France I give the preference to Suchet. Before his time Masséna was the first.' At another time he said of him, 'It is a pity that mortals cannot improvise men like him. If I had had two Marshals like Suchet I should not only have conquered Spain, but have kept it.' While making due allowance for the probability that the Emperor was influenced in this speech by the fact that Suchet alone relieved the gloom of the unsuccessful war in Spain, it is yet abundantly clear that the Marshal was a commander of no mean ability, for though he did not show the precocity of a Marmont, yet, as Napoleon himself said, 'Suchet was a man whose mind and character increased wonderfully.'

As a commander-in-chief, though acting in a small sphere and never having more than fifty thousand troops under his command, he showed that he possessed determination, insight, and great powers of organisation. From the first he saw that the one and only way to wear down the Spanish resistance was to capture the fortresses. Hence his operations were twofold - the conduct of sieges and the protection of his convoys from the guerrillas. He justified his reasoning; by 1812 he had captured no less than seventy-seven thousand officers and men and fourteen hundred guns and had pacified Aragon, Valencia, and part of Catalonia. Another great secret of his success lay in the fact that he knew how to profit by victory; the battle of Belchite followed on that of Maria; no sooner was Lerida captured than plans were made to take Mequinenza, and before that fortress was captured the siege train for Tortosa was got ready. Profiting by the depression of the enemy after the fall of Tortosa, he despatched columns to capture San Felipe and the Col of Balanquer. Thanks to his former training as chief of the staff, the Marshal was able with his own hand to draw up all the smallest regulations for siege operations, and for the government of Aragon and Valencia. The gift of drafting clear and concise orders and the intuition with which he chose his staff and column commanders explain to a great extent the reason why his operations in Catalonia, Aragon, and Valencia were so little hampered by the constant guerrilla warfare which paralysed the other French commanders in Spain. The indefatigable energy with which he made himself personally acquainted with every officer under his command, and his knowledge of, sympathy with, and care for his soldiers, always made him popular; while the burning enthusiasm which he knew how to infuse into French, German, and Italian like so stimulated his troops that he could demand almost any sacrifice from them. Thus it was that he himself created the morale which enabled him again and again to conquer against overwhelming odds.

As a man, moderation and justice lay at the root of his character, and they account largely for his success as a statesman. He had the difficult task of administering Aragon and Valencia for the benefit of the army under his command; yet he was remembered not with hate, but with affection, by the people of those countries. When any one inquired what was the character of the French general, the Spaniards would reply, 'He is a just man.' The same moderation which caused him to save Tarragona and Valencia from the fury of his troops taught him to devote himself to the welfare of his temporary subjects, and caused his hospital arrangements to receive the gratuitous praise of the Spanish and English commanders. At Saragossa his name was given to one of the principal streets, and on his death the inhabitants of the town paid for masses for his soul, while the King of Spain was only voicing the feelings of the people when he wrote to the Marshal's widow that everything he had heard in Spain proved how deservedly the Duke of Albufera had gained the affections of the people of Valencia and Aragon.

12

LAURENT GOUVION ST. CYR, MARSHAL

LAURENT GOUVION ST. CYR, the son of a small landowner of Toul, was born in that town on April 13, 1764. His father, who was a Gouvion, had married a St. Cyr, but the marriage had turned out an unfortunate one, and soon after the birth of the young Laurent a separation was agreed on. Consequently, from an early age, the boy lacked a mother's care. His father, many of whose relations were in the artillery, desired his son to enter the army, and with that object in view sent him to the Artillery College at Toul. But at the age of eighteen the future Marshal decided to abandon the career of arms for that of art, preferring the freedom of an artist's life to the dull routine of garrison service. Taking the bit between his teeth early in 1782, he set off for Rome, which he made his headquarters for the following two years, with occasional trips as far as Sicily. The year 1789 found Laurent Gouvion established in Paris with a great knowledge of art and some considerable skill in technique. Steeped in classic lore, contemptuous of dull authority and full of youthful enthusiasm, he hailed with joy the outbreak of the Revolution. But by the end of 1792 the young painter was too keen a student of men and matters not to perceive 'the danger which menaced the Republic', and, like all other thinking men, 'was lost in astonishment, not to say at the imprudence, but the folly of the Convention, which instead of seeking to diminish the number of its enemies, seemed resolved to augment them by successive insults, not merely against all kings, but against every existing government.' In spite of this, when Europe threatened France, Laurent Gouvion was one of the first to enlist in the volunteers. His personality and former training at once made themselves felt; within a month of enlisting he was elected captain, in which grade he joined the Army of the Rhine under General Custine. On reaching the front the volunteer captain soon found scope for his pencil. In an army thoroughly disorganised a good draughtsman with an eye for country was no despicable asset. Gouvion was attached to the topographical department of the staff. He added his mother's name - St. Cyr - to his surname because of the constant confusion arising owing to the number of Gouvions employed with the army. After a year's hard work on the staff, during which he acquired a thorough grasp of the art of manoeuvring according to the terrain, and a good working knowledge of the machinery of an army, St. Cyr was promoted on June 5, 1794, general of brigade, and six days later general of division. His promotion was not unmerited, for it was his complete mastery of mountain warfare which had contributed more than anything else to the success of the division of the Army of the Rhine to which he had been attached. The soldiers had long recognised the fact, and when they heard the guns booming through the defiles of the Vosges they used to call one to the other, 'There is St. Cyr playing chess.' Like Bernadotte, at first he refused this rapid promotion; he feared it might lead to the scaffold, for death was then the reward of failure, and besides this, the Gouvions were classed among the ci-devant nobles. As a commander the new general speedily proved that, much as he admired liberty in the abstract, he would have nothing but obedience from his men. Tall of stature, more like a professor than a soldier, through all his career wearing the plain blue overcoat, without uniform or epaulettes, which were affected by the generals of the Army of the Rhine, St. Cyr soon became one of the best known generals of Republican France. As one of his most bitter enemies wrote of him, 'It was impossible to find a calmer man; the greatest dangers, disappointments, successes, defeats, were alike unable to move him. In the presence of every sort of contingency he was like ice. It may be easily understood of what advantage such a character, backed by a taste for study and meditation, was to a general officer.' In the army of the Rhine Desaix and St. Cyr were regarded as the persons whose examples should be followed. The austerity of their manner of life, their sincere patriotism and laborious perseverance, left an indelible mark on all with whom they came in contact. But though they had much in common they were really very dissimilar, for Desaix was intoxicated with the love of glory, full of burning enthusiasm, sympathetic to an extraordinary degree, exceedingly susceptible to the influence of the moment, while St. Cyr loved duty as the rule of his life, modelled his action by the strict laws of calculation, was absolutely impervious to outside influence, and never knew what it was to doubt his own powers. But with all his great gifts he had many faults; he was exceedingly jealous, and without knowing it he allowed his own interests to affect his calculations, consequently very early in his career his fellow-generals hated to have to work in co-operation with him, and he got the name of being a 'bad bedfellow'. Further, excellent as he was as a strategist and tactician, the details of administration bored him. He never held a review, never visited hospitals, and left the threads of administration in the hands of his subordinates; consequently, much as his troops trusted him in the field, they disliked him in quarters, because, while his discipline was most severe, he did nothing to provide for their needs or amusements.

From 1795 to the peace of Campo Formio St. Cyr shared the fortunes and vicissitudes of the Army of the Rhine, serving as a subordinate under Hoche, Jourdan, and Moreau. The battle of Biberach, in 1796, was his personal triumph. With one single corps he defeated three-fourths of the whole of the enemy's army and drove it in rout with a loss of five thousand prisoners. But in spite of this victory and numerous mentions in despatches, on being introduced to the Director Rewbell, after the treaty of Campo Formio, he was actually asked, 'In which army have you served?' An explanation was necessary, whereupon the Director, finding that the general understood and spoke Italian, sent him off at once to take command of the Army of Rome. On March 26, 1798, he arrived there and commenced his first independent command. His task was a difficult one. The officers of the army had risen in revolt against Masséna, who had made no attempt to pay them or their troops, but had spent his time in amassing a fortune for himself. The new general had orders to arrest certain officers and restore discipline. It was a task admirably suited to his talents, and within four days of his arrival the disaffected were arrested and the mutiny quelled. His next duty, according to the command of the Directory, was to remove the Pope from Rome; by a queer coincidence the officer entrusted to escort his

Holiness to Tuscany was a certain Colonel Calvin. So far St. Cyr, much against his wish, had carried out the orders of the Directory, but his next action was spontaneous and dictated by his own idea of justice. It was the hour of spoliation: a committee appointed by the Directory was busy in transporting to France all the masterpieces of Italian art, and the newly appointed Consuls of the Roman Republic were likewise fully engaged in acts of vandalism. When the general heard that the magnificent oblation of diamonds belonging to the Doria family had been purloined from the Church of St. Agnes to grace the necks of the wives of the bastard Consuls, he at once ordered the ostensoir to be returned to its owners. The Consuls appealed to the Directory; so after a command of four short months St. Cyr was recalled, only to be sent at once to resume his old position as a divisional commander in the Army of the Rhine.

From there in June, 1799, he was hurriedly despatched to Italy to aid Moreau, who was attempting to stem the victorious advance of the Austrians and Russians. He arrived in time to take part in the hard-fought fight of Novi, and to help to organise a stubborn resistance on the slopes of the Apennines. Before the battle of Novi he actually had a glimpse of the redoubtable Suvaroff himself. The Russian general, who trusted his own eyes more than the reports of his scouts, one day rode right up to the line of French vedettes clad in his usual fighting kit, a shirt and pair of breeches, and after a hurried reconnaissance returned to his camp and gave his celebrated order: 'God wishes, the Emperor orders, Suvaroff commands, that tomorrow the enemy be conquered.' Novi added lustre to St. Cyr's reputation; it was his strenuous resistance on the right flank and his admirable handling of the rear guard which prevented the victorious Allies from hurling the beaten French through the passes into the sea. But Novi was an easy task compared to what was to follow. The passes of the Apennines had to be held and Genoa covered with a handful of men dispirited by defeat and half mutinous from want of necessary food. It was a rabble, not an army; there was no commissariat, no pay chest, no store of clothing. Meanwhile Genoa lay smouldering in rebellion at his rear. The task suited the man; by a series of clever feints and manoeuvres in the valley of the Bormida, he outwitted the enemy and gradually restored the morale of his troops, and was able to hurry back to Genoa with three battalions at the psychological moment when mutiny and rebellion were showing their head. With absolute calmness he told the civic authorities to prepare quarters for eight thousand troops, of which the few with him were the advance guard. The authorities, staggered by his sudden appearance, never doubted the arrival of this fabulous force, and subsequently St. Cyr was able to occupy all the strongholds in the town with the handful of troops he had with him, and then at his leisure to arrest the ringleaders of the rebellion. Meanwhile, the judicious establishment of free soup kitchens in the streets alleviated the necessities of the mob. Scarcely was Genoa pacified when the general was confronted by a much more serious event. Famine had driven the soldiers to mutiny, and even the very outposts withdrew from contact with the enemy, and announced their intention of returning to France. It was only by raising a forced loan from the Ligurian Government, and delivering a most touching appeal to their patriotism, that he was able to persuade the mutineers to return to their duty, telling them that if they left the colours, he intended, 'with the generals, officers, and non-commissioned officers to hold the positions occupied by the army.' Further to encourage them he began a series of small engagements, which restored their morale and led up to the battle of Albano, where he inflicted so severe a defeat on the Austrians that Genoa was for a considerable time relieved from all danger. The First Consul, on hearing of the victory of Albano, at once sent St. Cyr a sword of honour, a Damascus blade in a richly engraved sheath, with the pommel encrusted with diamonds, which had originally been intended for the Sultan.

But though thus rewarded by receiving the first sword of honour ever given by the First Consul, he was never a *persona grata* with Napoleon. Accordingly at the beginning of 1800 he was withdrawn from the Army of Italy and sent as lieutenant to Moreau, who was to operate in the valley of the Danube while Bonaparte reserved the theatre of Italy for himself. It was most unfortunate for St. Cyr that he was supposed to belong to the Moreau faction, for day by day the struggle between that general and the First Consul became more bitter. Moreau took no trouble to conceal his dislike of Bonaparte, and on hearing a rumour that the First Consul intended to take command of the Army of the Rhine and install him as second in command, he lost his temper and told his staff at dinner 'that he did not want a little tin Louis XIV with his army, and that if the First Consul came he would go.' Meanwhile great friction arose between the general and his new commander-in-chief. St. Cyr, proud of his late achievements, severely criticised the plans and organisation of his chief, who was extremely indignant at the idea that anybody should doubt his ability to manage an army of one hundred and thirty thousand men, and at the same time to command in person the reserve corps of twenty-five thousand; so Moreau belittled St. Cyr's achievements. St. Cyr at D'Engen, Mosskirch, and Biberach showed his accustomed skill as a tactician, but failed to keep in touch with the columns on his right and left, and increased his reputation as a jealous fighter. The second battle of Biberach was a masterpiece of audacity, and to his dying day the general, when recalling his success, always maintained, 'On that day I was a man.' During the operations round Ulm relations became still more strained, and St. Cyr was glad to seize the excuse of a wound to demand his return to France. The First Consul took the line which he always pursued with those whom he disliked but feared. He rewarded St. Cyr by making him a Councillor of State, and at the same time he got him out of the way by sending him on a diplomatic mission to Spain. The general remained at Madrid till August, 1802, and then after a short period of leave at Paris he was despatched in 1803 to command the army at Faenza which was to occupy the kingdom of Naples after the rupture of the treaty of Amiens. During the two years spent in command of the army of occupation he had many opportunities of showing his patience and diplomatic skill. The court of Naples had to be treated with all honour but watched with the greatest care, every effort had to be made to maintain outwardly an appearance of great cordiality, while Napoleon's demands had to be insisted on to the letter. The situation was further complicated by the continued interference of Murat, who commanded the Army of Italy, and who desired to have the Army of Naples under his control. The strictest discipline had to be maintained among the troops to prevent the Neapolitans having any handle to use against the army of occupation. So successfully did St. Cyr keep his troops in hand that the Neapolitan minister wrote in his next despatch to the Queen, 'Madame, we can make nothing of that point; these men are not soldiers, they are monks.' In spite of many an anxious moment these two years in Naples were pleasant years for the general, who delighted in the congenial society of the many men of letters who were attached to his army, for, as Paul Louis Corné wrote of him, 'He is a man of merit, a learned man, perhaps the most learned of men in the gentle art of massacre, a pleasant man in private life, a great friend of mine.' But there was one great disappointment connected with this Neapolitan command, for in 1804 St. Cyr found his name excluded from the list of Marshals, and the empty title of colonel-general of the cuirassiers and the Grand Cordon of the Legion of Honour in no way made amends for this disappointment.

The outbreak of the war with Austria in the autumn of 1805 caused Napoleon to withdraw the army of occupation from Naples, and St. Cyr hastened north in time to help Masséna drive the Austrians out of Styria and Carinthia. He greatly distinguished himself at Castel Franco, where with a smaller force he captured the whole of a column of the enemy under the Prince de Rohan. A month later he was sent back in haste with thirty thousand men to reinvade Naples, which Napoleon had given as a kingdom to his brother Joseph, but on hearing that he was to act as a subordinate to Masséna he threw up his command and withdrew to Paris. This independent conduct increased Napoleon's dislike for him, and he was peremptorily ordered, to return to Naples, where he remained till August, 1806.

It was not till two years later that the Emperor once again employed St. Cyr on active service. But the task he then called upon him to perform was one that would make any general, who was anxious about his reputation, hesitate to undertake. For Napoleon sent him with a motley force of some forty-eight thousand Swiss, Italians, and Germans to restore French prestige in the mountainous country of Catalonia, and ended his orders with the words, 'Preserve Barcelona for me; if it is lost I cannot retake it with eighty thousand men.' In Barcelona lay the French general, Duhesme, who had been hustled into that town by the Spanish regulars and guerrillas after the news of the great French disaster at Baylen. It was absolutely vital to the French to relieve Duhesme before lack of provisions caused him to surrender, but before any advance could be made it was necessary to seize the fortress of Rosas, which lay on the flank of the road from France to Barcelona; this post St. Cyr successfully took by assault under the very guns of Lord Dundonald's fleet. But still the problem of relieving Barcelona was a difficult one. There were two alternative lines of advance: the first and easier lay along the coast, but exposed to the guns of the English fleet; the other road was a mere track through the mountains, and was accordingly extremely difficult owing to the excellent opportunities it gave to the guerrillas. But St. Cyr, keeping his seventeen thousand men well in hand and taking every precaution against ambushes, successfully broke through the lines of regulars and guerrillas, relieved Barcelona, and pushed on down the coast towards Tarragona. His further advance was stopped by the rapid reorganisation of the Spanish armies in Catalonia, and it became clear that until Gerona, which commanded the mountain road to France was taken, the French forces in the south would always be in danger of having their communications cut. Accordingly the Emperor ordered him to return to assist General Verdier to capture this important town. Gerona had at one time been a fortress, but it was now simply covered with a feeble rampart. But the courage of the townspeople and their patriotism was fired by the example of Saragossa, and their spirit was animated by their governor, Alvarez, whose order, 'Whoever speaks of capitulation or defeat shall be instantly put to death,' was received with shouts of delight. Owing to quarrels between St. Cyr and Verdier, to the stubbornness of the defence, and above all to the constant success of the Spanish General Blake in throwing provisions into the town, the siege, which commenced by sap and assault gradually drifted into a mere blockade, and lasted for six and a half months. At last the Emperor, angry at the constant bickering between the commanders and at the protracted siege, superseded St. Cyr by Marshal Augereau. However, it did not suit that Marshal to take over his command until there seemed a reasonable prospect of success, and accordingly he waited at Perpignan for news of the approaching end of the siege. At last St. Cyr in disgust threw up his command without waiting for the arrival of Augereau The Emperor marked this act of insubordination by sending him under arrest to his country estate and depriving him of all his appointments. Accordingly one of the few French generals who never sustained a defeat in Spain passed the next two years of his life in disgrace without employment, while day by day the French arms were suffering reverses in the Peninsula.

It was not till 1812 that the Emperor recalled St. Cyr to active employment and gazetted him to the command of the sixth corps, which, together with the second corps under the command of Marshal Oudinot, was employed on the line of the Dwina to cover the communications of the forces advancing on Moscow. The campaign in Russia showed the general at his best and at his worst. In the operations round Polotsk his great tactical ability enabled him with the forces under his command to foil again and again the efforts of the Russian commander, Wittgenstein, but owing to his want of supervision before the winter arrived the sixth corps, which entered Russia twenty-five thousand strong, had been reduced to two thousand six hundred bayonets. It was not till his corps had almost disappeared at he bestirred himself and compelled his subordinates to look after the well-being and provisions of their men. Moreover, when placed under the command of Marshal Oudinot, while carrying out to the letter all orders transmitted to him, he invariably refused to aid him with his advice, and even during the first battle of Polotsk, when asked his opinion, he merely bowed and said, 'My Lord Marshal!' as though be would say, 'As they have made you a Marshal, you must know more about the matter than a mere general like me; get out of it as best you can.' But as soon as a wound caused Oudinot to retire from the field be at once seized the reins of command, and so great was the influence and confidence that he inspired that in a few hours the army which Oudinot had left scattered and depressed with its back to a river, was advancing victoriously and sweeping all before it. But, good soldier as he was when left in supreme command, he unfortunately would not act in co-operation with others, and when at the end of October Victor, with twenty-five thousand troops, arrived to reinforce him, he seized the opportunity of a wound to throw up his command and return to France. As one of his critics says, 'All that St. Cyr needed to be a consummate commander was a smaller share of egotism, and the knowledge to attach men and officers to him by attending to their wants.'

Still, Napoleon recognised his services against Wittgenstein by at last making him a Marshal.

An attack of typhus and a burst blood vessel deprived the Emperor of his new Marshal's assistance until after the armistice of Dresden. This was the first occasion on which the two had actually come into close contact, and Napoleon quickly saw that 'thrawn' and jealous as St. Cyr undoubtedly was, his clearness of brain made his advice of the highest importance, while St. Cyr speedily fell under the charm of the great Emperor. Accordingly all through the campaign Napoleon constantly came to him for advice, which was never withheld. Remembering also his great reputation as a master of mountain warfare, the Emperor entrusted him with the duty of holding the highland passes leading by Pirna on to Dresden, while he himself hurried off to Silesia. In the great battle round Dresden the Marshal's twenty thousand raw recruits played their part nobly. Napoleon, to cover his own mistakes, laid the blame of Vandamme's disaster on St. Cyr and Marmont, but in his private letter to the Marshal he placed the blame on Vandamme, as he wrote, 'That unhappy Vandamme, who seems to have killed himself, had not a sentinel on the mountain nor a reserve anywhere.' When the Emperor fell back on Leipzig he entrusted the defence of Dresden to St. Cyr, leaving him twenty-two thousand troops and provisions for eight days. After a siege of a month the Marshal was compelled for lack of powder to surrender with the honours of war, but the Allies, after the evacuation of the town, refused to carry out the terms of the surrender, and retained him and his troops as prisoners of war; consequently he took no part in the campaign of 1814. During the Hundred Days he remained quietly at his country estate, but on the second Restoration he was called upon to undertake the duties of Minister of War, to disband the old army and to organise the new forces of France; his tenure of office was short, as he refused to serve a ministry which proposed to cede French territory to the enemy. In May, 1817, on the accession of a Liberal ministry, he once again took office, and during this period he laid the foundation of the General Staff of the Army, but in November, 1819, he resigned, and lived in retirement till he died at Hyères on March 17, 1830.

During his hours of leisure the Marshal wrote his Memoirs, which he intended to aid the future historian of the French wars. These Memoirs show how clear and cutting his judgments were, both of men and matters, and his criticisms throw many useful lights on Napoleon's character and his methods of warfare, while they also to a great extent reveal his own character. No one who reads them can doubt that St. Cyr was a great strategist, while his powers as a tactician are proved by his never-failing success on the field of battle. But in spite of these talents the Marshal's actual record as a soldier is spoiled by his defects of character. A great believer in living by rule, he had two maxims which he ever clung to. First, that in war acts of kindness are too often harmful; second, the old adage of Machiavelli, 'That a victory destroys the effect of the worst operation, and that the man who knows how to give battle can be pardoned every fault that he may have before committed in his military career.' It is to these two maxims that we must attribute the want of supervision he showed over his troops and his absolute lack of cordiality towards his fellow Marshals and generals, which gave him the nickname of the 'Bad bed-fellow'. For that he did not lack the talents of an organiser is shown by the way, when roused, he provided for his troops in Russia, and also by the success of his efforts when Minister of War. But of all his gifts undoubtedly the most useful was his absolute coolness: no matter how badly the fight went, no matter if he were run away with in his carriage and carried straight through a brigade of the enemy's horse, he never was ruffled, never lost his clear grip on the situation. His bitter enemy, Macdonald, well summed up his character in answer to Louis XVIII's questions as to whether he was lazy. 'I am not aware of it,' said the Duke of Tarentum. 'He is a man of great military capacity, firm, honest, but jealous of other people's merit. In the army he is regarded as what is called a 'bad bed-fellow.' In the coldest manner possible he allowed his neighbours to be beaten, without attempting to assist them, and then criticised them afterwards. But this opinion, not uncommon among soldiers, is perhaps exaggerated, and he is admitted to have calmness and great capabilities.'

13

BON ADRIEN JEANNOT DE MONCEY, MARSHAL, DUKE OF CONEGLIANO

THE glamour of war appeals strongly to most men, to some it calls with irresistible demand. Such a one was the Duke of Conegliano. Born on July 31, 1754, at Palise, a little village of Besançon, the son of a well-to-do lawyer, Bon Adrien Jeannot loathed scholarship and loved adventure. When but fifteen years old the future Marshal ran away from school and enlisted in the Conti regiment of infantry. After six months' service he reluctantly agreed to the purchase of his discharge by his father; very soon ran away again to enlist in the regiment of Champagne. He served with this regiment till 1773, when, finding that his hopes of gaining a commission were disappointed, he once again bought himself out. A few months, however, spent in the study of the law only served to increase his hatred of a sedentary life and to kindle once more his old ambition, and he again enlisted as a private, this in the gendarmerie. But now fortune was more kind, after four years' service he achieved his desire and was gazetted, in 1779, as sub-lieutenant in the dragoons of Nassau Siegen. It was not, however, till April, 1791, that he gained his captaincy, which had cost him twenty-three years' hard service; but now promotion came rapidly, and in three years' time he rose to the rank of general of division.

In 1793 Moncey's regiment of dragoons formed part of the Army of the Western Pyrenees. In the first engagement with the enemy he had the good fortune to distinguish himself. The Spanish commander-in-chief, Bonaventura Casa, led a charge of horse against the ill-disciplined recruits and volunteers who formed the mass of the French army covering St. Jean Pied de Porte. The miserable French infantry broke, with cries of 'We are betrayed!' and it was Moncey who, rallying a few brave men, stopped the charge of the enemy's horse. Energetic, clear-witted, and self-confident, he soon became a man of mark. In February, 1794, he was promoted general of brigade, and six months later general of division, in which capacity, in August of that year, he was mainly instrumental in forcing the lines of Fontarabia; on the proposition of Barrère he was, a few days later, appointed by the Convention commander-in-chief of the Army of the Western Pyrenees. In October he fully justified his selection by forcing the famous pass of Roncesvalles, so intimately connected with the names of Charlemagne and the Black Prince. This action, which made good a footing in Spain, was extremely brilliant; the position, strong by nature, had been made almost impregnable by months of hard labour. Moreover, the French troops were badly handicapped by the difficulty of getting food; but, by now, they were very different from the ill-trained levies of 1793. The turning column, which had four days' hard mountain climbing and fighting on three biscuits per man, found nothing to eat, when the pass was forced, save a little flour, for the Spanish had burnt their magazines. In spite of this there was no grumbling, and the men, as their general reported, pressed on with cries of 'Vive la République!' Moncey, like Napoleon, knew how to use the great driving force of hunger. He thoroughly deserved the thanks which he received from the Convention, and he fully earned them again when, early in 1795, he drove the Spanish army in flight across the Ebro, for it was his magnificent forward movement which forced Spain to accede to the treaty of Basle.

From Spain the general was transferred to the Army of the Côtes de Brest. A year later he was posted to the command of the eleventh military division at Bayonne, and he still there when, in October, 1799, Bonaparte returned m Egypt and overthrew the Directory. No politician, it mattered little to Moncey who governed France, as long the honour of the country was maintained and he saw active service. Accordingly he gladly accepted from the new government the position of lieutenant to Moreau, the commander-in-chief of the Army of the Rhine. But he did not serve long under his new chief, being detached in May at the head of sixteen thousand to cross the Alps by the St. Gothard Pass, as part of the great stroke aimed at the Austrian lines of communication in Italy. His corps formed a flank guard to the main Army of the Reserve, which crossed St. Bernard under Napoleon himself. In the operations which succeeded the battle of Marengo the First Consul made full use of Moncey's great experience in mountain warfare, and sent him to the Valtelline to join hands with Macdonald, who was crossing the Alps by the Splügen Pass. Thereafter his division formed the left wing of the French army under Brune. After a brilliant series of skirmishes in the mountains, Moncey drove the flying enemy into Trent, but he was robbed of complete victory by the Austrian general, Laudon, who sent a message to say that Brune and Bellegarde had made an armistice. Unfortunately for the French their general, the soul of honour, suspected no deceit, and thus the Austrians were saved from annihilation or absolute surrender.

After the peace of Lunéville General Moncey was appointed Inspector-General of gendarmerie, and on Napoleon's elevation to the throne was created, in 1804, Marshal, Grand Officer of the Legion of Honour, and in 1808 Duke of Conegliano. Moncey invariably spoke his mind, and for this reason was no favourite with the Emperor; further, in comparison with his fellow Marshals, he was an old man, so from 1800 to 1808 he was not employed on active service. But on the invasion of Spain, Napoleon determined to make use of the Duke of Conegliano's knowledge of that country, and ordered him to proceed there with the Army of Observation of the Ocean, which he was then commanding at Boulogne. This army became the third corps of the newly formed Army of Spain. It was composed almost entirely of recruits, and when Murat marched into Madrid at the head of the third corps, the poor physique of these 'weak and weedy privates' had a very bad effect on the situation, for the Spaniards thought they could easily defeat such troops. From Madrid the Marshal was sent to capture Valencia, which had broken out into revolt against the French. Though old, the Duke of Conegliano was still active and vigorous. After a month's continuous fighting across mountain passes and rivers he reached Valencia; but he found the town in a state of defence. As Napoleon said on hearing of his check, 'A city of eighty thousand inhabitants, barricaded streets, and artillery entrenched at the gates cannot be taken by the collar.' Accordingly there was nothing for it but to retreat, and this the Marshal did in such a masterly manner that the failure of his expedition produced but little bad effect on the French cause. When, after Baylen, Joseph held his council of war at Madrid, Moncey alone stood out for the bold course of cutting communication with France and concentrating around the capital; but he was overruled, and the French fell back on the line of the Ebro.

As soon as Napoleon arrived in Spain he vented his anger indiscriminately on all those Marshals who had served under Joseph, but his greatest displeasure fell on Moncey, for the Duke of Conegliano did not believe that Spain could be gained by hanging all those who resisted, and had actually received the thanks of the junta of Oviedo, who considered him 'a just and honourable man', and published a manifesto saying, 'We know this illustrious general detests the conduct of his companions.' Accordingly, in the eyes of the Emperor he had been guilty of bungling and slackness, if not of something worse, and he was therefore subjected to the cruel affront of being placed under the orders of Lannes, a junior Marshal. Though much annoyed, as a soldier he could only obey, and the Emperor's decision was to some extent justified, as Lannes won the battle of Tudela with the same troops which Moncey had not dared to lead against the enemy. Three months later the Marshal was once again superseded by Lannes, and this time recalled and sent to France. The ostensible reason for this was that in the Emperor's opinion he had not pressed the siege of Saragossa. With a desire to avoid bloodshed he had tried to induce the Spaniards to capitulate by entering into negotiations, instead of pushing on his siege batteries. But his real offence was that he had not concealed his dislike of the seizure of Spain.

In 1812 his disgrace was deepened, for he expressed with equal frankness his hatred of the Russian campaign. Though never again employed at the front, the Emperor made use of him in 1809 in Holland, and in 1812 and 1813 he led the Army of Reserve; while in 1814 he was appointed major-general of the National Guard of Paris and made responsible for the defence of the capital. In the last dark days before the city capitulated Moncey, with six thousand citizen soldiers, fought bravely outside the Clichy gate.

On the Restoration the Marshal became a Minister of State and a member of the new Chamber of Peers, and was confirmed in his old appointment of inspector of gendarmerie. But on the return of

Napoleon he forgot the wrongs the Emperor had done him; he thought only of the glory Napoleon had once won for France; so he swore allegiance to the imperial government and was created a peer. But, on account of his age, the Emperor gave him no military command. To punish him for his desertion, Louis XVIII, on the second Restoration, appointed him president of the council of war for the trial of Ney. But the Duke of Conegliano wrote to the King boldly refusing to have anything to do with the trial of the hero of Moskowa. So angry was the King at his courageous act that he stripped the veteran of his marshalate and the title of duke, and sent him to prison for three months in the castle of Ham, the same prison which was later to receive the future Napoleon III. But time brought forgiveness. In 1819 the Marshal was restored to his honours, and in 1823 was actually once again employed on active service. It must have brought strange memories of the past to the veteran, who had been thought too old to fight at Waterloo, again to see service in Spain, where he had won his laurels in 1794 and had found naught but disgrace in 1808. So, in his seventieth year, he made his last campaign, not in command of a republican or imperial army, but as a corps commander in the royal army under the Due d'Angoulême. This time, however, there was but little call on his courage and ability, for the campaign brought no fighting and was merely a military promenade. On the fall of the Bourbon dynasty the Marshal took no active part in affairs, but as Governor of the Invalides in December, 1833, he had the honour to receive the remains of Napoleon when they were translated to France; and on his death nine years later, in 1842, at his special request, he was buried in the 'aisle of the brave', close to the tomb of the great Emperor.

14

JEAN BAPTISTE JOURDAN, MARSHAL

AMONG the recruits who enlisted in the Auxerrois regiment in 1778 was the son of the local doctor of Limoges, Jean Baptiste Jourdan. But sixteen years old, having been born on April 29, 1762, Jean Baptiste was attracted to the service by the desire to see America and to aid in the good cause against 'perfide Albion'. Returning to France in 1784, with all hopes of gaining a commission dashed to the ground by Ségur's ordinance, which excluded from commissioned rank all but those of noble birth, Jourdan took his discharge. The ex-sergeant married a marchande de modes, and set up a small drapery shop, but so humble was this venture that the future Marshal had to carry his stock in a valise on his back, and trudge from fair to fair to peddle his wares. As he went from village to village he retold his adventures and fired his listeners with the account of the glorious freedom of the New World, comparing it with the miserable restrictions which had driven from the army himself and many another fine soldier. When in the autumn of 1791 there came the call for volunteers, Jean Baptiste gladly left his counter and enlisted in the battalion of the Upper Vienne. His experience and ability soon marked him out for command, and he was chosen by his comrades as lieutenant-colonel. The opportunity he had long dreamed of had at last arrived, and he made the most of it. Methodical and industrious, with the lessons of handling and equipping irregulars which he had had in America, he made his battalion a pattern for the others, and was complimented by Lafayette on the admirable condition of his command. Serving under Dumouriez in the invasion of Belgium, he was present at Jemappes, and there proved that, in addition to powers of organisation, he possessed the capacity for leading in the field. Promotion came speedily when the guillotine cleared the way in the higher ranks by removing the incompetent and unfortunate.

By May, 1793, he had gained the grade of general of brigade; two months later he became general of division. His first opportunity of distinguishing himself in high command came six weeks later, when he was entrusted by Houchard with the command of the advance guard in the operations which ended in driving the English from the siege of Dunkirk. So well did he execute his orders at the battle of Handschötten that Carnot selected him to succeed his commander when Houchard was hurried off to the guillotine for failing to reap the full fruits of victory. Jourdan was fortunate in that Carnot, 'the organiser of victory', was responsible for the welfare of the French arms, and not the despicable Bouchotte. Carnot had grasped the fact that, if you are to defeat your enemy, you must bring superior moral and physical force against him at the decisive spot. Thanks therefore to him, Jourdan was able to mass superior weight, and at Maubeuge hurl himself on the scattered forces of the enemy, who were covering the siege of Valenciennes. But the victory of Maubeuge nearly cost him his head, as that of Handschötten had done for his predecessor. The Committee of Public Safety, with that incompetent rashness which those who know least of war most readily believe to be military wisdom, ordered him to pursue the enemy and conquer Belgium. It was in vain that he pointed out the strength of the Allies, his want of transport and stores, and the difficulty of undertaking a winter campaign with raw troops: reason was of no avail; his resignation was wrathfully accepted, and he was ordered to Paris to give an account of his actions. Face to face with the Committee, the General renewed his arguments, explained how the old battalions of regulars had dwindled down to some two hundred muskets apiece; how the new levies possessed neither arms nor clothing; how some battalions were armed with pikes, some merely with cudgels; and finished by offering, as a proof of his zeal for the Republic, to go to La Vendée and fight against the rebels. The truth of his statement and his obvious disinterestedness won the day, and, though for the moment he was refused a new command, his life was saved. Moreover, the Committee of Safety profited by his advice, and during the winter the Army of the North was reclothed and equipped. Thanks partly to his suggestion, the battalions of the line were brigaded with the volunteers, and this reorganisation produced the magnificent regiments which Napoleon found to hand when he commenced his career in Italy.

Jourdan's time of inactivity was but short. He had proved his worth in the field, and France needed every capable soldier. Moreover, he had made open testimony of his republicanism in the Jacobin Club, swearing before the Tribune that 'the sword which he wore should only be unsheathed to oppose tyrants and defend the rights of the people.' So, in March, 1794, he was sent to take command of a new army which Carnot had been raising during the winter. By June this new force of one hundred thousand, known to history as the famous Army of the Sambre and Meuse, had established itself on the Meuse and taken Charleroi. Coburg, the commander-in-chief of the Allies, anxious about his communications, hurried to oppose this successful advance, and on June 25th was fought the battle of Fleurus, which caused the Allies to evacuate France, ended the Reign of Terror, and was the starting-point for the long period of offensive warfare which was at last brought to an end twenty-one years later on the field of Waterloo. At Fleurus Jourdan proved his ability as tactician, and the victory was due to the moral courage with which he threw his last reserve into the fray. Backed by the Army of the North under Pichegru, he then swept over Belgium, and by the autumn the republican armies had crossed the Rhine.

During the next year Jourdan was engaged in the Rhine valley. But in 1796 he was ordered to advance through the Black Forest on Ratisbon, and there join another French army under Moreau, which was moving down the right bank of the Danube. Against this defective strategy he protested in vain, and, as be had expected, was driven back by the able measures of the Austrian general, the Archduke Charles. After this misfortune he was placed on the unemployed list, and, for some time, had to find an outlet for his energies in the field of politics. Entering the Council of Five Hundred as the representative of the Upper Vienne, he was warmly received by the republican party, and voted against the proposed re-establishment of the Catholic religion, and supported the coup d'état of the 18th Fructidor, by which the royalist councillors were driven into exile. Full of fiery zeal for the Republic, a rhetorical speaker ready to appeal to the gallery, swearing on his sabre the oath of fidelity, he nevertheless had a cool head for business, and it was at his suggestion that in September, 1798, the celebrated law was passed whereby conscription became the sole method of recruiting for the army. Jourdan introduced the law with a flourish of trumpets, assuring the Council that 'in agreeing to it they had decreed the power of the Republic to be imperishable,' while as a matter of fact they were forging the weapon which was to place their country at the mercy of the first adventurer who had the courage and capacity to make himself dictator. In 1799 foreign danger once again caused him to be entrusted with a military command, and once again he was opposed by his old adversary, the Archduke Charles, and driven back in retreat across the Rhine. Thereon the Directory superseded him by Masséna, and he returned to the Council of Five Hundred, and in September posed his memorable resolution, 'that the country is in danger. Italy under the yoke, the barbarians of the north our very barriers, Holland invaded, the fleet treacherously given up, Helvetia ravaged, bands of royalists indulging in every excess, the republicans proscribed under the name of Terrorists and Jacobins.' Such were the outlines of his picture. 'One more reverse on our frontier,' he added, 'and the alarm bell of royalty will ring over the whole surface of France.' But France had had enough of Terror, and knew that she could evolve her safety by other means than that of the guillotine. Six weeks later Bonaparte returned from Egypt.

From the advent of the Consulate a blight fell over Jourdan's career. Napoleon could never forgive him for the obstinacy with which he had opposed him on the 18th Brumaire. True, in 1800 he appointed him Governor of Piedmont, and in 1804 created him Marshal. He could not withhold the bâton from the general who had in 1794 driven the enemy from the sacred soil of France, who, more often than any other general, had commanded in chief the armies of the Republic, and who, in spite of numerous defeats, had established a reputation as one of the most brilliant of the generals of republican France. But though he gave him his bâton Napoleon thought but little of his military ability, and called him 'a poor general'; for in his eyes success, and success alone, was the test of merit, and he could see nothing in a general who, from his capacity for emerging with credit from defeat, was surnamed 'The Anvil'. But it was not this which caused Napoleon to snub the gallant Marshal: it was his ardent republicanism and well-known Jacobin sentiments which made him so hateful to the Emperor. But though Napoleon treated him shamefully, and did all he could to cast him into ill repute, the Marshal showed he had a soul above mere personal ambitions, and served France faithfully. At St. Helena the fallen Emperor confessed: 'I certainly used that man very ill: he is a true patriot, and that is the answer to many things urged against him.' From 1805 to 1815 Jourdan's life was full of mortification. When the war broke out against Austria in 1805 he was in command of the army in Italy, but was at once superseded, under the plea that his health was bad, and that he did not know the theatre of war like Masséna. However cleverly the pill was gilded, the Marshal knew that it was the Emperor's distrust which had lost him the command. But, though Napoleon disliked him, Joseph was his friend, and in 1806 the new King of Naples applied to be allowed to take him with him to Italy as his major-general and chief of the staff. When in 1808 Joseph exchanged the crown of Naples for that of Spain the Marshal accompanied him, and when, in 1809, Napoleon hurriedly left Spain to return to Paris, he appointed him chief of the staff to King Joseph. The major-general's task was a difficult one. He had no executive authority: his duty was simply to give advice to the King, and to transmit such orders as he received; but unfortunately neither Joseph nor he had the power to enforce orders once given, for although certain French corps had been placed at the disposal of the King, and were supposed to obey his orders, their commanders had still to communicate with Berthier and to receive through him the decrees of the Emperor. Hence there was a dual authority, and, to make matters worse, Napoleon did not attempt to veil his contempt of Joseph's military ability. At the same time he cast aspersions on Jourdan's skill, and showed his open dislike to the Marshal by omitting his name from the list of French Marshals in the 'Almanack,' under the pretence that he had been transferred to the Spanish establishment and was no longer a Frenchman. Consequently the other Marshals paid but little attention to the King or the major-general. At the battle of Talavera Jourdan's advice was utterly disregarded and his orders entirely neglected, and still he had to bear the blame, and endure the whole Napoleon's wrath. In despair, broken down in health, he applied to be relieved of his duties, and returned home to private life. But in 1812, when the Emperor was summoning his vast army for the invasion of Russia, being short of officers, he sent the Marshal back to his old post in Spain. The task had been a hard one in 1809, it was harder still in 1812. The flower of the French troops were now withdrawn for the Russian campaign. The authority of the King was more feeble than ever, and years of warfare had transformed the English army into a perfect fighting machine. The Spaniards were now past masters in guerrilla warfare, while the iniquitous scheme of making war support war had subverted discipline and broken the morale of the French army. With admirable lucidity the Marshal drew up a memoir showing the state of affairs in Spain, and pointing out what was at fault; but memoirs written for Joseph could not alter evils which flowed directly from Napoleon's having broken the golden canon of the 'unity of command'. With three practically independent commanders-in-chief who refused to acknowledge the controlling authority of the King, who were too jealous of each other to work with mutual accord, disaster was bound to follow. The temporary co-operation of all three drove the English back on Portugal at the end of 1812. But in 1813 the disaster in Russia had caused the Emperor to make further heavy drafts on the force in Spain. Jourdan could only advise a steady retirement towards France. The culminating blow at Vittoria was no fault of his. Struck down by a fever the day before the action, he was unable to give his advice at the critical moment. So Joseph had to fight Vittoria without the assistance of the chief of his staff, and with subordinates who not only despised, but disobeyed him in the presence of the enemy. It was no wonder that defeat easily turned into rout. The whole of the French baggage was captured, and in the flight the Marshal had the misfortune to lose his bâton, which was picked up by the 87th Regiment and sent to England.

After 1813 Jourdan's career came to a close. Napoleon heaped reproaches on him, and refused him further employment, entirely oblivious of the fact that it was he himself who was responsible for the Spanish disaster, and that the Marshal had done all that was possible. On the Emperor's abdication the old Jacobin took the oath of allegiance to King Louis, and remained true to his allegiance during the Hundred Days. Time had chastened and mellowed his fiery republicanism, and seeing that a Republic was impossible, he preferred the chance of constitutional liberty under a monarchy to the tyranny of the Empire. In 1817, as a reward for his services, he was created a peer of France. But though he accepted the Restoration in preference to the Empire, all his sympathies were liberal, and no one had a greater dislike for the reactionary policy of Charles X. In 1830 he gladly accepted the new liberal constitution of Louis Philippe, the old Philippe, Égalité of the days of Jemappes. The new monarch appointed his former comrade governor of the Hospital of the Invalides, and there, among his old fellow-soldiers of the revolutionary wars, the Marshal breathed his last on November 23, 1833, in his seventy-second year.

15

CHARLES PIERRE FRANÇOIS AUGEREAU, MARSHAL, DUKE OF CASTIGLIONE

THE future Duke of Castiglione was born in Paris on November 11, 1757. His father was a mason by trade and his mother, a native of Munich, kept a furniture shop in the Faubourg Saint Marceau. From his earliest youth Pierre François, handsome and long-limbed, hot-blooded and vain, thirsted after adventure. At the age of seventeen, on his mother's death, he enlisted in the carabineers. A keen soldier and a fine horseman, he soon became sergeant, and within a few years gained the name of being one of the best blades in the army; but in upholding this reputation Sergeant Augereau constantly fell into disgrace with the authorities. Though a blusterer by nature and full of bravado, the sergeant was certainly no coward. On one occasion a noted professional duellist thought that he could intimidate him. Accordingly, he swaggered into a café, where Augereau was talking to some friends, and plunged himself down on the table at which the sergeant was sitting, and, lolling back till he almost leant against him, began to boast how, on the previous day, he had accounted for two sergeants of the Garde Française. This was sufficient insult to cause a challenge, but Augereau preferred to let the challenge come from his adversary, and, accordingly, undoing the leather of his would-be opponent, he quietly poured the whole of a cup of scalding coffee down the inside of his breeches. Having thus taken the upper hand of the quarrel, he so completely mastered the spirit of the bully that he had little difficulty in disposing of him in the duel which followed. An unfortunate incident cut short his career in the carabineers. One day a young officer, losing his temper with him on parade, threatened to strike him with his whip. Thereon, Augereau in fury snatched the whip from the officer, who at once drew his sword and attacked him. Augereau at first confined himself to parrying, but at last, being wounded, he thrust out and killed his opponent. The colonel, well aware that it was not the sergeant's fault, arranged for his escape across the frontier. After wandering about Constantinople and the Levant, Augereau passed some years as sergeant in the Russian army, and served under Suvaroff at the taking of Ismailia, but, getting tired of service in the East, he deserted and escaped to Prussia. There he enlisted, and, owing to his height and proficiency in drill, was transferred to the guards. His captain held out hopes of a commission, but these were dashed, for when he was brought to the King's notice Frederick asked who he was. 'A Frenchman, sire,' was the reply. 'So much the worse,' answered the King; 'so much the worse. If he had been a Swiss, or a German, we might have done something for him.' Augereau, on hearing this, determined to quit the Prussian service. Desertion was the only way of escape, but the Prussians, by offering heavy rewards for recapture, had made desertion almost impossible. Luckily, he was not the only guardsman dissatisfied with the Prussian service, and he had little difficulty in getting together about sixty of the boldest of the regiment, and, seizing a favourable opportunity, he marched off his squad with their arms and ammunition, and, beating off all attacks from the peasants and detachments of soldiers who tried to stop them, he safely convoyed his comrades across the frontier to Saxony. After this escapade Augereau settled down as a dancing and fencing master at Dresden, but on the amnesty, at the birth of the Dauphin, he returned to France and regained his rank in his old regiment. His adventurous life and his natural aspirations soon made him tire of always holding a subordinate position, and in 1788 he applied to be sent, as one of the French instructors, to help in the reorganisation of the Neapolitan army. There he soon gained a commission. In 1791 he fell in love with the daughter of a Greek merchant, and, as her father refused to listen to him, he quietly married her and carried off by ship to Lisbon. In Portugal his freedom of speech, and approval of the changes which were happening in France, caused the authorities to hand him over to the Inquisition, from whence he was rescued by a French skipper and conveyed, with his wife, to Havre.

Augereau returned to France ready to absorb the most republican doctrines. His banishment, after killing the officer, had always seemed unfair; his long subordination and the harshness of military discipline had rankled in his soul; physically, he knew himself superior to most men, and by his wits he had found himself able to hold his own and make his way in nearly every country in Europe; so far birth had seemed to be the only barrier which cut him off from success. But now caste was hurled aside, and France was calling for talent; good soldiers were scarce: Augereau saw his opportunity, and used it to the full. A few months spent fighting in La Vendée taught him that renown was not to be gained in civil war, and, accordingly, he got himself transferred to the Army of the Pyrenees, where he rose in six months from simple captain to general of division. From the Pyrenees he was transferred with his division to Italy, and covered himself with glory at Loano, Millesimo, and Lodi. But it was his conduct at Castiglione which once and for all made his reputation; though it is not true, as he boasted in 1814 after deserting the Emperor, that it was only his invincible firmness which caused Bonaparte to fight instead of retreat for Bonaparte was concentrating to fight, and his abandonment of the siege of Mantua, against which Augereau so wildly protested, was but part of the preparation for victory. Though he would not listen to Augereau's strategic advice, he had enough confidence in him to leave the first attack on Castiglione entirely in his hands. According to the Marshal's Memoirs, Bonaparte was afraid of attacking. 'I wash my hands of it and go away,' he said. 'And who will command if you go?' asked Augereau. 'You,' retorted Bonaparte. And well he did his work, for not only did he defeat the fifteen thousand Austrians at Castiglione, but he restored the fallen confidence of his soldiers and refreshed the morale of the whole army. Napoleon never forgot this service, and when detractors saw fit to cast their venom at Augereau, he answered, 'Let us not forget that he saved us at Castiglione.' From Castiglione onwards the soldiers of Augereau's division would do anything for their commander. It was not only that they respected his tactical gifts, and had complete confidence in him in the hour of battle, but they loved him for his care of them. In time of peace a stern disciplinarian, with a touch of the drill sergeant, he was ever ready to hear their complaints, and never spared himself in looking after their welfare, while in war time he was always thinking of their food and clothing; but, above all, he gave them booty. Adventurer as he was by nature and training, he loved the spoils of war himself, and, while the 'baggage wagon of Augereau' was the by-word in the army, he saw to it that his men had their wagons also well loaded with plunder. His courage was a thing to conjure with; at Lodi he had been one of the numerous generals who rushed the bridge; but at Arcola, alone, flag in hand, he stood on the bridge and hurled taunts and encouragements at his struggling troops, and for three continuous days exposed himself, the guiding spirit of every assault and forlorn hope. While adding to his reputation as a stern and courageous fighter, a clever tactician, and a born leader of men, Augereau's opinion of himself increased by leaps and bounds. He was in no way surprised when, after Leoben, Bonaparte entrusted him with a delicate secret mission to Paris. In his own opinion no better agent could have been found in the rôle of a stern, unbending republican and fiery Jacobin. Bonaparte told him he would represent the feeling of the Army of Italy, and help to bring to nothing the wiles of the royalists. So the general arrived at Paris full of his mission and of his own importance, to the delight of his father - the old mason - who saw him ride into the city covered with gold lace to present sixty stands of captured colours to the Directory. Once in Paris, the fighting general's threats against the Clicheans were turned into deeds. Though he protested that 'Paris has nothing to fear from me: I am a Paris boy myself,' on September 4, 1797, he quietly drew a cordon of troops round the Tuileries, where the Councils sat, and arrested and banished all whose political opinions opposed his own. Relying on the promises of Barras, he now thought that he would become a Director, in place of either Carnot or Barthélemy, who had been deposed. But he soon found, to his sorrow, that he was not the great politician he had believed himself to be, but merely the dupe of Bonaparte and others, who had allowed him to clear the ground for them and to incur the consequent odium. His immediate reward was the command of the Army of the Rhine. Full of bitterness, he arrived at his new headquarters 'covered with gold embroidery, even down to his short boots', and thought to debauch his soldiers and get himself accepted as dictator by telling how, in the Army of Italy, everybody had a pocketful of gold. But the Directory, though unable to curb a Bonaparte, had no fears of the 'Fructidor General', and very soon deprived him of his command, and sent him to an unimportant post at Perpignan, on the Spanish frontier.

For two years Augereau remained at Perpignan, where he had time to understand the causes of his failure. Though completely dominated by Bonaparte while in his presence, he had not the guileless heart of a Lefèbvre, and he began to perceive how the wily Corsican had used him and betrayed him. Accordingly, when Bonaparte returned from Egypt he read his design of becoming Dictator, and, true to his Jacobin principles, at first resolved to fight him to the death; when, however, he found generals, officers, and men going over to Bonaparte, he hastened off to make his submission, saying reproachfully, 'When you were about to do something for our country, how could you forget your own little Augereau?' But though he made his submission, again and again his Jacobin principles made themselves felt. Forced to accompany Bonaparte to the first mass held in Paris after the Concordat, Augereau attempted to slip out of the carriage during the procession to Nôtre Dame, and was ignominiously ordered back by one of the First Consul's aides-de-camp; but he revenged himself by laughing and talking so loudly during the service that the priest could hardly be heard. But Napoleon knew his man and his price: a Marshal's baton and a princely income did much to control his Jacobin proclivities. As early as 1801, Augereau invested part of his savings on the beautiful estate of La Houssaye, where, when not actively employed, he spent his time dispensing lavish hospitality, and delighting his friends and military household with magnificent entertainments, himself the life and soul of the whole party, enjoying all the fun and the practical jokes as much as the youngest subaltern. However he gained his money, he spent it freely and ungrudgingly. When the First Consul tried to put Lannes in an awkward position by ordering him at once to replace the deficit of three hundred thousand francs, caused by the magnificent uniforms he had ordered for the guard, Augereau, as soon as he heard of it, hurried to his solicitors and told them to pay that sum to General Lannes's account. When Bernadotte, whom he scarcely knew, asked him to lend him two hundred thousand francs to complete the purchase of an estate, he at once assented; and when Madame Bernadotte asked him what interest he would require, he replied, 'Madame, bankers and money-lenders, no doubt quite rightly, draw profit from the money they lend, but when a Marshal is fortunate enough to oblige a comrade, the pleasure of doing him a service is enough for him.'

In the scheme for the invasion of England the Marshal's corps, which was stationed round Brest, was destined for the seizure of Ireland, so when the Grand Army was turned against Austria his divisions were the last to arrive on the theatre of operations, and were directed to the Tyrol, where they forced General Jellachich and most of his army to surrender. In the following year the Marshal greatly distinguished himself at Jena and Pultusk; but at Eylau, though not owing to his own fault, he suffered a reverse. The Emperor had placed him in the centre of the first line and ordered him to advance against the Russian centre. The fog and snow were so thick that the French could not see the foe until they came within two hundred yards of them; the enemy suddenly opened fire on them with massed batteries; in a moment Augereau's staunch divisions were cut to bits by the hail of grape, and, owing to the smoke and snow, they could not see their foes; they tried to hold their ground and reply to the fire, but at last they wavered and broke. The Marshal, so ill with fever that he had to be tied to his horse, did his utmost to stop the rout, but in vain; at last, wounded and sick at heart, he had to return and report his failure. The Emperor, wishing to cover his own mistake, laid all the blame for the ill-success of the day on Augereau, and breaking up the remnants of his corps among the other Marshals, he sent him home. Afraid, however, of arousing his enmity, and mindful of his past services, next year he created him Duke of Castiglione; but he never entrusted him again with an important command in the field. In 1809 the Marshal was sent to Spain to supersede St. Cyr at the siege of Gerona. He had lost his lust for fighting, and was soon recalled for not showing sufficient energy. In 1812 he commanded part of the reserve of the Grand Army in Prussia. In 1813 he was in command of a corps of recruits in Germany, and was present at Leipzig, but all through the campaign he grumbled against his troops. When reproached for slackness, and told that he was not the Augereau of Castiglione, he turned on Napoleon, crying out, 'Ah, give me back the old soldiers of Italy and I will show you that I am!' Still, he had no heart for the war, and after the catastrophe at Leipzig he broke out into open revolt, cursing the Emperor and telling Macdonald that 'the idiot does not know what he is about...the coward, he abandoned us and was prepared to sacrifice us all, but do not imagine that I was fool enough to let myself be killed or taken prisoner for the sake of a suburb of Leipzig.' In spite of this, in 1814 Napoleon was so hard pressed that he was forced to employ him. He sent him to Lyons with orders to prevent the Allies from debouching from Switzerland, and, if possible, to fall on the line of communication of Schwartzenberg's army, which was threatening Paris; and he, implored him 'to remember his former victories and to forget that he was on the wrong side of fifty.' But old age and luxury had snapped the once famous spirit of the Duke of Castiglione, and his operations round Lyons were contemptible. As Napoleon said at St. Helena, 'For a long time Augereau had no longer been a soldier; his courage, his early virtues, had raised him high above the crowd, but honour, dignity, and fortune had forced him back into the ruck.' Accordingly, as soon as he heard of the capitulation of Paris he hoisted the white cockade and issued a proclamation saying 'Soldiers you are absolved from your oaths; you are so by the nation, in which the sovereignty resides; you are still more so, were it necessary, by the abdication of a man who, after having sacrificed millions to his cruel ambition, has not known to die as a soldier.' Soon after this he met his former Emperor and benefactor on his way to exile at Elba, and bitter conversation ensued, in which, in reply to the Emperor's recriminations, the Marshal asked, 'Of what do you complain: has not your insatiable ambition brought us to this?'

Yet when the Emperor returned to Paris Augereau threw up his command in Normandy and hastened to proffer his allegiance. But Napoleon would have none of it, and refused him place or preferment. After Waterloo the Bourbons also showed him the cold shoulder; so the Marshal retired to his country seat of La Houssaye, where he died on June 11, 1816, of dropsy on the chest. Born and bred a Paris boy, he had lived as such, and of such were his virtues and his vices. Physically brave, yet morally a coward; vain, blustering, yet kind-hearted; full of boisterous spirits, greedy, yet generous; liberal by nature, hating control, yet a severe disciplinarian; a firm believer in the virtue of principles, yet ever ready to sacrifice his principles on the altar of opportunity, Augereau, in spite of his many faults, knew how to win and keep the love of his soldiers and his friends. A leader of men rather than a tactician or strategist, he played on the enthusiasm of his soldiers by example rather than precept. Unfortunately for his reputation, his moral courage failed him at the end of his career, and he added to the imputation of inconstancy the crime of ingratitude.

16

GUILLAUME MARIE ANNE BRUNE, MARSHAL

GUILLAUME MARIE ANNE BRUNE, poet and warrior, was born on May 13, 1763, at Brives-la-Gaillard. His father, who belonged to a legal family, destined his son to follow in his footsteps, and after giving him a good education, sent him to finish his study of law at the College of France at Paris. But the boy's taste did not lie among the dull technicalities of law. Artistic and emotional by temperament, he early threw himself heart and soul into literature. At the age of eighteen he published his first work, half prose, half verse, in which he described a holiday in Poitou and Angoumois. But his father viewed with suspicion his son's literary aspirations, and the breach between them widened when Guillaume married a young burnisher of metal, Angélique Nicole Pierre, the orphaned daughter of a miller from Arpajon, who had captivated him by her beauty, and then nursed him through a dangerous illness. The young couple were thrown entirely on their own resources, and Angélique had to continue her burnishing, while to ensure the publication of his works Brune took to the trade of printer. But in spite of poverty and hard work the marriage was a happy one, for Angélique's beauty, and purity of mind and character were the necessary complement to her husband's artistic desires. While engaged in his literary work Brune met the celebrated Mirabeau who introduced him to his friends, Camille Desmoulins and Danton. Generous by nature, and smarting under the social disgrace which followed his marriage, the poet, turned printer, threw himself heart and soul into the philosophy of the day: when the Revolution broke out he hailed the new era with delight, but, like many another visionary, he failed to see the cruel necessities which the Revolution was bringing in its train. Following the example of his friend Camille Desmoulins, on September 15,1789, he started a newspaper, the *Magazin Historique ou Fournal*

Général, and followed up speculation by editing, in collaboration with Gauthier, the *Fournal de la Cour*; but owing to the violent politics of Gauthier, Brune broke his connection with the paper in August, 1790. As the Revolution grew in violence and blind disorder, and hate took the place of his dream of platonic justice, eager to escape from cruelty and lust, the printer hastened to console himself among those who were hurrying to the frontier to fight the enemy as the only means of getting away from the chaos at home. In August, 1791, he enlisted in the volunteers of the Seine and Oise, and within a few weeks his activity, zeal, and talent for administration caused his comrades to elect him adjutant-major. Early in 1792 he joined the staff of the army as assistant adjutant-general, and, owing to the influence of Danton and his political friends, was recalled from Thionville to Paris in September, 1792, as commissary general, to direct and organise the newly raised battalions of volunteers. But when he arrived in Paris on September 5th, and found the streets swimming in blood and Danton gloating over his work, disgusted with Paris and its savage population, he at once applied for active service, and was back at the camp of Meaux in time to take part in Dumouriez's campaign of Valmy. Though he recoiled from their methods, his friendship with Danton and Camille Desmoulins stood him in good stead; as adjutant-general he served at Neerwinden, and after that battle was one of the five general officers chosen to rally the scattered troops of the Army of the North. In July he was ordered to Calvados to assist in crushing the Girondists. After his success in Normandy his friends offered him a post in the ministry at Paris, but 'he loved liberty fair and free, as she existed in the army but not as she was adored in Paris, to the sound of the tocsin and the beat of the générale, and fierce songs of death trolled out by cannibals.' Accordingly he returned to the Army of the North in time to fight under Houchard at Handschötten. But he had to pay the penalty for his friendship with the Terrorists, for just as he was setting out full of delight to fight the English at Dunkirk, owing to the exigencies of political strife he was hurriedly recalled to give the Girondists their coup-de-grâce at Bordeaux.

Brune returned to the capital in 1794 in time to witness the fall of his patron, Danton; but fortunately for him Barras took him under his protection, and in October, thanks to his influence, he became commandant of Paris. For a whole year the general held this post, and on October 5th commanded the second column while Bonaparte with the first column ended the reaction of the Terror with a few rounds of grape shot. Still under the patronage of Barras, Brune spent the year 1796 in pacifying .the Midi, and his work there has been admirably portrayed in Alexandre Dumas' 'Les Compagnons de Jéhu,' where he figures as General Rolland. From this vexatious and wearisome struggle against hostile countrymen he was summoned to Italy at the beginning of 1797, and was present with Masséna's division at the battle of Rivoli. Under Masséna, he fought through the campaign which ended at Leoben, and attracted the notice of Bonaparte by his courage and goodwill: in reward for his services he was created general of division. From Italy the general, with his division, was sent in October to join the Army of England; while marching north it was suggested that he should take the post of ambassador at Berlin; but when the troops heard of this offer they asked the adjutant-general to write to their commander, saying, 'Listen general: your division charges me to tell you not to give fighting; the division will bring you honour, and that is much better than an embassy.' However, there was to be question of an embassy, for on February 7, 1798, the Directors sent him to take over the command of the French troops whose duty it was to annex Switzerland to France.

This was the general's first independent command; and though the campaign added to his military reputation, unfortunately it left a stain on his honour. The war was entered on merely with the desire of capturing the Swiss treasury at Berne, and thus providing funds for Bonaparte's Egyptian expedition. Brune had learned his lesson in Italy, so the campaign was short, in spite of the difficulty of the country and the patriotism of the Swiss. Writing to Bonaparte, the general explained the cause of his success: 'From the moment I found myself in a situation to act, I assembled all my strength to strike like lightning: for Switzerland is a vast barrack, and I had everything to fear from a war of posts. I avoided it by negotiations which I knew were not sincere on the part of the Bernese, and since then I have followed out the plan which I traced to you. I think always I am still under your command.' The crushing of the Swiss peasantry and the capture of Berne were followed by the hour of spoliation; no less than one million seven hundred thousand pounds were wrung from the wretched Swiss. Brune himself kept his own hands clean and was, as he wrote, 'constantly paring the nails of rascals and taking the public treasure from them'; but the fact that he was officially responsible for the spoliation and that his own share of the plunder was thirty-two thousand pounds caused his name to be loathed throughout the length and breadth of Switzerland, and 'to rob like a Brune' became a proverb, which was eagerly seized on by his detractors.

The Directors, pleased with his operations in Switzerland, despatched Brune, on March 31, 1798, to take command of the Army of Italy. His task was a difficult one, for at Rome and Mantua the starving troops had mutinied, while the contractors and agents of the Directors were amassing huge fortunes. To complicate the situation the general was encumbered by a civil Commission, whose duty it was to supervise the governments of the Cisalpine Republic. Trouvé, the moving spirit of the Commission, had but one idea, to curb the growing democratic spirit of the Piedmontese. The commander-in-chief, whose love of freedom had not yet been blunted, violently opposed Trouvé, and at last forced his views on the Directory, and Trouvé was replaced by Fouché. But it was too late; the mischief had been done. The Piedmontese would no longer bear the French control: 'This then,' they cried, 'is the faith, the fraternity, and the friendship you have brought us from France!' In spite of Brune's efforts to restore confidence they had lost all faith in French honour, and on December 6th his successor found himself forced to expel, at the point of the bayonet, all senators opposed to the French interest.

Leaving Italy in November, Brune found himself sent at the beginning of 1799 to Holland, where danger was threatening: it was evident that England was going to make an effort to regain for the Prince of Orange his lost possessions. In spite of this knowledge, as late as August the French commander could only concentrate ten thousand men under General Daendals to oppose an equal force of English under Abercromby when they landed on the open beach at

Groete Keten. Though as strong as the enemy, General Daendals made the most feeble attempt to oppose the landing. Day by day English and Russian reinforcements poured into Holland, till at last they numbered forty-eight thousand. But the Duke of York, the English commander-in-chief, had a hopeless task. With no means of transport, no staff, and an army composed of hastily enrolled militia recruits and insubordinate drunken Russians, his only chance of success lay in a general rising of the Dutch; for early in September the French forces were numerically as strong as his own. Abercromby's opinion was that defeat would mean utter disaster: 'Were we to sustain a severe check I much doubt if the discipline of the troops would be sufficient to prevent a total dissolution of the army': while the English opinion of the Russians was that they were better at plundering than at fighting. As a militiaman wrote, 'The Russians is people as has fear of God before their eyes, for I saw some of them cheeses and bitter and all badly wounded, and in particklar one man had an eit day clock on his back, and fiting all the time which made me to conclude and say all his vanity and vexation of spirit.' In spite of this the English had some considerable tactical success, and drove the French back towards Amsterdam; but lack of provisions compelled them at the beginning of October to fall back on their entrenched position on the Zype. Fortunately Brune, who had been much impressed by the fighting powers of the enemy, did not understand how difficult it would have been for them to re-embark their forces if he pressed an attack. He allowed some staff officers to throw out hints of an armistice and convention, which were eagerly accepted, for on October 20th the English had only three days' provision of bread. With Masséna's victory at Zurich and the embarkation of the Allies after the convention of Alkmaar, the ring of foes which had so gravely threatened France was snapped asunder, and Brune, although he had shown but little resource or initiative during the fighting in Holland, and had failed to diagnose the extremity of the enemy, was hailed, along with Masséna, as the saviour of the country, and his tactical defeats were celebrated as the victory of Bergen.

From Holland the conqueror of the English was despatched, early in 1800, by the First Consul to quell the rising in La Vendée, where his former experience of guerrilla warfare in Switzerland stood him in good stead and he soon brought the rebels to their knees. During the Marengo campaign he commanded the real Army of Reserve at Dijon, but in August, when Bonaparte found it necessary to replace Masséna, he despatched Brune to take command of the Army of Italy. Unfortunately the future Marshal's genius was more suited to the details of administration and the direction of small columns than to the command of large forces in the field. Though at the head of a hundred thousand men, and supported admirably by Murat, Marmont, Macdonald, Suchet and Dupont, he failed conspicuously as a commander-in-chief. His movements at the crossing of the Mincio were hesitating and slow, and he neglected to seize the opportunity which Dupont's successful movements presented to him. At Treviso, as in Holland, he showed only too clearly his limitations: he held the enemy in the hollow of his hand, but, failing to see his advantage, he once again signed an armistice which permitted the foe to escape out of his net.

On his return to France the First Consul regarded him with suspicion. His well-known republican opinions did not harmonise with Bonaparte's schemes of self-aggrandisement. The First Consul had a very poor estimate of his military ability, but the people at large still hailed him as the saviour of Holland and France. Bonaparte treated him like all those whom he suspected but whom he could not afford to despise, and under the pretext of a diplomatic appointment he practically banished him to Constantinople. Diplomacy was not Brune's forte, and after eighteen months' residence in Turkey he was obliged to quit the Porte, which had fallen entirely under Russian influence.

The general was still abroad when the Emperor created his Marshals: his appointment of Brune, like his appointment of Lefèbvre, was part of his scheme for binding the republican interest to his dynasty, for his opinion of the Marshal's talent was such that he scarcely ever employed him in the field. From 1805 to 1807 Brune was occupied in drilling the troops left at Boulogne. In May, 1807, he was appointed to command the reserve corps of the Grand Army, and when in July the King of Sweden declared war on Napoleon, he was entrusted with the operations round Stralsund, and captured that fortress and the island of Rügen. During this short campaign the Marshal had an interview with Gustavus of Sweden, and tried to point out to him the folly of fighting against France. A garbled account of this interview, full of unjust insinuations, came to Napoleon's ears. In anger the Emperor sent for Brune and taxed him with the false accusations. The Marshal, furious that his good faith should be suspected, refused any explanation and merely contented himself with repeating: 'It is a lie.' The Emperor, equally furious at his obstinacy, deprived him of his command. The result of this quarrel was that for the next five years Brune lived at home in disgrace. On the Restoration he made his submission to Louis XVIII, and received the cross of St. Louis. But in 1815, on the return from Elba, he answered the Emperor's summons, for Napoleon could no longer afford the luxury of quarrelling with generous Frenchmen who were willing to serve him. Remembering the Marshal's talent for administration and a war of posts, he offered him the command of the Midi. Brune hesitated; Napoleon had treated him disgracefully, but in his generosity he was ready to overlook all that; still, he knew well that the Empire was not the Republic: yet he preferred Napoleon's régime to that of the Bourbons, and at last he accepted, but set out for his new duties depressed and not at all himself. The difficulties he had to contend with were enormous; the Austrians and Sardinians were massing on the frontiers, the allied fleet commanded the Mediterranean, while Provence was covered by bands of brigands who called themselves royalists. Marseilles, the fickle, which had given France, and the Republic the 'Marseillaise,' was no red-hot Legitimist. So the news of Waterloo and of Napoleon's abdication came as a relief to the harassed Marshal, who was only too glad on July 22nd to hand over Toulon to the English. Thereon, in obedience to the command of the King, he set out for Paris.

Well aware of the disorder in the Midi, the Marshal asked Lord Exmouth, the commander of the British squadron, to take him by sea to Italy, so that he might escape the danger which he knew threatened him from the hatred of the royalists. Unfortunately for the fame of England, Lord Exmouth refused in the rudest terms, calling him 'the prince of scamps' and a 'blackguard'. Accordingly he set off by land, receiving a promise of protection from the royalist commander, but no escort. With his two aides-de-camp he reached Avignon in safety, but there he was set on by the mob, chased into a hotel and shot in cold blood, and his body thrown into the Rhône; a fisherman by night rescued the corpse, and for many years the body of the Marshal reposed in the humble grave where the kind-hearted fisherman had placed it. Meanwhile the Government sanctioned the story that he had committed suicide. But at last the persistence of his widow compelled an inquiry, when the truth was revealed, and it was proved without doubt that the murder had been connived at by the authorities. The inquiry further revealed that the real cause of the Marshal's death was not so much the measures he had taken to stamp out the bands of royalists during his command in the Midi, as his old connection with Camille Desmoulins and Danton. In spite of the fact that he was not in Paris during the September massacres, and that he was constantly employed with the army, rumour said that it was Brune who had carried round Paris the head of the Princess Lamballe on a pike, and the cunning revival of this story by the leaders of the White Terror had roused the mob to commit the outrage. The story was absurd. The archives of the War Office proved beyond doubt that he not in Paris at the time of the execution of the Princess. Strange to say, the Marshal himself years before seems to have foretold his own death when, writing about the Terrorists, he composed the following lines:

> Against one, two hundred rise,
> Assail and smite him till he dies.
> Yet blood, they say, we spare to spill,
> And patriots we account them still.
> Urged by martial ardour on,
> In the wave their victim thrown,
> Return their frantic joy to fill;
> Yet these men are patriots still.

Though his faithful wife had forced the authorities to remove the stain of suicide from the Marshal's fair fame, it was not till 1839, the year after her death, that at last a fitting monument was raised at

Brives-la-Gaillard to the memory of the Marshal, who, whatever his failings as a commander might be, had lived a staunch friend, a true patriot, a courageous soldier; and had twice received grateful thanks of the Government, and had twice been acclaimed as the saviour of his country.

17

ADOLPHE ÉDOUARD CASIMIR JOSEPH MORTIER, MARSHAL, DUKE OF TREVISO

ÉDOUARD MORTIER was born near Cambrai on February 13, 1768. His father, a prosperous farmer, gave the future Marshal a fair education. Becoming a man of some importance on the outbreak of the Revolution, he was able in 1791 to secure for his son a commission in the volunteer cavalry of the north. Extremely tall, heavily built, slow of speech, 'with a stupid sentinel look', the yeoman captain of 1791 gave the casual observer but little sign of promise. But in spite of those rather weary looking eyes, young Mortier was possessed of a burning enthusiasm and a dauntless courage. From his first engagement at Quiévrain, in April, 1792, where he had a horse killed under him, to the day he and Marmont surrendered Paris in 1814, every skirmish or engagement in which he took part bore testimony to his extraordinary bodily strength and bravery. Nature having also endowed him with a kindly temperament, it was not to be wondered at that his men swore by him, and were ready to follow him anywhere. But in spite of many gallant actions and numerous mentions in despatches, promotion came but slowly; for Mortier spent the first six years of his service with the armies of the Sambre and Meuse and of the Rhine, and had to compete against such men as Soult, Ney, St. Cyr, Kléber, and Desaix, who were on a higher mental plane. Still, he was recognised as one who was bound to rise, and was one of those whom Kléber singled out for commendation when he wrote to the Directory saying, 'With such chiefs a general can neglect to count the number of his enemies'; and well he might, for on the day after he wrote his report, Mortier, with a single battalion four squadrons of cavalry, having been ordered to try and drive two thousand of the enemy out of a strong position on the Wisent, attacked them with such vivacity that, to the surprise of everybody, in an hour he drove them in flight.

After the campaign in 1798 Jourdan sent up his name for the command of a brigade; but he preferred the colonelcy of the twenty-first regiment of cavalry. However, a few months later, on February 22nd, he was promoted general of brigade. It was in this capacity that he served under Masséna in the celebrated campaign in Switzerland. At the second battle of Zurich he did yeoman service; by a vigorous demonstration he held the enemy near the town while Masséna completed his turning movement; he further distinguished himself by his vigour and resource during the pursuit of the Russians; thus he won his promotion to general of division on September 25, 1799. When Bonaparte became First Consul, Mortier found no cause for dissatisfaction with the change of Government; no politician, he was ready to accept any strong government. Fortunately for him his dogged character and his fighting record attracted the First Consul's attention. Bonaparte saw in him a man without guile, a soldier who would accept any order from his chief, and execute it instantly without questioning. Still, it was a great piece of fortune for the general of division, who had hitherto held no independent command in the field, that he lay with his troops near the Vaal, at the time that the First Consul determined to punish England for her suspicion of him by seizing Hanover. With twenty thousand men General Mortier issued from Holland, fell suddenly on the Hanoverian troops at Borstel on the Weser, and forced Count Walmoden to sign a convention whereby the Hanoverian army was to retire behind the Elbe and not to bear arms against the French as long as the war continued. The English Government refused to ratify it, so Mortier at once called on Walmoden to resume hostilities; but so unequal was the contest, that the Hanoverian general was forced to accept a modified form of the former convention. Thereon Mortier hurriedly occupied Hamburg and Bremen, and closed the Elbe to English commerce. But brilliant as his operations had been in the field, as military governor of the ceded provinces he established a reputation for great rapacity, which followed him throughout his career.

Napoleon, however, winked at his general's peculations so long as they did not affect his treasury, and he showed his approbation of his successful campaign by making him one of the four commandants of the Guard, and including him, in 1804, among the first creation of Marshals. Next year Mortier marched to Germany in command of a division of the Guards. When after Ulm the army was reorganised for the advance on Vienna, a new corps, composed of the division of Dupont and Gazan, was entrusted to the Marshal. The duty he was to perform was difficult; he was to cross the Danube at Linz and, unsupported save by a flotilla of boats, hang on the Russian rear, while the rest of the army marched on Vienna by the right bank of the river. The Emperor impressed on him the necessity for caution, and warned him that he must throw out a ring of vedettes and keep somewhat behind Lannes's corps, which was marching in advance of him on the other side of the river. Unfortunately the Marshal, in his eagerness to inflict loss on the Russians, whom he believed to be flying in complete rout, neglected all warnings and pushed recklessly forward. At Dürrenstein (near the castle where Richard Coeur de Lion was imprisoned by the Archduke of Austria) he fell into a trap. The enemy allowed him to pass the defile of Dürrenstein with Gazan's division, knowing that Dupont was many miles in the rear, and then closed in on him on front and rear. With but seven thousand men, surrounded by thirty thousand Russians, it seemed that the Marshal was lost. But he kept his head, and at once turned about to try and break back and join Dupont, who he knew would hurry to his support. Firing at point-blank range, struggling bayonet against bayonet, the small French force worked its way towards the defile. Darkness fell, but still the fight continued, and at last Dupont's guns were heard at the other side of the gorge. But by then two-thirds of Gazan's division had fallen, three eagles were taken, and Mortier himself, conspicuous by his towering height, owed his safety to his skill with his sabre. His officers had begged him to escape across the river by boat, lest a Marshal of France should become a prisoner in the hands of the despised Russians; this he indignantly refused. 'No,' he said, 'reserve this resource for the wounded. One who has the honour to command such brave soldiers should esteem himself happy to share their lot and perish with them. We have still two guns and some boxes of grape; let us close our ranks and make a effort.' But still the Russians pressed the devoted column, and now all the ammunition was expended and the survivors were preparing to sell their lives dearly, when Dupont's men at last hurled the enemy aside, and amid cries of 'France! France! you have saved us!' the undaunted remnant of Gazan's division threw themselves into the arms of their comrades. On the morrow the sorely battered corps was recalled across the Danube, but the Emperor could not lay all the blame on Mortier, for it was his own mistake in strategy in dividing his army by the broad Danube which had really caused the disaster.

In 1806 the Marshal acted independently on the left of the Grand Army, and after occupying Cassel and Hamburg, where his cruel exactions greatly increased his reputation for rapacity, he was entrusted with the operations against the Swedes. In 1807, however, he was called up to reinforce the Grand Army in time to take part in the decisive battle at Friedland. In July, 1808, Napoleon rewarded him by creating him Duke of Treviso. A month later he despatched him to Spain in command of the fifth corps, which was composed of veterans of the Austrian and Prussian campaigns, very different from the recruits of the third corps and other corps in Spain. But in spite of this magnificent material the Marshal did not distinguish himself. The severe reverse he had received at Dürrenstein seemed to have killed his dash. His physical bravery remained the same as ever, but his moral courage had deteriorated, and in Spain his manoeuvres were always halting and timid. At Saragossa he did not press the siege with the vehemence Lannes showed when he superseded him; but at the battle of Ocaña be showed that during a combat his nerve was as good as ever. The first lines of the French, broken by the fire of the Spanish battery, had begun to waver; the Marshal was slightly wounded, but at the critical moment he rode up to Girard's division, which was in reserve, and leading it through the intervals of the first line, he caught the victorious enemy at a disadvantage, and completely turned the fortunes of the day. The remainder of the Duke of Treviso's service in the Peninsula was spent under the command of Marshal Soult, either in front of Cadiz or as a covering force to the troops occupied in that siege. From Spain he was recalled in 1812 to command the Young Guard in the Russian campaign. When the French evacuated Moscow the Marshal, at the Emperor's commands, had the invidious duty of blowing up the Kremlin. During his retreat he showed himself worthy of his post of commander of the Young Guard, and in 1813, in the same capacity, he fought throughout the campaign, taking his share in the battles of Lützen, Bautzen, Dresden, Leipzig, and Hanau. After Dresden he incurred, along with St. Cyr, the wrath of the Emperor for not having aided Vandamme. But the fact remains that the blame of the disaster at Külm rests entirely on Napoleon and Vandamme. No orders were sent to Mortier or St. Cyr till after the disaster had occurred, and Vandamme had not taken the most elementary precautions against surprise. In 1814 the Marshal fought gallantly at Montmirail and Troyes, but, like Victor and Ney, he showed but little ingenuity. When Napoleon made his last dash eastward, he left Mortier and Marmont to hold off the Prussians from Paris. The Duke of Treviso, though far senior to the Duke of Ragusa, bowed to his superior genius, and in the operations ending in the surrender of Paris he carried out his junior's ideas with great generosity and without the least show of jealousy.

Like the rest of the Marshals, the Duke of Treviso made his submission to the new Government. On the return of Napoleon he for a time kept true to his oath to the Bourbons. When the Duke of Orleans, who shared with him the command of the north, on leaving Lille, wrote to him, 'I am too good a Frenchman to sacrifice the interests of France, because now misfortune compels me to quit it. I go to hide myself in retirement and oblivion. It only remains for me to release you from all the orders which I have given you, and to recommend you to do what your excellent judgment and patriotism may suggest as best for the interests of France,' the Marshal, in spite of his decoration of St. Louis and his seat as a peer of France, once again returned to his old allegiance. The Emperor greeted him warmly and created him one of his new peers, and in June sent him to the frontier in command of the Young Guard; but an attack of sciatica forcing him to bed, he escaped the disaster of Waterloo. On the second restoration he lost for the time his honours and dignities, but refused to re-purchase them at the price of sitting as judge on Marshal Ney; however, in 1819 he was reinstated in all of them.

It was not till the accession of the July monarchy that the Duke of Treviso once again played a prominent part. In 1831 his old friend, the Duke of Orleans, now become King, made him Grand Chancellor of the Legion of Honour, and in November, 1834, called on him to accept the onerous task of head of the Government and Minister of War. To help his friend and sovereign the Duke accepted the responsibility, but soon found that he was unequal to the task. A frank and loyal soldier, of unimpeachable honour, integrity, and character, he could shine in the field, but not in the forum. His fine, lofty figure, commanding air, military bearing, and frankness were of no avail in the Chamber of Peers, where what was wanted was a subtle spirit which could discern and influence the drift of parties, a clear, facile tongue, and an apparent acquaintance with any subject which might come up for discussion. These were the very qualities in which the Marshal was most lacking. Slow-witted by nature, with a limited vocabulary and a bad delivery, he soon found himself unfitted for the post, and resigned in February, 1835. But unfortunately for him he still retained his position as Grand Chancellor, and in this capacity he attended Louis Philippe on his way to the ill-fated review of July 29th. As the procession arrived at the boulevard of the Temple, the Marshal complained of the heat; his staff tried to persuade the old soldier to go home, but he refused, saying, 'My place is by the King, in the midst of the Marshals, my comrades in arms.' Scarcely had he spoken when Fieschi hurled the fatal bomb, which missed the King and the princes, but killed the Marshal and many another soldier.

The Duke of Treviso, while doing his duty by his sovereign, met his death like a soldier, though not on the field of battle. As with Davout, the key to his character was his dogged determination; but though he resembled the Prince of Eckmühl on the battlefield, he had not his powers of organisation, nor his clear insight into matters of policy and strategy. But he had other qualities which Davout lacked. He was kind-hearted, and beloved by his men. His simplicity and faithfulness appealed to Napoleon, and to all who came in contact with him, and it was for this reason that the Emperor entrusted him with the Young Guard. What distinguished him from many of the other Marshals was his lack of jealousy, and the generous way in which he co-operated with his comrades in arms. When the funeral procession passed down the Rue Royale on its way to the Church of the

Invalides, with four Marshals on horseback holding the corners of the pall, men felt, and felt rightly, that France had suffered a loss, for one was gone who, peasant-born, had in his high position known how to retain the simple virtues of a peasant, whose one vice was the peasant vice of avarice, and who, with this exception, had never allowed place or power to interfere with what he thought was his duty.

18

JEAN BAPTISTE BESSIÈRES, MARSHAL, DUKE OF ISTRIA

FIDELITY and conscientiousness are great assets in life's race, and to these Jean Baptiste Bessières added great presence of mind and considerable dash. It is not therefore surprising that, in an age when disinterestedness and reliability were notably absent among public men, his force of character pushed him above the ordinary adventurers, and caused him to become one of Napoleon's most trusted lieutenants. The Marshal was born at Prayssac in 1768. His father, a surgeon, brought up his son in his own profession. But the outbreak of the Revolution opened a wider field to the audacious young Gascon. Early in 1792 Jean Baptiste quitted Cahors and the medical profession, and started off to Paris as one of the newly enrolled 'garde constitutionnelle'. His fidelity and courage were soon put to the test. He aided the royal family in the flight to Varennes, and consequently had to seek safety in retirement. But the life of a soldier was as the breath of his nostrils, and three months later he managed to enlist in the 22nd Chasseurs, a corps which formed part of the Army of the Pyrenees. There his courage and ability made him conspicuous. Within three months of enlisting he was promoted sub-lieutenant. The year 1793 proved a disastrous one for France. Defeat followed defeat. But Jean Baptiste never despaired, and when success ultimately smiled on the French arms, he had established a reputation as a daring and capable squadron commander. Still, like many another of the successful soldiers of the age, Bessières owed his quick promotion to his early friendship with the great Corsican. It was Murat who called Napoleon's attention to the future commander of the Imperial Guard, and Bonaparte, with his eagle eye, at once appreciated his qualities. When the young chief formed his special bodyguard, called the Guides, he placed him at their head. The new corps was composed of the choicest troops, and formed the nucleus of the Imperial Guard. Henceforward Bessières became his chief's confidant and inseparable friend. It was the rare fidelity that he displayed to his master and his constant attention to detail, his intuitive knowledge of his commander's requirements, and his energy in carrying out his plans, rather than great military genius, which accounted for the Emperor's life-long appreciation of the commander of his Guides.

At Lonato and Castiglione Bessières proved the correctness of the young Corsican's judgment. At Roveredo he broke through the centre of the Austrian infantry, and, with six others, captured two of the enemy's guns. At the first battle of Rivoli, in accordance with his general's commands, he laid an ambuscade in the marsh on the Austrian left, which proved the decisive factor in the battle. In the following year he again distinguished himself at the second battle of Rivoli and at the siege of Mantua. As a reward for his services Bonaparte sent him to Paris with the official despatches and the stands of colours won from the enemy, and at the end of the campaign promoted him full colonel, and as a further mark of his confidence appointed him tutor and instructor to his stepson, Eugène. Bessières accompanied Bonaparte to the East, and served by his side in Egypt and Syria.

The commander of the Guides was among the chosen body of friends who accompanied Bonaparte on his secret return to France, and in Paris he helped Murat, Lannes, and Marmont to win over the army, and took a prominent part in the coup d'état of the 18th Brumaire. Immediately after becoming First Consul Napoleon created the consular Guard, composed of four battalions of infantry and two regiments of cavalry. He placed at the head of the infantry Lannes, and at the head of the cavalry Bessières. With the cavalry of the Guard Bessières took part in the famous march across the Alps and in the drawn battle of Marengo. Faithful as he had proved himself in war, he showed his fidelity in peace by exposing the plot of the artist, Caracchi, and thus by ties of gratitude bound himself closer to the First Consul. Tall, good-looking, with a graceful figure and a charming smile, the commandant of the Guard captivated everybody by his intelligence and his distinguished bearing, which had a piquant flavour by reason of his adherence to the queue and powder of a bygone age.

Rejecting the brilliant match proposed by the First Consul, he chose as his bride Mademoiselle Lapezrière, a young lady of a royalist family. The couple were married by a nonjuring priest, and, far from incurring displeasure, were greatly complimented, for Bonaparte already desired the Concordat with the Pope, and saw in the bride a useful supporter of his scheme. Madame Bessières was a great social success: a favourite of Napoleon and a close friend and confidant of Josephine; everywhere she was welcomed for her beauty, her force of character, and the charm of her manner.

During the year of peace and the preparation for the invasion of England, Bessières accompanied the First Consul on all his numerous expeditions. To his credit be it said, he protested loudly against the ill-judged execution of the Duc d'Enghien. When the First Consul became Emperor he enrolled his friend among his new Marshals, not for his military genius, but as a reward for his fidelity, for none knew better than Napoleon how lacking the new Marshal was in many of the requisites of a great commander.

In 1805 the cavalry of the Guard formed part of the Grand Army, and their commander, by his able backing of Murat, had his share in helping to win the battle of Austerlitz. During the interval between the Austrian and the Prussian campaigns the Marshal was busily occupied in Paris in reorganising and expanding the Guard, and, as usual, was in close touch with the Emperor. In the Prussian campaign Bessières had his first taste of an independent command, and gained great credit for his masterly manoeuvring in Poland, where with a weak force he kept the enemy in complete ignorance of the movements of the French, and covered the conjunction of the various corps of the army.

After the peace of Tilsit he was entrusted with the delicate mission of negotiating a marriage between Princess Charlotte of Würtemburg and Prince Jerome, the new King of Westphalia. Hardly had he returned to Paris when he was hurried off again on active service, this time to Spain.

It was just a week before the disaster of Baylen that Marshal Bessières was confronted with a most serious problem. The Spanish levies from Old Castile, under Cuesta, had effected a junction with the levies of Galicia, under Blake, and were threatening to overwhelm the weak force of ten thousand men with which the Marshal was attempting to put down the guerrilla warfare in the northern provinces. Bessières had not been the great Emperor's confidant for nothing, and he at once saw that, unless he took the initiative, his force was doomed, for the enemy were in overwhelming strength, and every day added to their numbers. He knew well how ill-disciplined their forces were, and he determined to try the effect of a surprise. Everything fell out as he wished. On July 14th he found the Spanish armies in position outside Medina del Rio Seco, some few miles east of Valladolid. The Spaniards, not knowing whether the French were advancing from the direction of Valladolid or Burgos, had placed the army of Blake on the Valladolid road, and that of Cuesta on the Burgos road. Accordingly the Marshal was able to surprise and defeat Blake, and then to turn and inflict a similar defeat on Cuesta. So far his dispositions had been excellent, but, as General Foy said, 'He could organise victory, but he could not profit by it,' for he was paralysed by the extent of the guerrilla warfare with which he was faced, and after a short but bloody pursuit he called off his troops. Still, he had accomplished much; for the time he had dispersed all organised resistance in the northern provinces, and had opened the road to Madrid for King Joseph.

But Baylen and Vimeiro proved that the war in the Iberian Peninsula was still only in its first stage. Joseph had hastily to evacuate Madrid, and, in spite of having twelve thousand French troops under his command, Bessières could effect nothing. The Spanish armies of Cuesta and Blake once again took shape; and, like the other French generals, the Marshal had to fall back on the line of the Ebro. Such was the situation in October when the Emperor himself appeared on the scene. The situation changed like magic at the touch of a master hand. The French troops, strung out in a great semicircle on the Ebro, were quickly concentrated. Blake and Cuesta were each defeated by an overwhelming combination of the different French armies. Meanwhile, the Emperor, recognising the limitations of his faithful friend, superseded him by Soult, but gave him the command of the Guard and of the reserve cavalry, under his own immediate supervision, and took him back to France when he gave up the pursuit of the English.

Napoleon desired to take the Guard with him on the Austrian campaign, and, as several regiments were still in Spain, others had to be enrolled to take their places. These regiments were entirely organised by Bessières, and formed the nucleus of what was later called the Young Guard. The Marshal's duty during the Austrian campaign of 1809 was the same as in Spain: the command of the Guard and of the reserve cavalry. During the famous Five Days' Fighting he proved again that no troops in Europe could resist the charges of the heavy cavalry of the Guard, and that he himself had almost as great a command of the technique of cavalry tactics as his famous friend and instructor, the King of Naples. At Aspern and Essling the cavalry of the Guard and the reserve cavalry covered themselves with glory by their dashing charges. Again and again, with cries of 'Vive l'Empereur', the glittering masses of cuirassiers attempted to break down the stern handful of indomitable Hungarians who guarded the Austrian batteries. When the bridges were broken, and the retreat to the island of Lobau was the only hope for the army, Bessières, with the remains of cavalry, so severely punished the enemy that the retirement was effected in safety. At Wagram, when all seemed lost, Napoleon called on his old comrade to sacrifice himself with his cavalry. As the cuirassiers of the Guard trotted past to debouch on their heroic mission, the Emperor, waving his sword, cried out, 'No sabring. Give point, give point!' The needed time was gained, and the gallant Marshal was wounded. But at the end of the day, when the troopers, after their great effort, could no longer face the unbroken lines of slowly retreating Austrians, Napoleon, chagrined at his failure, met his cavalry and their commander with reproach: 'Was ever anything seen like this? Neither prisoners nor guns! This day will be attended with no result.'

The Emperor's ill-humour was only temporary. When his most trusted lieutenants were grumbling and longing for peace in which to enjoy the spoil they had collected in war, when Bernadotte and Fouché were openly intriguing against him, Napoleon could ill afford to disregard his most faithful friend. Accordingly, immediately after Wagram he despatched the newly created Duke of Istria to Belgium to take over the command of the French troops who were opposing the ill-fated English expedition to the isle of Walcheren. When the Marshal returned from Belgium to Paris he found that the Emperor had made all arrangements for the divorce of Josephine and for his second marriage. Bessières was placed in a very awkward position. Prince Eugène was his greatest friend. Josephine had always been most kind to him and the Duchess, but he could not help them in any way, and, to make matters worse, the Emperor insisted on coming and staying with him at his country house at Grignon.

Meanwhile the war in Spain was spoiling many great reputations. Reinforcements were urgently required, so the Emperor decided to give his Young Guard their baptism of fire in Spain. Accordingly, at the commencement of 1811 he despatched them with Bessières, their commander, to operate on the northern lines of communication. The ill-success of the French was palpably due to two causes. There was no commander-in-chief on the spot - the Emperor was in Paris - and there was no other Marshal whom all the others would obey. Secondly, there was a great want of concentration; as Bessières wrote to Berthier: 'All the world is aware of the vicious system of our operations, everyone sees that we are too much scattered. We occupy too wide an extent of country: we exhaust our resources without profit and without necessity: we cling to dreams. We should concentrate our forces; retain certain points d'appui for the protection of our magazines and hospitals, and regard two-thirds of Spain as a vast battlefield, which a single victory may either secure or wrest from us.' Unfortunately the Marshal was human, like his comrades, and instead of loyally backing up Masséna, he came to an open rupture with him on the question of supplies, and by his inaction at Fuentes d'Onoro he caused the French to lose that battle. Though he made good his excuses before Napoleon, and secured the disgrace of the Prince of Essling, in the opinion of the Duke of Wellington it was Bessières's refusal to lend Masséna assistance which was entirely responsible for the French defeat. Moreover, sound as were his views on the method of conducting war, he had not the personality to impress them on others or the application to put them into practice, and his whole time was occupied in attempting to make head against the guerrilla warfare. His methods were rough and barbarous, and reacted against the French, for he avenged the ill deeds of the guerrillas on their families and women folk, and visited with military execution any village which failed to meet his onerous requisitions. So the Spaniards retaliated with revenge, the weapon of the weak, that 'wild kind of justice'. The Marshal's blunders were cut short by his recall to Paris at the beginning of 1812 to reorganise the Guard prior to the Russian campaign.

The Duke of Istria accompanied the Emperor to the front. His individual share was restricted by the fact that the King of Naples was with the army. But during the retreat he led the van and did yeoman service in restoring order among the disheartened troops.

Early in 1813 he was recalled from Ebling to reorganise the Guard and the reserve cavalry. The task tried to the utmost the Marshal's great administrative capacity, for not only was there the question of men and equipment, but above all he was confronted with the difficulty of providing remounts. In spite of all his efforts it was impossible to find anything like enough horses for the cavalry, for the guns had to be supplied first.

The Marshal's share in the campaign was short. At Lützen, on the eve of the first engagement, he was greatly depressed and possessed by a presentiment of death, which proved only too true, for scarcely had the battle opened when he was struck by a bullet which inflicted a mortal wound.

The Duke of Istria has always been among the more unknown of the Marshals. The reason for this is clear. As commander of the cavalry of the Guard and organiser of the Young Guard, his greatest work was done in the office at Paris, disciplining, organising, equipping, and supervising the instruction of these picked troops. His greatest talents were those of administration. As a cavalry leader in the field he was overshadowed by the brilliant and more striking King of Naples. Still, as a subordinate he possessed some sterling qualities, as is proved by his actions during the Great Five Days, and by the fierce fight at Aspern-Essling. As an independent commander he was a failure. Again and again his moral courage seemed to desert him at the critical moment. In Spain, at Medina del Rio Seco, at Burgos, and at Fuentes d'Onoro, he could not brace himself to take the responsibility of throwing his whole weight into the action. Like many another general, he was sound, but he was unable to rise to the height of those great commanders who intuitively know when to stake their all. Consequently, although he undoubtedly possessed the true military eye, as is shown by the wonderful way he covered the junction of the French corps along the Vistula, and by his clearly written despatch on the errors of the war in Spain, his military reputation always suffered when he had not his great chief close at hand to stiffen his determination. Napoleon knew full well his weakness, and the reproaches he hurled at him at Wagram were not altogether without ground. Still, the Emperor was aware that Bessières's advice was always valuable, because of his clearness of vision and his absolute lack of all bias and prejudice; and while he made allowances for his lack of moral courage, he always listened to him attentively. The army believed that it was his frantic appeal, 'Sire, you are seven hundred leagues from Paris,' which deterred the Emperor at Moskowa from throwing the Guard into the action, and thus permitted the Russians to escape absolute annihilation. As a man the Marshal was loved and respected by all for his absolute disinterestedness and straightforwardness. He was adored by his troops, while he possessed the qualities which enabled him to succeed in the difficult task of establishing an iron discipline in the Guard. It was due to him that, in the Imperial Guard, there was none of that lawlessness which made the Pretorians of Rome a danger to the Empire. When not unnerved by responsibility the Marshal was tenderhearted to an extreme. At Moscow he was foremost in saving the wretched inhabitants from the flames; during the horror of the retreat he dashed back alone to a deserted camp on hearing the cries of an infant. But when frightened he could be cruelty itself, as is shown in his terrible decrees against the Spanish guerrillas. Yet even in Spain his justice was appreciated, and in many a village in Castile, on the news of his death, masses were sung for his soul. Though he lacked the highest moral courage, his physical bravery was proven on many a stricken field from Valladolid to Warsaw. At St. Helena the great Emperor gave his friend a noble epitaph - 'He lived like Bayard, he died like Turenne.'

19

CLAUDE VICTOR PERRIN, MARSHAL, DUKE OF BELLUNO

NOT specially dowered by fortune with talents for war, but possessed of a resolute character, a high sense of honour, great courage, and that intrepidity which Napoleon maintained was so absolutely essential for high command, the Duke of Belluno is a striking instance of how large a factor is character in the struggle of life which ends in the survival of the fittest. Born on December 7, 1764, at La Marche, among the mountains of the Vosges, Victor Perrin enlisted as a private, at the age of seventeen, in the artillery regiment of Grenoble. The artillery was the finest arm of the old royal army, for there, and there alone, merit, not favour, was the key to promotion. Accordingly the future Marshal served his apprenticeship to arms under officers who knew their service and loved it. Ten years spent in the ranks under those who maintained strict discipline and were themselves punctilious in matters of duty, who exercised careful supervision over their men and matériel, and made a serious study of their profession, the art of war - these years with their example were not thrown away on the young soldier. When, in 1791, the upheaval of the Revolution threatened to subvert the service, Claude Victor, now a sergeant, in disgust at the licence prevailing among the troops, applied for his discharge. Seven months of civil life proved enough for the sturdy ex-sergeant, and in October he enrolled himself in the volunteers of the Drôme, where in nine months he forced himself by strength of character to the command of his battalion, for, as Napoleon aptly said, 'the times of revolution are the occasions for those soldiers who have insight and courage.' After six months' drill under the hand of the ex-artilleryman, the volunteers of the Drôme were able to hold their own on the parade ground with the best regiments of the line. Well might their commander be proud of his battalion. In the fighting on the Var, Victor's volunteers greatly distinguished themselves, but it was at Toulon that they first showed their real worth. It was well for the colonel that he had brought his troops to a high pitch of morale, for, on starting to attack Mount Faron, General Dugommier summoned him aside. 'We must take the redoubt,' he said, 'or -' and he passed his hand in a suggestive way across his throat. In this attack, alone of all the corps engaged, the men of the Drôme stood their ground when the English made their counter-attack; amid cries of 'Sauve qui peut!' they alone replied steadily to the murderous fire of the enemy, and as quietly as on parade they covered the rout and slowly withdrew in good order. Three weeks later came the opportunity of Victor's life in the assault on the 'Little Gibraltar', the seizure of which position forced the English to evacuate Toulon. The attack was planned by Bonaparte, and Victor had the good fortune to be chosen as one of the leaders; he was already the firm friend of the Corsican captain of artillery, and he now won his boundless admiration by his reckless bravery and his capacity for making his troops follow him. The two wounds which he received in the charge which carried the palisades were a cheap price to pay for the rank and glory which he was later to gain as a reward for the way in which he flung his shattered column against the second line of defence. His immediate recompense was the post of general of brigade in the Army of the Eastern Pyrenees.

From the Spanish campaign Victor returned, in 1795, to Italy with an enhanced reputation and some knowledge of mountain warfare which was to stand him in good stead later. When, in 1796, Bonaparte took command of the Army of Italy, he found Victor still general of brigade, but reputed one of the bravest men in that army of heroes. The campaign of 1796 brought him still more to the front. Dego, Mondovi, Peschiera, San Marco, Cerea, and the fights round Mantua proved his courage and capacity to exact the most from his troops, but it was his manoeuvring on January 16, 1797, at Saint Georges, outside Mantua, which proved his real ability, for there, with but two French regiments, he forced the whole division of General Provera, seven thousand strong, to lay down its arms. Bonaparte chose the conqueror of Provera to lead the French army to invade the Papal States. This was Victor's first independent command, but, owing to the poor condition of the Papal troops, it was no severe test of his ability; still, it gained for him his step as general of division, and confirmed his chief's high opinion of him.

During the year following the peace of Campo Formio, General Victor held several posts in France, but was back again in Italy in 1799, to take part in the disastrous campaign against the Austrians and Russians. Detached by General Moreau to aid Macdonald on the Trebbia, he, for the first time, showed that jealousy which was such a blemish in his character, and during the retreat he paid so little attention to orders that he was almost overwhelmed by the enemy. Not from cowardice, but from his desire to escape Macdonald's control, he abandoned his guns, and withdrew into the mountains to try to join Moreau; but Macdonald saved the guns, and sarcastically wrote to his insubordinate lieutenant that he had secured the guns but found neither friend nor foe.

Victor was serving under Masséna when Bonaparte returned from Egypt. Stern Republican, sprung from the ranks, he hated the idea of a dictatorship, and did not hide from superiors or inferiors his dislike of the coup d'état of the 18th Brumaire. Indeed, so subversive of discipline became his attitude and his speeches to his soldiers, that Masséna was forced to remove him from his command and report him to the First Consul. In retirement and disgrace at Monaco, he saw with dismay the armies of the Allies surging up to the French frontier. Putting aside all personal animosity, he wrote to his former friend and commander, with no complaints, or prayers to be reinstated, but giving a clear exposition of the state of affairs in Italy, and of the means necessary to restore the prestige of the French arms, and actually proposing the plan, which the First Consul had already conceived, of crossing the Alps and falling on the communications of the enemy. Bonaparte was greatly struck with this letter. Perhaps also he called to mind his former friendship, in the days when the old ex-artillery sergeant used to walk round his batteries at Toulon, and doubtless he remembered his stubborn courage and tenacity in the fights round Mantua; at any rate, he summoned him to Paris, received him with marks of affection, and sent him off at once to command a division of the Army of Reserve. But though he forgave him outwardly, Bonaparte was too shrewd a judge of men not to see that his old comrade was always dangerous when not employed. While busy drilling and supervising his troops the general had no time to think about politics and the theories of government. So, as First Consul and Emperor, Napoleon saw to it that the ex-artilleryman had plenty of employment. During the Marengo campaign the general gained fresh honours. Luckily it was his old friend, Lannes, with whom he had to co-operate; and Lannes willingly acknowledged his loyal aid at Montebello, for on the day he received his dukedom he embraced Victor, saying, 'My friend, it is to you I owe my title!' At Marengo he again had to work with Lannes, and it was due to their admirable co-operation and stubbornness that the retreat did not become a rout, and that Desaix had time to return to the field, and allow the First Consul to fight another battle and turn a defeat into a victory.

But though Napoleon gave him his due share of the glory of Marengo, and mentioned him first in despatches and presented him with a sword of honour, he yet remembered his former hostility, and, while constantly employing him, took care to keep him as much as possible out of France. So for two years after Marengo General Victor held the post of commander-in-chief in the Army of Holland. Then in 1802 he was appointed Captain-General of Lousiania. But fortune here defeated the First Consul's intentions, and the expedition to America never sailed. Victor was sent back to his post in Holland, and kept there till February, 1805, when he was appointed Minister Plenipotentiary at the Danish court.

During these years it was clear to everybody that he was in disgrace, and it was due to the boldness of his friend, Marshal Lannes, that he was recalled to active service and once again given a chance of distinguishing himself. In September, 1806, owing to the promotion of his chief staff officer, Lannes had to find a new chief of the staff for his corps, and he applied to the Emperor to be allowed to appoint General Victor. Napoleon hesitated for a moment, then, mindful of the number of troops under arms, and the necessity of employing really efficient officers on the staff, he acquiesced in the Marshal's choice, saying, 'He is a really sound man and one in whom I have complete confidence, and I will give him proof of this when the occasion arrives.' Jena and Pultusk added to the general's distinguished record, and the Emperor began to treat him once again with favour, and in January, 1807, entrusted him with the new tenth corps of the Grand Army. Soon after he had taken over his new command he had the bad luck to be captured by a patrol of the enemy while driving with a single aide-de-camp near Stettin. Luckily for him he had by now completely won back the goodwill of the Emperor. Napoleon at once set about to effect his exchange, and in a few days he was back again with his corps. At the beginning of June, when Bernadotte fell ill, the Emperor summoned him to the front to take command of the first corps, and it was in this capacity that he was present at the battle of Friedland, and in that terrible struggle he won his bâton. Rewards now came speedily, for after Tilsit he was entrusted with the government of Prussia, and in 1808 created Duke of Belluno.

From Prussia the Marshal was summoned, in the autumn of 1808, to take command of the first corps of the Army of Spain, and for the next three years he saw continuous service in the Peninsula. During the first few months of his career there fortune smiled upon him. At Espinosa he dealt General Blake a smashing blow; later he led the van of the army under Napoleon in the march on Madrid, and forced the enemy's entrenched position in the pass of the Somosierra by a charge of his Polish lancers. From Madrid he was despatched to the south to keep the enemy at some distance from the capital, and at Ulces and Medellin he proved that the Spanish generals were no match for him and his seasoned troops. But unfortunately he smirched the fame of these victories by the licence he permitted his soldiers: at Ulces he allowed the town to be sacked, and executed sixty-nine of the most prominent of the citizens, including some monks, while he ordered all prisoners who were unable to march to be shot. At Medellin the French bayoneted the Spanish wounded. Further, like many another commander, he did not scruple to make the most of his successes in his reports, and the Spaniards assert that he eked out his trophies by taking down the old battle-flags of the knights of Santiago from the church of Ulces. After Medellin his successes ended. Placed under the command of Joseph and Jourdan, whom he despised; in great straits to feed his army in a country which was really a wilderness; worried by constant contradictory orders, it was in no pleasant mood that he at last found himself under the personal command of King Joseph at Talavera. Anxious to maintain his independence and to show off his military skill, he attempted by himself to surprise the English wing of the allied army. Consequently he committed King Joseph and Jourdan to an action which they did not wish to fight, and by refusing to co-operate with the other corps commanders he brought defeat upon the French army, for, as Napoleon wrote to Joseph, 'As long as you attack good troops, like the English, in good positions, without reconnoitring them, you will lead your men to death en pure perte."

After Talavera Victor's independent career came to an end; he was placed under the orders of Marshal Soult and sent to besiege Cadiz, before which place he lay till he was summoned to take part in the Russian campaign. But before leaving Cadiz he fought one more action against the British when General Graham seized the opportunity of Soult's absence to attempt to break up the siege; and he had once again to acknowledge defeat, when at Barossa the little column of four thousand British turned at bay and boldly attacked and defeated nine thousand chosen French infantry under the Marshal himself.

In Russia the Duke of Belluno was saved some of the greatest hardships, for his corps was on the line of communication, and it was not till the day before the battle of the Beresina that he actually joined the retreating army, in time to earn further glory by covering the passage of the river, though at the cost of more than half his corps. During 1813 he fought at Dresden and at Leipzig, and at the commencement of 1814 was entrusted with the defence of the Vosges; but he soon had to fall back on the Marne. At Saint Dizier and Brienne he bore himself bravely, but at Montereau he fell into disgrace; he neglected to hold the bridge on the Seine, and thus completely spoiled Napoleon's combination. The Emperor was furious, and deprived him of the command of his corps and told him to leave the army. But the Marshal refused to go. 'I will shoulder my musket,' said he; 'Victor has not forgotten his old occupation. I will take my place in the Guard.' At such devotion the Emperor relented. 'Well, Victor,' he said, stretching out his hand, 'remain with us. I cannot restore to you your corps, which I have bestowed on Girard;

but I give you two divisions of the Guard.' However, the Marshal did not long occupy his new position, for he was severely wounded at Craonne and forced to go home.

On Napoleon's abdication the Duke of Belluno swore allegiance to the Bourbons and kept it, for, on the return of Napoleon from Elba, he withdrew to Ghent with Louis XVIII. On the second Restoration he was created a peer of France and nominated one of the four major-generals of the Royal Guard. Though never an imperialist, and at heart a republican, it was Napoleon's treatment of him at Montereau which recalled the old grievance of his disgrace in 1800 and turned him into a royalist. The Marshal earned the undying hatred of many of his old comrades by the severity he displayed when 'charged with examining the conduct of officers of all grades who had served under the usurpation.' But, though steadfast in his adherence to the monarchy, the Duke of Belluno still clung to his liberal ideals, and it was for this reason that in 1821 Villèle invited him to join the Cabinet as Minister for War. It was a strange position for the ex-sergeant of artillery, but he filled it admirably, and brought considerable strength to the Ministry, in that as a soldier of fortune, a self-made man, he conciliated the Liberals, and as a resolute character, a firm royalist, and a man of intrepidity and honour, he had the confidence and esteem of the Conservative party. It was during his term of office that a French army once again invaded Spain, and thanks in no small degree to his knowledge of the country and to his business capacity that it suffered no reverse. When the Bourbon dynasty fell in July, 1830, the Duke of Belluno took the oath of allegiance to the new Government, but never again entered public life, and on March 1, 1841, he died in Paris at the age of seventy-seven.

20

EMMANUEL DE GROUCHY, MARSHAL

WHEN the Revolution broke out in 1789 the young Count Emmanuel de Grouchy was serving as lieutenant-colonel in the Scotch company of the Gardes du Corps. Born on October 23, 1766, the only son of the Marquis de Grouchy, the representative of an old Norman family which could trace its descent from before the days of William the Conqueror, Emmanuel de Grouchy had entered the army at the age of fourteen. After a year's service in the marine artillery he had been transferred to a cavalry regiment of the line, and on his twentieth birthday had been selected for the Gardes du Corps. A keen student of military history and devoted to his profession, the young Count had read widely and thought much. Impressionable and enthusiastic, a philosophical liberal by nature, he eagerly absorbed the teaching of the Encyclopedists. As events developed, he found that his position in the Gardes du Corps was antagonistic to his principles, and, at his own request, at the end of 1791 he was transferred to the twelfth regiment of chasseurs as lieutenant-colonel commanding. After a few months' service with this regiment he was promoted brigadier-general, and served successively under General Montesquieu with the Army of the Midi, and under Kellermann with the Army of the Alps. At the commencement of 1793, while on leave in Normandy, he was hurriedly despatched to the west to take part in the civil war in La Vendée. No longer Comte de Grouchy but plain Citizen-general Grouchy, for the next three years he saw almost continuous service in the civil war, with the exception of a few months when, like all ci-devant nobles, he was dismissed the service by the decree of the incompetent Bouchotte. But Clanclaux, who commanded the Army of La Vendée, had found in him a most useful subordinate and a sound adviser; and accordingly, at his instance, the ci-devant noble was restored to his rank, and sent back as chief of the staff to the Army of the West, and in April, 1795, promoted general of division. Clear-headed, firmly convinced of the soundness of his opinions, without being bigoted or revengeful, Grouchy saw that the cruel methods of many of the generals did more to continue the war than the political tenets of the Vendéens and Chouans, and he used his influence with Clanclaux, and later with Hoche, to restrain useless reprisals and crush the rebellion by overwhelming the armed forces of the rebels, not by insulting women and shooting prisoners. The problem to be solved was a difficult one, as he pointed out in a memoir written for Clanclaux. 'It is the population of the entire country which is on your hands, a population which suddenly rushes together to fight, if it is strong enough to crush you; which hurls itself against your flanks and rear, and then as suddenly disappears, when not strong enough to resist you.' His solution of the difficulty was to wear down resistance by light mobile columns, and to starve the enemy out by devastating the country. In September, 1795, on Clanclaux's retirement, the Commissioners attached to the Army of the West wished to invest Grouchy with the command, but the general refused the post; for, clear counsellor and good adviser as he was, he lacked self-confidence, and knew that he was not fit for the position. It was this horror of undertaking responsibility which dragged him down during all his career, and which, on the two occasions when fortune gave him his chance to rise, made him choose the safe but inglorious road of humdrum mediocrity. In 1796 came his first chance: after a brief period of service with the Army of the North in Holland he was once again at his old work under Hoche in the west, when the Directory determined to try to retaliate for the English participation in the Chouan revolt by raising a hornet's nest in Ireland. At the end of December a force of fifteen thousand men under Hoche, with Grouchy as second in command, set sail for Ireland. Unfortunately the expedition met with bad weather, the ship on which Hoche sailed got separated from the rest of fleet, and, when Grouchy arrived at the rendezvous in Bantry Bay, he found the greater part of the expedition, but no general-in-chief. In spite of this he rightly determined to effect a landing, but had not the necessary force of character to ensure his orders being carried out, and six days' procrastination Admiral Bouvet, pleading heavy weather, refused to allow his ships to remain off the coast, and the expedition returned to France. If Grouchy had been able to get his orders obeyed, all would have been well, for on the very day after his squadron left Bantry Bay, Hoche himself arrived at the rendezvous. As Grouchy said, if he had only flung that Admiral Bouvet into the sea all would have been right. Where Grouchy hesitated and failed a Napoleon would have acted and conquered.

Hoche died, and Grouchy, who under his influence had disapproved of the policy of France towards the Italian States, at once accepted employment in Italy. He soon had to rue his decision, for he found himself entrusted with the task of using underhand means to drive the King of Sardinia from his country. Still, he obeyed his orders to the letter. During negotiations he secretly introduced French troops into the citadel at Turin and then seized the fortresses of Novara, Alessandria, and Chiasso. Meanwhile he terrified the unfortunate monarch by announcing the arrival of imaginary columns of troops, suborned the King's Council, and so worked on the feelings of the bewildered sovereign that he escaped by night from his palace and fled across the sea. But though their King had deserted them, the Piedmontese did not tamely submit, and for the next few months the general was busy tracking out and capturing the numerous members of the secret societies who were avenging their country by cutting the throats of Frenchmen. While striking with a heavy hand at these conspirators, Grouchy was level-headed enough to understand that the proper method of tackling the problem was to remove the grievance. In his opinion it was not the people so much as the Church which was opposed to the French, and accordingly he did his best to get Joubert to issue a proclamation that there should be no interference with religion. Still, the situation must have been galling to a man of culture and a theoretical liberal, for, while forcing democratic institutions on an unwilling people, he had at the same time to strip their capital of all objects of art; and while issuing proclamations for the freedom of religion he had to arrange for the passage of the Pope on his way to captivity. In May, 1799, the general was recalled from his governorship of Turin, for the Austrians and Russians were invading Lombardy and Joubert was concentrating his forces. The campaign, as far as Grouchy was concerned, was short, for while attempting to stem the flight of the left wing after the battle of Novi he was ridden over and captured by the Allies. Four sabre cuts, one bullet wound, and several bayonet thrusts kept him in hospital for some time; when he was well enough to be moved he was sent to Grätz, and it was not till a year later - in June, 1800 - that his exchange was effected. But he soon had his revenge on the Austrians, for in the autumn he was despatched to join the army under Moreau, which was operating on the Danube, and arrived at headquarters in time to take part in the battle of Hohenlinden. In the face of a blinding snowstorm Grouchy's division drove back the main column of the enemy, and after hours of murderous hand-to-hand fighting in the forest, he shared with Ney the honour of the last charge which drove the enemy in hopeless rout.

It was on his return from Hohenlinden that the ex-Count met Bonaparte. The First Consul, who aimed at conciliating the old nobility, made much of him, employed him on a confidential mission to Italy, and nominated him inspector-general of cavalry. This post admirably suited Grouchy, who was a horseman by nature and a cavalry soldier by instinct. Later, on the formation of the Army of the Ocean, he was appointed to the command of an infantry division in Marmont's corps in Holland, and it was with Marmont that he made the campaign of 1805. In October, 1806, he was summoned from Italy to a more important command. The Grand Army was advancing on Prussia, and Napoleon had need of capable leaders to command his vast masses of cavalry. Grouchy was entrusted with the second division of dragoons of the cavalry corps under Murat and played a prominent part in the battle of Prinzlow and the pursuit to Lübeck. At Eylau he had a narrow escape: his charger was killed in the middle of the mêlée and he was only saved by the devotion of his aide-de-camp; though much shaken, he was able to resume command of his division, and distinguished himself by his fierce charges in the blinding snow. At Friedland a chance occurred for which his capacity proved fully equal. Murat was absent at Königsberg trying to get across the enemy's rear, and Grouchy was in command of all the reserve cavalry at the moment the advance guard interrupted the Russian retreat. It was his admirable handling of the cavalry under Lannes's directions which held the Russians in check for sixteen hours, until Napoleon was able to concentrate his divisions and give the Russians the coup de grâce. The Emperor showed his gratitude by presenting the general with the Grand Cross of Baden, investing him with the Cordon of the Legion of Honour, and granting him the domain of Nowawies, in the department of Posen.

The following year, 1808, saw Grouchy, now a Count of the Empire, with Murat in Spain, acting as governor of Madrid. But when, in the autumn, Joseph evacuated all the western provinces, Grouchy, whose health had been much shaken by the Polish campaign, was granted leave of absence and took care not to be sent back, for he had seen enough of the Spanish to foresee the terrible difficulties of guerrilla warfare; moreover, the annexation of the country was contrary to his ideas of political justice. When the war with Austria was imminent Napoleon sent him to Italy to command the cavalry of the viceroy's army. With Prince Eugène he fought through Styria and Carinthia and distinguished himself greatly at the battle of Raab. At Wagram his cavalry was attached to Davout's corps, and his fierce charges, which helped to break the Austrian left, brought him again under the notice of the Emperor, who showed his appreciation by appointing him colonel-general of chasseurs.

In 1812 the Count was summoned once again to the field, to command the third corps of reserve cavalry with the Grand Army in Russia. At Moskowa his cuirassiers, sabre in hand, drove the Russians out of the great redoubt, but Grouchy himself was seriously wounded. During the retreat from Moscow he commanded one of the 'Sacred Bands' of officers who personally guarded the Emperor, but his health, never good, completely broke down under the strain and he was allowed to return straight home from Vilna. A year elapsed before he had sufficiently recovered to take the field, and it was not till the beginning of 1814 that he was fit for service. During the campaign in France, first under Victor and later with Marmont, he commanded the remnant of the reserve cavalry; but on March 7th at Craonne he was once again so badly wounded that he had to throw up his command.

During the Restoration Grouchy remained at his home; his relations with the Bourbons was not cordial, and he bitterly resented the loss of his title of colonel-general of chasseurs. Accordingly, when Napoleon returned from Elba and France seemed to welcome him with open arms, in spite of having accepted the Cross of St. Louis, he had no scruple in answering the Emperor's summons. He was entrusted with the operations against the Duc d'Angoulême round Lyons, but disliked the task, for he remembered the fate of the Duc d'Enghien, and in spite of Napoleon's protests that he only desired to capture the Duke in order to make the Austrians send back the Empress, Grouchy determined that, if possible, while doing everything to defeat the royalists, he would not capture d'Angoulême. Unfortunately, the Duke refused the opportunity to escape which was offered him, and Grouchy had to make him a prisoner. However, Napoleon, anxious to stand well with the powers of Europe, at once ordered him to be set free. At the same time he sent Grouchy to command the Army of the Alps, giving him his Marshal's baton. The new Marshal was delighted with his promotion; he had now served for twenty years as general of division, and although only forty-nine, had practically given up all hope of promotion. But scarcely had he reached his new command when he was recalled to Paris.

With Murat in disgrace and Bessières dead, the Emperor had no great cavalry leader on whom he could rely, and, remembering the new Marshal's exploits at Friedland and Wagram, and his staunchness in 1814, he determined to entrust him with the command of the reserve cavalry. Unfortunately for Napoleon and Grouchy, the exigencies of the campaign forced the Emperor to divide his army; so, while entrusting Ney with a part of his troops, with orders to pursue the English, and keeping the Guard and reserves under his immediate control, he gave Grouchy the command of two corps of infantry and one of cavalry; in all, some thirty-three thousand men. The appointment was an unfortunate one, for the Marshal, though in many respects a good cavalry leader, had never before had the command of a large body of mixed troops, and even his cavalry successes had been obtained when under the orders of a superior: at Friedland he was under Lannes; at Wagram under Davout; at Moskowa under Eugène; and in 1814 under either Victor or Marmont. But what was most unfortunate about the selection was that Grouchy had not enough personal authority to enforce his orders on his corps commanders, and the fiery Vandamme not only despised but hated him because he had received the bâton which he hoped was to have been his, while Girard was a personal enemy. At Ligny, where Napoleon himself supervised the attack, all went well, but from the moment fighting ceased difficulties began. Immediately after the battle the Emperor entrusted the Marshal with the pursuit of the Prussians, but Pajol, who commanded his light cavalry, carried out his reconnaissance in a perfunctory manner, and reported that the Prussians had retreated towards Namur. Grouchy received this news at 4 a.m. on June 17th, but he did not dare to disturb the Emperor's rest, and it was 8 a.m. before he could see him and demand detailed orders. Napoleon, trusting to Pajol's report, thought that the Prussians were absolutely demoralised and were leaving the theatre of war, and so he kept the Marshal talking about Paris and politics till 11 a.m. Consequently it was 11.30 before he received exact orders, penned by Bertrand, which told him to proceed to Gembloux, keeping his forces concentrated; to reconnoitre the different roads leading to Namur and Maestricht, and to inform the Emperor of the Prussians' intentions, adding, 'It is important to know what Blücher and Wellington mean to do, and whether they prefer to unite their armies in order to cover Brussels and Liège, by trying their fortunes in another battle.' Bad staff directions and heavy rains retarded the advance, and it took six hours for the troops to cover the nine miles to Gembloux, where at eight in the evening Grouchy heard that part of the Prussians had fallen back on Wavre, which meant that they might still unite with the English to cover Brussels. He at once reported this to the Emperor, adding that Blücher had retired on Liège and the ariillery on Namur. But, in spite of the fact that on the evening of the seventeenth Napoleon knew that this was a mistake, and that the Prussians were actually massed round Wavre, it was not till 10 a.m. on the morning of Waterloo that he sent to the Marshal informing him of the Prussians' concentration, and telling him that 'he must therefore move thither (i.e., to Wavre) in order to approach us, and to push before him any Prussians who may have stopped at Wavre.' This was the exact course which Grouchy had determined to pursue. It is therefore quite clear that neither the Emperor nor the Marshal had dreamed that Blücher would attempt to give any assistance to the English in their position at Waterloo. At 11 a.m., when his columns were just approaching Wavre, the Marshal heard the commencement of the cannonade at Waterloo. Girard entreated him to march to the sound of the cannon, but Grouchy had what he considered distinct orders to pursue the Prussians; he was now in touch with them, and with a force of thirty-three thousand men he did not dare to make a flank march in the face of what, he was becoming convinced, was the whole Prussian army. At 5 p.m. he received Napoleon's despatch, hastily written at 1 p.m., ordering him to turn westward and crush the Prussian corps which was marching on the Emperor's right rear, but by then his main force was heavily engaged at Wavre, and even if he had been able to despatch part of his force it could not have arrived at Mont St. Jean till long after the end of the battle.

On the morning of the nineteenth the Marshal was preparing to pursue Thielmann's corps, which, on the previous evening, he had driven from Wavre, when he heard of the catastrophe at Waterloo. He immediately stopped the pursuit, and, by rapid marching, reached Namur before the Allies could cut him off, and, by a skilful retreat, brought back his thirty-three thousand men to Paris before the enemy arrived at the gates. But instead of the thanks he had expected he found himself saddled with the blame of the loss of Waterloo. The disaster, however, clearly rested on the Emperor, whose orders were vague, and who had not realised the extraordinary moral courage of Blücher and the stubbornness of the Prussians, and if Napoleon did not foresee this he could not blame Grouchy for being equally blind. The Marshal did all that a mediocre man could do. He carefully carried out the orders given him, trusting, no doubt, too much to the letter, too little to the spirit. But long years spent in a subordinate position under a military hierarchy like that of the Empire were bound to stifle all initiative, and it was not to be supposed that the man who, twenty years earlier, had failed to rise to the occasion in Ireland would, after at last gaining his Marshal's bâton, risk his reputation by marching, like Desaix at Marengo, to the sound of the guns, across the front of an enemy vastly superior to himself, through a difficult country partially waterlogged and intercepted by deep broad streams, contrary to what seemed his definite orders.

The Marshal's career really ended on the abdication of the Emperor, though he was appointed by the Provisional Government to the command of the remains of the Army of the North, and in this capacity proclaimed the Emperor's son as Napoleon II. On gaining Paris he found himself subordinate to Davout, an old enemy. Accordingly he threw up his command and retired into private life. After his conduct during the Hundred Days he could expect no mercy from the returned Bourbons, and was glad to escape abroad. Included in the general pardon, he returned to France in 1818, but his marshalate was annulled, and he never regained his bâton, though on the accession of Charles X he was actually received at court. But though the King might forgive, his favourites and ministers could not forget, and in December, 1824, he was included among the fifty generals of Napoleon who were placed on the retired list, an action which General Foy shrewdly remarked was 'a cannon-shot charged at Waterloo, fired ten years after the battle, and pointed direct at its mark.' Like many another of the Marshals, the veteran retained his health and faculties for many years, and defended his character and actions and criticised his enemies with the same clear logic which had so powerfully contributed to his early advancement; for the ex-Marshal wielded the pen as easily as the sword. It was not till 1847 that death carried off the sturdy old warrior at the age of eighty-one.

21

FRANÇOIS CHRISTOPHE KELLERMANN, MARSHAL, DUKE OF VALMY

WHEN old institutions suddenly collapse with a crash; when all is confusion and chaos, and the lines of reconstruction are as yet veiled in uncertainty; when people suspect their old rulers and are shy of those who would set themselves up as their new directors, there comes an interval before genius and wile can organise their forces, when character, and character alone can shepherd the people scattered like sheep on the mountains. Such was the case in France in September, 1792. The old constitution had foundered, sweeping away in its ruin the order and discipline of the royal army. The officers had either fled or been deposed by their men, and such few as remained were held 'suspect'. The new officers, chosen by their fellows, had but little authority. The staff of the army was changed weekly to suit the whim of some civil or military self-seeker, at a time when France was at war with the great military powers of Europe. It was little wonder, therefore, that the Prussians and Austrians looked forward to the campaign of 1792 as a military promenade. They knew better even than the War Minister at Paris how debauched were the regular troops of France, how unreliable and contemptible were the few thousand old men and boys who rejoiced in the name of volunteers, and they never for a moment believed that the French generals would be able to force their men to stand and fight. But they had calculated wrongly. They had not learned that in war a man is everything; they had not grasped how deeply the spirit of discipline had been engrained in the old royal army. Fortunately for France she had two men of character to fall back upon; and aided by their example, on September 20th the regulars of France stood firm before the famous Prussian army. The two men were Dumouriez and Kellermann. Dumouriez had brains and character, Kellermann character and stolid imperturbability.

Descended from an old Saxon family long domiciled in Alsace, François Christophe Kellermann was born. at Strasburg on May 28, 1735. Entering the French army at the age of fifteen, he fought his way up step by step by sheer hard work and merit. Winning the Cross of St. Louis for distinguished cavalry work in the Seven Years' War, he was sent in 1766 on a mission to Poland and Russia, on the strength of which he was lent by the French Government to help the Confederates of Bar to organise their irregular cavalry. Returning to France, he slowly gained promotion, and in 1788 became major-general and was promoted lieutenant-general in March, 1792, mainly owing to his warm adoption of the revolutionary principles. Kellermann had not the gifts of a great commander, but he had what is sometimes better, the confidence of his men. He was notorious for his hatred of the old régime and had a high reputation as a cavalry commander: added to this, the firm belief he had in himself served to inspire confidence in others. Independent by nature, ambitious, cantankerous, jealous and conceited, Kellermann had not found his life in the army any too pleasant. Save in war time merit gained little reward; promotion came neither from the east nor the west, but from court favouritism. It thus happened that the rough Alsatian had always found himself subordinate to men who were really his inferiors, but who despised his want of culture and his provincial accent; for Kellermann knew no grammar, spoke through his nose and spelt as he spoke, even writing 'debuté' for 'deputé'. It was thanks to the friendship of Servan, the War Minister, that on August 25th he was summoned from the small column he had been commanding on the Lauter to succeed Lückner in command of the Army of the Centre. When he arrived at his new headquarters at Metz he found a woeful state of affairs. The Prussians and Austrians were sweeping everything before them, and at Metz he found a fortress without stores and an army without discipline. Luckily he had the advantage of Berthier, a staff officer of the highest order, Napoleon's future chief of the staff. The soldiers welcomed Kellermann, 'this brave general whose patriotism equals his talents', and whose civism was praised throughout all Alsace. Organisation was his first work, and his former experience of irregular warfare in Poland stood him in good stead. He immediately sent home the battalions of the volunteers of 1792, who were arriving without arms and in rags. He retained a few picked men from each battalion, to be used as light troops and pioneers. After weeding out undesirables and drafting reinforcements into his most reliable regiments, in three weeks he evolved a force of twenty thousand men capable of taking the field. While thus engaged he was ordered to join Dumouriez, who had been holding the Prussians in check at the defiles of the Argonne. On the evening of September 19th Kellermann effected his junction with Dumouriez near St. Menehould, and was attacked early next morning by the enemy under the Duke of Brunswick. The morning was wet and foggy, and the Prussians surprised the French and cut them off from the road to Paris. But instead of driving home their attack they thought to frighten them by a mere cannonade. Luckily the artillery was the least demoralised part of the French army, and under the able command of d'Abbéville, it not only replied to the Prussian guns, but played with great effect on the infantry, when at last Brunswick ordered an attack. Kellermann meanwhile sat on his horse in front of his infantry, and by his example and sangfroid managed to keep them in the ranks, though they were really so unsteady that when an ammunition wagon blew up, three regiments of infantry and the whole of the ammunition column fled in disorder from the field. But Kellermann galloped up in time to prevent the panic spreading. Meanwhile Dumouriez had hastened up reinforcements to secure Kellermann's flanks, and the Duke of Brunswick, seeing the French standing firm, and not being sure of his own men refused to allow the attack to be pressed home. Such was the cannonade of Valmy; the Prussians had thirty-four thousand men engaged, and lost one hundred and eighty-four men; the French had thirty-six thousand engaged out of a total of fifty-two thousand, and lost three hundred, and the greater proportion of this loss was due to Kellermann's bad tactics in massing his infantry close behind his guns.

Still, Valmy was one of the most important battles in the world's history, for it taught Europe that France still existed as a political unit, and it allowed her to effect her regeneration in her own way. Neither Kellermann nor Dumouriez at first understood what they had done. Dumouriez drew off his army to a better position to await events. But Valmy had restored the morale of the French and broken that of the Prussians, whom disease and bad weather further affected, and soon Brunswick was glad to negotiate and retreat to the Rhine. Kellermann's share in the great event is easily determined. He had most unwillingly joined Dumouriez, he had allowed himself to be surprised in the morning, and his tactics were so bad that his men suffered heavier loss than was necessary; but though it was Dumouriez who made good the tactical mistake and covered Kellermann's flanks, and d'Abbéville whose artillery caused the infantry attack to miscarry, it was Kellermann's reputation and example which kept the really demoralised infantry in line, and prevented them from running in terror from the field. It was the sight of the old Alsatian quietly getting on a fresh horse when his former one was killed, caring nothing though one of his coat-tails was carried off by a round shot, which breathed new life and courage into the masses of waiting men, and taught them to cry out, 'Vive la nation! Vive la France! Vive notre general!' So, though men might smile when they heard the old boaster talking of 'My victory', yet in their hearts they knew he had done much to save France.

While the Prussians retreated Kellermann was entrusted by Dumouriez with the pursuit; on his return to Paris his boasting habits brought him into trouble. The Terrorists, hearing him constantly talking of 'My men', 'My army', were afraid he was getting too powerful and he very nearly came to the scaffold. Restored to favour, he was employed with the Army of the Alps and the Army of Italy in 1794 and 1795, where he gained some success, although his plans were constantly interfered with by the Committee of Public Safety. In 1796 the Army of the Alps was made subordinate to the Army of Italy under Bonaparte, and the Directory wanted to associate Kellermann with Bonaparte, but the future conqueror of Italy would brook no equal, especially a cantankerous boaster. So he wrote to Carnot, 'If you join Kellermann and me in command in Italy, you will undo everything. General Kellermann has more experience than I, and knows how to make war better than I do; but both together we shall make it badly. I will not willingly serve with a man who considers himself the first general in Europe.' When, however, Bonaparte came to power he did not forget the old Alsatian: in 1800 he made him one of his Senators, and in 1804 he created him a Marshal, though not in the active list. But exigencies of warfare demanded that France should use all her talents, and in every campaign the Emperor entrusted the old warrior with the command of the Army of the Reserve. Sometimes on the Rhine, sometimes on the Elbe, sometimes in Spain, the old soldier taught the recruits of the Grand Army how to keep themselves and their muskets clean; and, in spite of age and infirmities, showed those talents of organisation which he had learned in Poland and earlier still in the Seven Years' War. In 1808, when creating his new nobility, the Emperor cleverly conciliated the republican party by creating the Marshal Duke of Valmy, and presenting him with a splendid domain at Johannisberg, in Germany. But when the end came in 1814, the Duke of Valmy, like the other Marshals, quietly accepted the Restoration, and the veteran republican, now in his eightieth year, was created a peer of France and accepted the command of the third military division. During the Hundred Days he held no command, and on the Restoration he retired into private life, and died at Paris on September 23, 1820. His body was buried in Paris, but his heart, according to his directions, was taken to Valmy and interred beside the remains of those who had fallen there, and a simple monument was placed over the spot with the following lines, written by the Marshal himself: 'Here lie the soldiers who gloriously died, and who saved France, on September 20, 1792. Marshal Kellermann, the Duke of Valmy, the soldier who had the honour to command them on that memorable day, twenty-eight years later, making his last request, desired that his heart should be placed among them.'

22

FRANÇOIS JOSEPH LEFÈBVRE, MARSHAL, DUKE OF DANTZIG

FRANÇOIS JOSEPH LEFÈBVRE, Marshal and peer of France, is best known to the ordinary reader as the husband of that Duchess of Dantzig who has been so unjustly caricatured in Monsieur Sardou's celebrated play as Madame Sans Gêne. Accordingly, the record of this hard-fighting soldier of the Empire has been cruelly buried in ridicule. The son of an old private soldier of the hussars of Berchény, who became in later life the wachtmeister of the little Alsatian town of Rouffach, François Joseph was born October 26, 1755. After his father's death he was entrusted, at the age of eight, to the care of his uncle, the Abbé Jean Christophe Lefèbvre. The abbé destined his nephew for the Church, but nature had dowered him for the camp, and after a severe tussle with the good abbé, Jean François set out with a light heart, a light purse, a few sentences of Latin, a rough Alsatian accent, and a fine physique to seek his fortune in the celebrated Garde Française at Paris. The year 1789 found him with sixteen years' service, one of the best of the senior sergeants of the regiment, married since 1783 to Catherine Hübscher, also from Alsace, by profession a washerwoman, by nature a philanthropist. Washing, soldiering, and philanthropy being on the whole unremunerative occupations, the Lefèbvres had to supplement their income, and Madame went out charring, while the sergeant taught Alsatian, which he called German, and occupied his spare moments in instructing his wife in reading and writing. But the Revolution suddenly changed their outlook. On September 1, 1789, Lefèbvre was granted a commission as lieutenant in the newly enrolled National Guard as a recompense for the devotion shown to the officers when the Guards mutinied. Within the next two years he further showed his devotion to the lawful authorities, and was twice wounded while defending the royal family. But in spite of personal attachment to the Bourbons, the Prussian invasion turned him into a republican, and the Republic, as idealised by the warm-hearted warriors of the armies of the Sambre and Meuse and of the Rhine, became the idol of his heart. From the siege of Thionville, in 1792, till he was invalided in 1799, Lefèbvre was on continuous active service. His extraordinary bravery, his knowledge of his profession, and his absolute devotion to his duty brought him quick promotion, for he became captain in June, 1792, lieutenant-colonel in September, 1793, brigadier two months later, and general of division on January 18, 1794. The stern battle of Fleurus in June, 1794, proved that the general of division was worthy of his rank, for it was his counter-attack in the evening which decided the fate of the day. The early years of the republican wars were times when personal bravery, audacity, and devotion worked marvels on the highly strung, enthusiastic republican troops, and Lefèbvre had these necessary qualifications, while his Alsatian accent and kind-heartedness won the devotion of his men. He was highly appreciated by his commander-in-chief, Jourdan, who, in his official report, stated 'that the general added to the greatest bravery all the necessary knowledge of a good advance guard commander, maintaining in his troops the strictest discipline, working unceasingly to provide them with necessaries, and always manifesting the principles of a good republican.' Unswerving devotion to duty - 'I am a soldier, I must obey' - was the guiding principle of his career, and accordingly each commander he served under had nothing but praise for the thoroughness with which he did his work, from the enforcement of petty regulations to the covering of a defeated force. But in spite of this the ex-sergeant knew his worth and did not fear to claim his due. When Hoche, in his general order after the battle of Neuweid, stated that 'the army had taken seven standards of colours,' Lefèbvre naïvely wrote to him, 'It must be fourteen altogether, for I myself captured seven.' But Hoche had both humour and tact, and made ample amends by replying, 'There were only seven stands of colours as there is only one Lefèbvre.'

By 1799 seven years' continuous fighting had begun to tell on a physique even as strong as Lefèbvre's, and the general applied for lighter work as commander of the Directory Guard, and later, for sick leave; but the commencement of the campaign against the Archduke Charles, in the valley of the Danube, once again stimulated his indefatigable appetite for active service. Though suffering from scurvy and general overstrain, he took his share in the hard fighting at Feldkirche and Ostrach, but a severe wound received in the latter combat at last compelled him to leave the field and go into hospital.

On his return to France he was entrusted by the Directory with the command of the 17th military district, with Paris as its headquarters. The task was a difficult one, as the numerous coups d'état had shaken both public morality and military discipline. Among other unpleasantnesses the commander of Paris found himself on one occasion forced to place a general officer in the Abbaye, the civil prison, for flatly refusing to obey orders. But, difficult as his task was, the situation became much more complicated by the sudden return of Bonaparte from Egypt. Bonaparte arrived in Paris with the fixed determination to assume the reins of government. It was clear to so staunch a republican as Lefèbvre that all was not well with the Republic under the Directory, and it seemed as if Bonaparte, shimmering in the glamour of Italy and Egypt, was the sole person capable of conciliating all parties and of bringing the state of chronic revolution to an end. Directly he met the famous Corsican the simple soldier fell an easy victim to his personality; while Bonaparte was quick to perceive what a great political asset it would be if Lefèbvre, the republican of the republicans, the embodiment of the republican virtues, could be bound a satellite in his train. On the morning of the 18th Brumaire, the commander of the Paris Division was the first to arrive of all the generals whom the plotter had summoned to his house; he was puzzled to find that troops were moving without his orders, and he entered in considerable anger. Bonaparte at once explained the situation. The country was in danger, foes were knocking at the door, and meanwhile the Republic lay the prey of a pack of lawyers who were exploiting it for their own benefit without thought of patriotism. 'Now then, Lefèbvre,' said he, 'you, one of the pillars of the Republic, are you going to let it perish in the hands of these lawyers? Join me in helping to save our beloved Republic.

Look, here is the sword I carried in my hand at the battle of the Pyramids. I give it to you as a token of my esteem and of my confidence.' Lefèbvre could not resist this appeal; his warm and generous nature responded to the artful touch; grasping the treasured sword with tears in his eyes, he swore he was ready 'to throw the lawyers in the river'. With a sigh of relief Bonaparte put his arm through Lefèbvre's and led him into his study, and for the next fourteen years he remained, as he thought, the confidential right-hand man of the great-hearted patriot, but in reality the tool, dupe, and stalking-horse of a wily adventurer.

The general accompanied Napoleon to the Tuileries and listened to the carefully chosen words: 'Citizens, Representatives, the Republic is perishing; you know it well, and your decree can save it. A thousand misfortunes on all who desire trouble and disorder. I will oust them, aided by all the friends of liberty . . . . I will support liberty, aided by General Lefèbvre and General Berthier, and my comrades in arms who share my feelings . . . . We wish a Republic founded on liberty, on equality, on the sound principles of national representation. We swear this: I swear this; I swear in my own name and in the name of my comrades in arms.' Later in the day, during the struggle at the Orangerie, it was Lefèbvre who saved Lucien Bonaparte and cleared the hall with the aid of some grenadiers.

From the 18th Brumaire Napoleon, as First Consul, and later as Emperor, held in Lefèbvre a trump card whereby he could defeat any attempted hostile combination of the republicans. Hence it was that, at the time of the proclamation of the Empire, he included him in his list of Marshals, to prove as it were that the Empire was merely another form of the Republic. Later still, for the same reason, when he was making his hierarchy stronger, he created him one of his new Dukes.

The immediate reward for Lefèbvre's support during the coup d'état was a mission to the west to extinguish the civil war in La Vendée. The general was lucky in surprising a considerable force of rebels at Alençon, and soon fulfilled his work, and received the further reward of a seat as Senator, which brought in an income of 35,000 francs a year. When the list of Marshals was published he was bracketed with Kellermann, Pérignon, and Serurier as 'Marshals whose sphere of duty would lie in the Senate.' As such, at the coronation of the Emperor in Notre Dame he held the sword of Charlemagne, while Kellermann carried the crown. Strong in his trust of him, Napoleon had, in 1803, created him Praetor of the Senate. But fortune did not destine that he should long enjoy his honours in peace. Thanks to his magnificent physique a few years of rest entirely restored his health. The wound, which in 1799 had threatened to incapacitate him permanently, had completely healed, and in 1806 he once again found himself on active service. The Emperor knew well that the Marshal was a sergeant-major rather than a strategist, and accordingly placed him at the head of the Guard, where his powers of discipline could be utilised to the full without calling on him to solve any difficult problems. At Jena the Guard had plenty of hard fighting such as their commander loved. A few days later the Marshal proved that the Guard could march as well as fight, when, at nine o'clock on the evening of October 24th, the regiments marched into Potsdam after covering forty-two miles since the morning.

Early in 1807 the Emperor entrusted the Marshal with the siege of Dantzig, a strong fortress near the mouth of the Vistula, well-garrisoned by a Prussian force of fourteen thousand under Marshal Kalkreuth. Lefèbvre, conscious of his lack of engineering skill, was afraid of undertaking the task but the Emperor promised to send him everything necessary, and to guide him himself to the camp of Finkenstein, and ultimately said goodbye to him with the words, 'Take courage, you also must have something to speak about in the Senate when we return to France.' The siege lasted fifty-one days, during which the Marshal took scarcely a moment's rest: ever in the trenches, heading every possible charge, calling out to the soldiers, 'Come on, children, it's our turn to-day,' or 'Come on, comrades, I am also going to have a turn at fighting.' Such treatment worked wonders with the fiery French, but the sluggish men of Baden, who formed a considerable part of his force, were not accustomed to be so hustled, and the Marshal's camp manners grated on the Prince of Baden, who considered 'that the Marshal's staff was mostly composed of men of little culture, and that his son held the first place among those who had no manners.' The Emperor had to write to his fiery lieutenant, 'You treat our allies without any tact; they are not accustomed to fire, but that will come. Do you think that our men are as good now as in 1792 - that we can be as keen to-day after fifteen years' war? Pay what compliments you can to the Prince of Baden . . . you cannot throw down walls with the chests of your grenadiers . . . let your engineers do their work and be patient . . . Your glory is to take Dantzig; when you have done that you will be content with me.' It was hard for the Marshal to show patience, for he knew but one way to do a thing, and that was to go straight at it as hard as he could. As one of the privates said, 'The Marshal is a brave man, only he takes us for horses.' With Lannes and Mortier sent to reinforce him, it was still more difficult to show patience. But the end came, and on the fifty-first day of the siege Marshal Kalkreuth surrendered, and the two other Marshals had the generosity to allow Lefèbvre to enjoy alone all the honours of the conquest.

In the next year the Emperor had determined to strengthen his throne by the creation of a new nobility. It was important to see how Republican France would greet this scheme, and accordingly Napoleon determined to include Lefèbvre among his new Dukes. One day the Emperor sent an orderly officer with orders to say to the Marshal, 'Monsieur le Duc, the Emperor wishes you to breakfast with him, and asks you to come in a quarter of an hour.' The Marshal did not hear the title and merely said he would attend. When he entered the breakfast-room the Emperor went up to him, shook hands with him, and said, 'Good-morning, Monsieur le Duc; sit by me.' The Marshal, hearing the title, thought he was joking. The Emperor, to further mystify him, said, 'Do you like chocolate, Monsieur le Duc?' 'Yes, sire,' replied the Marshal, still mystified. Thereon the Emperor went to a drawer and took out a packet labelled chocolate; but when the Marshal opened the box he found it contained one hundred thousand écus in bank notes. While in the army the new Duke was warmly congratulated on his honours, at Paris the smart ladies and Talleyrand did their best to annoy the Duchess. Numerous were the cruel tales they spread of her lack of breeding and of her Amazon ways; how, when the horses bolted with her carriage, she seized the coachman by the scruff of his neck and by main force pulled him off the seat and herself stopped the runaways. But, quite unmoved, the

Duchess pursued her course, visiting the sick, giving away large sums to charities, lending a helping hand to any friend in difficulties, and as usual prefacing her remarks by 'When I used to do the washing.'

When, in the autumn of 1808, Napoleon realised how serious was the Spanish rising, he despatched his Guard to the Peninsula under the Duke of Dantzig. But the war brought few honours to any one, and the Marshal proved once again that he could neither act independently nor assist in combinations with patience. He nearly spoiled Napoleon's whole plan of campaign by a premature move against Blake, prior to the battle of Espinosa. From Spain the Guard was hurriedly recalled on the outbreak of the Austrian campaign of 1809. The Marshal, in command of the Bavarian allies, did yeoman service under Napoleon's eye during the great Five Days' Fighting. He was present also at Wagram, and immediately after that battle was despatched to put down the rising in the Tyrol. During the Russian campaign he once again commanded the Guard, taking part in all the hard fighting of the advance and also in the horrors of the retreat. Though in his fifty-eighth year the tough old soldier marched on foot every mile of the way from Moscow to the Vistula, and shared the privations of his men, watching over his beloved Emperor, his little 'tondu de caporal,' with the care of a woman, himself mounting guard over him at night and surrounding him with picked men of the Guard. To add to the trials of that dreadful campaign the Duke lost at Vilna his eldest son, a most promising young soldier who had already reached the rank of general. This blow and the strain of the retreat were too much for him, and he was unable to assist the Emperor in the campaign of 1813. But when the Allies invaded the sacred soil of France the old warrior put on harness again and fought at Montmirail, Arcis-sur-Aube and Champaubert, where he had his horse killed under him. At Montereau he fought with such fury that 'the foam came out from his mouth'.

While the Marshal was spending his life-blood in the field, the Duchess in Paris was fighting the intrigues of the royalist ladies. When an insinuation was made that the Duke might be won over from the Emperor, the Duchess despatched a friend to the army commanding him 'to return to the army and tell my husband that if he were capable of such infamy I should take him by the hair of his head and drag him to the Emperor's feet. Meanwhile, inform him of the intrigues going on here.' On April 4th the end came. The Marshals refused to fight any longer, and, after Napoleon's abdication, Lefèbvre, with the others, went to Paris to treat with Alexander. The Emperor was gone, but France remained, and it was thanks to Kellermann and Lefèbvre that Alsace was not wrested from her, for they so strongly impressed Alexander by their arguments that he decided to oppose the Prussians, who desired to strip France of her eastern provinces.

The Marshal swore allegiance to the Bourbons and duly received the Cross of St. Louis and his nomination as peer of France. With the year's peace came time for reflection, and he began to see that 'son petit bonhomme de Sire,' as he called Napoleon, had merely used him as a political pawn in his endeavour to bind the republicans to the wheel of the imperial chariot. Accordingly, when the Emperor returned from Elba he was not among those who rushed to meet him. Still, although he had no personal interview with the Emperor during the Hundred Days, he so far compromised himself as to accept a seat in the Senate. For this conduct he was under a cloud for the first years of the second Restoration, but in 1819 he was pardoned and restored to his rank and office.

From 1814 to the day of his death the Duke of Dantzig spent the greater part of his time at his estate at Combault, in the department of the Seine and Marne, dispensing that hospitality which he and his wife loved to shower on all who had met with misfortune, and many a poor soldier and half-pay officer owed his life and what prosperity he had to the generous charity of the Duke and Duchess of Dantzig. His death on September 14, 1820, two days after that of his old friend Kellermann, was due to dropsy, arising from rheumatic gout brought on by the strain of the Russian campaign.

The greatness of the Duke of Dantzig lay not so much in his soldierly capacity as in his personal character. His military renown rested largely on his ability to carry out, without hesitation and jealousy, the commands of others. By his personality he was able to maintain the strictest discipline and exact the last ounce from his troops without raising a murmur. His men loved him, for they knew that he shared all their hardships and that his fingers were soiled with no perquisites or secret booty. It was no empty boast when he wrote to the Directory asking 'bread for himself and rewards for his officers'. Though raised to ducal rank he never lost his sense of proportion and delighted to give his memories of 'when I was sergeant' to his friends and to the officers of his staff. Still, he was intensely proud of his success, which he had won by years of hard work, and he knew how to put in their place those whose fame rested solely on the deeds of their ancestors, telling a young boaster, 'Don't be so proud of your ancestors; I am an ancestor myself.' Though he ever looked an 'old Alsatian camp boy', even in his gorgeous ducal robes; though his manners were rough and he would not hesitate to refuse a lift to a lady to a review, with the words, 'Go to blazes; we did not come here to take your wife out driving' - he was the true example of the best type of republican soldier, fiery, full of theatrical zeal, absolutely unselfish, and animated solely by love of France.

23

NICOLAS CHARLES OUDINOT, MARSHAL, DUKE OF REGGIO

NICOLAS CHARLES OUDINOT, the son of a brewer of Bar-le-Duc, was born on April 23, 1767. From his earliest days he showed that spirit of bravado which later distinguished him among the many brave men who attained the dignity of Marshal. Though kind-hearted and affectionate, his fiery character led him into much disobedience, and his turbulent nature caused many a sorrowful hour to his parents. Still it was with sore hearts that, despite their entreaties, they saw him march gaily off in 1784 to enlist in the regiment of Médoc. But two years later he returned home, tired of garrison duty, and, greatly to his parents' delight, entered the trade. When, in 1789, the good people of Bar-le-Duc began to organise a company of the National Guard, young Oudinot was chosen as captain, and for the next two years threw himself heart and soul into politics, to the neglect of the brewery. But much as he approved of the spirit of the Revolution, he was no advocate of mob rule, and he used his company of citizen soldiers to put down all disturbances in the town. Later still, in 1794, when invalided home from the front, he used a short and sharp method with an enthusiastic supporter of the Terror; in his anger he seized a large dish of haricot and effectually stopped the praises of Hébert by hurling it in the Jacobin's face. In September, 1791, the call to arms summoned the fire-eating captain of the National Guard to sterner scenes. He at once entered the volunteers, and it was as a lieutenant-colonel of the third battalion of the Meuse that he set out on active service which was to last almost continuously for twenty-two years, and from which he was to emerge with the proud rank of Marshal, the title of Duke, and the honourable scars of no less than thirty-four wounds.

His campaigning began auspiciously with the action at Bitche, when, with his battalion of volunteers, he captured seven hundred Prussians and a standard. The hard fighting in the Rhine valley in 1793 added greatly to his reputation; but it was at Morlantier in June, 1794, that his gallant action made his name resound throughout the French armies. The division of General Ambert was attacked on both flanks. Oudinot with the second regiment of the line formed the advance guard, but, not perceiving the plight of the main body, he continued to advance. The enemy surrounded him with six regiments of cavalry. Forming square, he repulsed every assault, and ultimately fought his way back to camp with but slight loss, and recaptured eight French standards which the enemy had seized when they surprised Ambert's division. Ten days later he was promoted general of brigade. But, in spite of his glorious exploit, the officers of the regiment of Picardy, the senior regiment of the old royal army, were disgusted at being commanded by a young brigadier, as yet but twenty-seven years old, and sprung from the ranks. Calling the disaffected officers together, the general thus addressed them: 'Gentlemen, is it because I do not bear an historic name that you wish to throw me over for your old titled chiefs, or is it because you think I am too young to hold command? Wait till the next engagement and then judge. If then you think that I cannot stand fire I promise to hand over the command to one more worthy.' After the next engagement there were no more murmurs against the general, and officers and men were ready to follow him to the death. While Oudinot thus won the love and respect of his command, he requited them with equal love. But his way of showing it was characteristic of the man. As he used to say in later years, 'Ah, how I loved them; I know full well I loved them! I led them all to death.' For in his eyes a glorious death on the field of battle was what the true soldier desired above all things. In August, 1794, a fall from his horse which broke his leg placed him in hospital for some months, and he could not return to the front till September, 1795. He arrived in time to take part in the capture of Mannheim, but a month later, at Neckerau, he was ridden down by a charge of the enemy's cavalry, receiving five sabre cuts and being taken prisoner. After three months' captivity at Ulm he was exchanged. The campaigns of 1796 and 1797 on the Danube added to the number of his wounds. In

1799 he served under Masséna in Switzerland, and gained his step as general of division. His new commander formed so high an opinion of his capacity that he appointed him chief of his staff, and took him with him when transferred to the Army of Italy. It was a new rôle for the fiery Oudinot, but he played it well, and Masséna gave him but his due when he wrote to the Directory, 'I owe the greatest praise to General Oudinot, my chief of the staff, whose fiery nature, though restrained to endure the laborious work of the office, breaks out again, ever ready to hand, on the field of battle; he has assisted me in all my movements, and has seconded me to perfection.' During the disastrous campaign in Italy in 1800 he earned the further thanks of his chief. He it was who broke the blockade at Genoa, and penetrating through the English cruisers, successfully carried the orders to Suchet on the Var, and returned to the beleaguered city to share the privations of the army. By now his name was well known to friend and foe alike, and his chivalrous nature was admired, even by his enemies. But an episode occurred during the siege which, for some time, caused his name to be execrated by the Austrians. The French had captured three thousand prisoners during the sorties round Genoa. At the command of Masséna, Oudinot wrote to General Ott to explain that, owing to famine, it was impossible to give them nourishment, and asking him to make arrangements for feeding them. Ott replied that the siege would end before they could starve. With their own soldiers dying of hunger at their posts, the French could spare but little food for the miserable prisoners, and when the town capitulated there was hardly one left alive. But the burden of this calamity falls on General Ott and Masséna, and not on Oudinot, who could only carry out the orders he received.

After the surrender, Oudinot went home on sick leave, but was back in Italy in time to take part in the last phase of the war under General Brune. On December 26th, at Monzembano, he had an opportunity of showing his dashing courage. An Austrian battery, suddenly coming into action, threw the French into disorder. Oudinot dashed forward, collected a few troopers, galloped across the bridge straight at the Austrian guns, and captured one of them with his own hands. A few days later he was sent home to Paris with a copy of the armistice signed on January 16, 1801. Arriving in Paris, the general was received with great warmth by the First Consul, who gave him a sword of honour and the cannon which he had captured at Monzembano.

During the years of peace which followed the treaty of Lunéville, General Oudinot fell entirely under the influence of Napoleon. His frank, chivalrous nature was captivated by the bold personality of the Corsican, so great in war, so attractive in peace. The First Consul rewarded his affection by giving him the posts of inspector-general of infantry and cavalry. While not engaged in these duties, or in attendance at the court of Paris, the general spent his leisure hours at his home at Bar-le-Duc. There he was the idol of the populace; his bust adorned the hôtel de ville, and his fellow-citizens were never tired of singing his praise and repeating the stories of his marvellous adventures and daring escapades. But no one who first saw him could believe that this was Oudinot, the hero of all these marvellous tales. There was nothing of the swashbuckler about this aristocratic-looking man, spare, of medium height, whose pale, intellectual face, set off by a pair of brown moustaches, revealed a rather gentle, gracious expression, over which flashed occasionally a fugitive smile. It was only those piercing, flashing eyes which revealed his real character. Still, it was easy to understand how, with his heroic exploits, he had fascinated both friend and foe, and gained for himself the title of the young Bayard. By his first wife the general had two sons and two daughters. The daughters married early, Generals Pajol and Lorencz, but it was his sons who were his pride. He had sent for his eldest boy, at the age of eight, to accompany him on the Zurich campaign, and the lad had at that age to perform all the duties of a subaltern officer. During the year of peace both boys were constantly with their father, who spent his time superintending their military studies and building for himself a house at Bar-le-Duc. From this patriarchal life he was recalled in 1804, to take command of the chosen division of picked grenadiers which had been organised at Arras by Junot. The division, so well known to history as 'Oudinot's Grenadiers,' or the 'Infernal Column', was composed of selected men from every regiment, and next to the Guard, was the finest division in the imperial army. In the campaign of 1805 the division formed part of Lannes's corps, and covered itself with distinction at Ulm, and again at Austerlitz, where Oudinot was present, though not in command. He had been wounded at Hollabrünn, and sent to hospital, and his division entrusted to Duroc, the Grand Marshal of the palace. But when he heard of the approaching engagement, the fire-eating soldier could not be held back, and on the eve of the battle he arrived in camp. Duroc chivalrously offered to give up command, but Oudinot, who was satisfied as long as he saw fighting, would not hear of this. 'My dear Marshal,' he said, 'remain at the head of my brave grenadiers; we will fight side by side.' After the treaty of Pressburg he was sent to Switzerland, to take possession of Neuchâtel, which had been ceded to France by Prussia, to form a fief for Marshal Berthier. The Neuchâtelois were furious at being treated as mere pawns in the game, and trouble was expected. Fortunately Oudinot possessed great common sense. He saw that a timely concession might bind the proud Swiss to their new lord. The people of Neuchâtel depended almost entirely on their trade with England, and he wrung from Napoleon the promise that this trade should not be interfered with. So grateful were the Swiss that they passed a law making Oudinot a citizen of Neuchâtel. The general returned from his diplomatic triumph in time to command his grenadiers in the Prussian campaign of 1806, and gained fresh laurels at Jena, Ostralenka, Dantzig and Friedland. At Dantzig, with his own hand, he killed a Russian sergeant who had caught a French cavalry colonel in an ambush. At Friedland he was with Lannes when the Marshal surprised the Russian rear, and held them pinned against the town until Napoleon could draw in his troops and overwhelm them. From six in the evening till twelve next day the grenadiers fought with stubborn tenacity. At last the Emperor arrived on the field. Oudinot, with his coat hanging in ribbons from musket shots, his horse covered with blood, dashed up to the Emperor, 'Hasten, Sire,' he cried; 'my grenadiers are all but spent; but give me some reinforcements and I will hurl all the Russians into the river.' Napoleon replied, 'General, you have surpassed yourself: you seem to be everywhere; but you need not worry yourself any more. It is my part to finish this affair.'

After Friedland came the peace of Tilsit, but even peace has its dangers. Soult, Mortier and the grave Davout were at times carried away by Oudinot's extravagant spirits, and used to amuse themselves after dinner by extinguishing the candles on the table with pistol shots. During the day the general spent his time in his favourite pursuit of riding. His horses were always thoroughbreds, and nothing stopped him once he had decided to take any particular line. So one day, while attempting to jump the ditch of a fort, instead of going round by the gate, his horse fell with him, and he broke his leg and had to be sent home. His officers and comrades gave him a farewell dinner. At dessert a pâté appeared, from which, when opened by General Rapp, a swarm of birds fluttered out, with collars of tricolour ribbon, with the inscription 'To the glory of General Oudinot.'

On returning home the Emperor, in addition to presenting him with the pipe of Frederick the Great, had granted him the title of count and a donation of a million francs. With part of this sum Oudinot bought the beautiful estate of Jeand Heurs. In 1808 he was selected as governor of Erfurt during the meeting of the Czar and Napoleon, and had the honour of being presented to Alexander by the Emperor, who said, 'Sire, I present you the Bayard of the French army; like the 'preux chevalier,' he is without fear and without reproach.' The year 1809 brought sterner interludes, and Oudinot was present in command of his grenadiers during the Five Days' Fighting, and at Aspern-Essling. On the death of Lannes he was promoted to the command of the second corps, and in that capacity played his part at Wagram. During the early part of the battle it took all his self-restraint to stand still while Davout was turning the Austrian left, but when he saw the French on the Neusiedel he could no longer control his impatience, and without waiting orders he hurled his corps against the enemy's centre, receiving in the attack two slight wounds. The next day the Emperor sent for him. 'Do you know what you did yesterday?' 'Sire, I hope I did not do my duty too badly.' 'That is just what you did - you ought to be shot.' But the Emperor overlooked his impetuosity, and a week later rewarded him for his service by presenting him with his baton, and a month later created him Duke of Reggio.

The Duke was fortunate in not being selected for duty in Spain.

His next service was in 1812, when he commanded a corps on the lines of communication in Russia. This was his first independent command, and it proved that, though a good subordinate, a dashing soldier and a capable diplomatist, he did not possess the qualifications of a great general. At Polotsk the day went against the French, but when a wound caused the Marshal to hand over his command to St. Cyr, that able officer easily stemmed the Russian advance and turned defeat into victory. The Marshal, however, made up in zeal what he lacked in ability; a few weeks later, hearing that St. Cyr was wounded, he hastened back to the front. It was owing to his gallant attack on the Russians that the Emperor was able to bridge the Beresina. But, while driving off the enemy who were attempting to stem the crossing, he was again wounded. Thanks to the devotion of his staff, he was safely escorted back to France and escaped the last horrors of the retreat. In 1813 the Duke fought at Bautzen, and after the armistice of Dresden was despatched to drive back the mixed force of Swedes and Prussians who were threatening the French left under Bernadotte. The action of Grosbeeren proved once again that the Duke of Reggio had no talent for independent command, and the Emperor superseded him by Marshal Ney, whom he loyally served. Emerging unscathed from the slaughter at Leipzig, he fought with his accustomed fury all through the campaign of 1814 without adding to his reputation as a soldier. On Napoleon's abdication the Duke swore allegiance to the Bourbons, who received him with warmth, as in the early years of the revolutionary wars he had shown great humanity to the captured émigrés. Louis XVIII nominated him colonel-general of the royal corps of grenadiers, and gave him command of the third military division, with headquarters at Metz. It was there that the Marshal first heard of the Emperor's return from Elba. He at once set out to try and intercept his advance on Paris, but his troops refused to act against their former leader. Thereon Oudinot threw up his command and returned to Jeand Heurs. On his arrival at Paris, the Emperor told his Minister of War, Davout, to summon the Duke of Reggio to court, thinking that, like many another, he would forget his oath to the Bourbons. But the Duke was of different stuff; he had sworn allegiance to Louis XVIII at Napoleon's command, but he could not break his oath. On his arrival the Emperor greeted him with the question, 'Well, Duke of Reggio, what have the Bourbons done for you more than I have done, that you attempted to intercept my return?' The Marshal replied that he had plighted his oath. The Emperor told him to break it and take service with him, recalling past favours. The Marshal was much affected, but firm. 'I will serve nobody since I cannot serve you,' he said, 'but trust me enough not to spy on me with your police: save me that degradation. I could not endure it.' So the interview ended, and the Marshal returned to Jeand Heurs.

On the second Restoration Oudinot became a great favourite of the Bourbons. The King made him a peer of France, presented him with the order of St. Louis, created him one of the four major-generals of the Royal Guard and commandant-in-chief of the National Guard. When the heir to the throne, the Duke of Berri, married a Neapolitan princess, the second wife of the Marshal became her chief lady, and the Oudinots, husband and wife, served the royal family with the greatest fidelity. The Marshal once again saw service when, in 1823, he commanded the first corps of the army which invaded Spain. It was through no fault of his that Charles X lost his throne, for he was patriotic enough to tell him how unfortunate was the disbanding of the National Guard and his other ill-advised actions.

After the fall of the Bourbon dynasty in 1830, the Duke of Reggio never again entered public life, although in 1839 Louis Philippe created him Grand Chancellor of the Legion of Honour, and in 1842 governor of the Invalides. It was in this honoured position that the Duke breathed his last on September 13, 1847, in his eighty-first year.

The Duke of Reggio was fortunate in his career; he never saw service in Spain, and he seldom held independent command, for which his fiery temper and impetuosity unfitted him. It was his gallantry and intrepidity which won for him his baton. In a subordinate position he could usually control himself enough to obey orders, in a sub ordinate position also he could do good staff work, and his quick impetuous brain teemed with ideas which were useful to his superiors. But by himself he was lost. Napoleon well knew his shortcomings. In 1805 the Emperor was holding a review; Oudinot's horse was restive and refused to march past, whereon he drew his sword and stabbed it in the neck. That evening at dinner the Emperor asked, 'Is that the way you manage your horse?' 'Sire,' replied Oudinot, 'when I cannot get obedience that is my method.' But it was seldom that his impetuosity resulted in cruelty, and the wounded at Friedland and in many another action had cause to bless him. The hero of Friedland, the saviour of the émigrés, and the administrator of Neuchâtel was loved not only in the French army, but also among the enemy. At Erfurt there was a poor Saxon gardener who delighted to cultivate a rose which he called Oudinot; when asked the reason he replied, 'The general has made me love the war which has ruined me.' The Duke of Reggio turned his face steadily against plundering, and would reprimand any officer who recklessly rode over a field of wheat.

Old age did not change his character. Happy in his family relations, adored by his young wife, he was universally beloved, and it was with great grief that, on September 13, 1847, Royalist, Orleanist, Imperialist, and Republican learned that he whom the soldiers called 'The Marshal of the Thirty-Four Wounds' had passed away.

24

DOMINIQUE CATHERINE DE PÉRIGNON, MARSHAL

AMONG the few men of moderate opinion who were chosen in 1791 to represent their country in the Legislative Assembly was Dominique Catherine de Pérignon. The scion of a good family of Grenade, in the Upper Garonne, neither an ultra-royalist nor ultra-republican, he was a man of action rather than a talker. One year spent among the self-seekers of Paris was sufficient to prove to him that his rôle did not lie among the twisting paths of partisan statesmanship, and gladly, in 1792, he heard the summons to arms and left the forum for the camp. Now thirty-eight years old, having been born on May 31, 1754, this was not his first experience of soldiering; he had held a commission for some years in the old royal army and had served on the staff. He was, for this reason, at once elected lieutenant-colonel of the volunteer legion of the Pyrenees. His bravery and his former military training soon caused him to rise among the mass of ignorant and untrained volunteers who formed the Army of the Pyrenees. Luckily for France, she was opposed on her western frontier by an army which knew as little of war as her own, led by officers of equal ignorance, without the stimulus of burning enthusiasm and the dread power of the guillotine; had it been otherwise, Perpignan and the fortresses covering Provence would soon have been in the hands of the enemy.

With all Europe threatening the eastern frontier and civil war at home, the Government could spare but few troops, and these the least trained, for the defence of the west. Accordingly, in the opening fights of the campaign ill-conceived plans and panics too frequently caused the defeat of the French, and it was often only the personal example of individuals which saved the army from absolute annihilation. From the first engagement Pérignon made his mark by his coolness and courage. The French attack on the Spanish position at

Serre had been brought to a halt by the fierce fire of the enemy, and, as the line wavered, a timely charge of the Spanish horse threw it into confusion. Pérignon, commanding the first line, rushed up and seized the musket and cartridges of a wounded soldier, and collecting a few undaunted privates, quietly opened fire on the Spanish cavalry, and by his example shamed the runaways into returning to the attack. For this he was created general of brigade on July 28, 1793. By September the enemy had opened their trenches round Perpignan, and Pérignon was entrusted with a night sortie. On approaching the Spanish line a fusillade of musketry swept down five hundred of his little force, and his men at once halted and opened fire; but Pérignon believed in the bayonet. With stinging reproaches he again got his men to advance, and sweeping over the enemy's entrenchments, he drove them in rout and captured their camp. He thus won his promotion as lieutenant-general.

In November of 1794 Dugommier, the French commander-in-chief, fell mortally wounded at the battle of Montagne-Noire, and Pérignon was at once appointed his successor. Though no great strategist or tactician, he was an able leader of men, and had the faculty of enforcing obedience to his orders. Trusting entirely to the bayonet, he forced the fortified lines of Escola, making his troops advance and charge over the entrenchments with shouldered arms, without firing a shot. The fortresses of Figueras and Rosas alone barred the advance of the French into Catalonia. So demoralised were the enemy that Figueras, with all its immense stores, nine thousand troops and two hundred pieces of artillery, capitulated to a mere summons. But Rosas stood firm, covered on the land side by the fort of Le Bouton on the top of a precipice, and on the sea side swept by the guns of the Spanish squadron anchored in the roads. The fort of Le Bouton was called 'l'imprenable'. But Pérignon was not frightened by names; although greatly hampered by the civil Commissioners with the army, and held by them as 'suspect', he determined to capture Le Bouton and Rosas. Le Bouton was dominated by a perpendicular rock two thousand feet high. It was certain that if batteries could be established on this precipice Le Bouton could be taken. But the artillerymen believed that it was impossible to construct a road to haul guns up to this height. 'Very well, then, it is the impossible that I am going to do,' replied the obstinate little general, and after immense toil a zigzag road was constructed and the guns hauled by hand to the summit; after a severe bombardment Le Bouton was carried by an assault. But still Rosas held out; the weather was very severe and the snow came above the soldiers' thighs, and the engineers declared that it was impossible to construct siege works unless a certain outlying redoubt was first taken. 'Very well,' said the general, 'make your preparations. Tomorrow I will take it at the head of my grenadiers.' So at five o'clock the next morning, February 1, 1795, the grenadiers, with their general at their head, marched out of camp and, under a murderous fire, by eight o'clock captured the outlying redoubt, so after a siege of sixty-one days Rosas was captured. It was the personality of their general which had taught the French soldiers to surmount all difficulties. Absolutely fearless himself, full of grim determination, he taught his soldiers how to acquire these virtues by example, not by precept, ever exposing himself to danger, showing absolute callousness, until his men were shamed into following his example. On one occasion during the siege a shell fell at his feet with the match still fizzling; he was at the moment directing some troops who were exposed to the fire. The men called out to him to get out of the way of the explosion, and throw himself flat, but he paid no attention to the bomb and quietly went on giving his orders, for he knew how his example would steady his troops; meanwhile someone dashed up and extinguished the match before the bomb could explode.

The peace of Basle prevented Pérignon from gaining any further success in Spain, and the Directors, out of compliment, appointed him ambassador to the court of Madrid, where his good sense and moderation did much to strengthen the peace between the two countries. In 1799 he was sent to command a division of the Army of Italy, and commanded the left wing at the battle of Novi. While attempting to cover the rout he was ridden over by the enemy's horse, and taken prisoner with eight honourable sabre wounds on his arms and chest. When the Russian surgeon was going to attend to his wounds, thinking more of others than of himself, he said to him, 'Do not worry about me; look first after those brave men there, who are in a worse plight than I.' After a few months his exchange was effected and he returned to France, severely shaken in health and not fit for further active service, to find Bonaparte First Consul. Though not one of his own followers, Bonaparte recognised the services he had rendered to his country, and arranged for his entry into the Senate, and in 1802 appointed him Commissioner Extraordinary to arrange the negotiation with Spain, a delicate compliment to Pérignon, who had made his name on Spanish soil. Further to recall his Spanish victories, in 1804 the Emperor created him honorary Marshal, not on the active list, and later gave him the title of Count. But though Napoleon did not think that the Marshal was physically fit to command again in the field, he entrusted him in 1801 with the government of Parma and Piacenza, and in 1808 sent him to Naples to command the French troops stationed in the kingdom of his brother-in-law, Murat. The task was a difficult one, for Murat was no easy person to get on with, and Southern Italy, from the days of Hannibal, has been a hard place in which to maintain military virtues. But the Marshal, with his sound common sense, gave satisfaction both to Napoleon and to King Joachim, and at the same time kept a tight hand over his troops; when, however, in 1814, Murat deserted the Emperor, the old Marshal withdrew in sorrow to France, to find Paris in the hands of the enemy. Like the other Marshals he accepted the Restoration and was created a peer of France. Being himself of noble birth, and an ex-officer of the old royal army, Louis XVIII appointed him to investigate the claims, and verify the services of the officers of the old army who had returned to France at the Restoration. When, in 1815, Napoleon returned from Elba, the Marshal, who was at his country house near Toulouse made every effort to organise resistance against him in the Midi. During the Hundred Days he remained quietly at his home, and on the second Restoration was rewarded with the command of the first military division, and created Marquis and Commander of the Order of St. Louis. But he did not long enjoy his new honours, for he died in Paris on December 25, 1818, aged sixty-four.

25

JEAN MATHIEU PHILIBERT SERURIER, MARSHAL

AFTER thirty-four years' service to be still a captain, with no probable chance of promotion: such was the lot of Serurier when the Revolution broke out in 1789. Born on December 8, 1742, he had received his first commission in the militia at the age of thirteen, and from there had been transferred to the line. His war service was not inconsiderable, including three campaigns in Hanover, one in Portugal, and one in Italy; he had been wounded as far back as the action of Wartburg in 1760, but there was no court influence to bring him his majority. With the Revolution, however, fortune quickly changed. The years of steady attention to duty, of patient devotion to, and loving care of his men, brought their reward, and when promotion became the gift of the soldiers and not of the courtiers, the stern old disciplinarian found himself at the head of his regiment. In the hand-to-hand struggles which distinguished the early campaigns in the Alps, he soon acquired a reputation for bravery and the clever handling of his men. By June, 1795, he had risen to be general of division, in which capacity he distinguished himself on July 7th by the way he led his division at the fight for the Col de Tenda, and for the modesty with which he attributed all his success to his soldiers. A month later he saved the whole army at the Col de Pierre Etroite.

When under the cover of driving rain and mist the enemy surprised the French line of picquets at midnight and had all but seized the position, it was Serurier who, collecting three hundred and fifty men, hurled himself against the enemy's column of fifteen hundred bayonets, and by sheer hand-to-hand fighting held them in check for six hours, and at last repulsed them with the loss of a considerable number of prisoners.

With the halo of this action still surrounding him, in March, 1796, he first came into direct connection with Bonaparte. The new commander-in-chief quickly took measure of his tall, stern subordinate. While recognisin to the full his bravery, the excellent discipline he knew how to maintain, and the high regard in which he was held by his division, he saw that the iron of years of subordination had entered into the old soldier's soul, and that, while he could be relied on to obey orders implicitly, he never could be trusted with an independent command. Still, what Bonaparte most required from his subordinates was immediate obedience and speedy performance of orders and consequently Serurier played no insignificant part in the glorious campaign of 1796. At Mondovi he showed his stubbornness, when the Sardinian general turned at bay and, as Bonaparte wrote to the Directory, the victory was due entirely to Serurier. When the Austrians were driven into Mantua, Bonaparte entrusted him with the siege. The Austrian forces in the fortress numbered some fourteen thousand; Serurier had but ten thousand to carry on the siege, although the usual estimate is that a besieging force should be three times as strong as the besieged; but by his clever use of the marshes and bridges he was able to hold the enemy and open his trenches and siege batteries. It was no fault of his that, on the advance of Würmser, he had to abandon his guns and hasten to Castiglione, for Bonaparte had given him no warning of the sudden advance of the Austrian relieving force. After Castiglione he returned to his task round Mantua and gallantly repulsed all sorties. When the end came he had the honour of superintending the surrender, and of receiving the parole from the gallant old Marshal Würmser and the Austrian officers. In the advance on Vienna his division distinguished itself in the terrible march to Asola; but, as Bonaparte said, 'the wind and the rain were always the crown of victory for the Army of Italy.' At Gradisca Serurier captured two thousand five hundred prisoners, eight stands of colours, and ten pieces of artillery, and again crowned himself with glory at the Col de Tarvis. In June Bonaparte sent the old warrior to Paris to present twenty-two captured stands to the Directory, and in his despatches, after enumerating his triumphs from Mondovi to Gradisca, he finished by saying, 'General Serurier is extremely severe on himself, and at times on others. A stern enforcer of discipline, order, and the most necessary virtues for the maintenance of society, he disdains intrigues and intriguers'; he then proceeded to demand for him the command of the troops of the Cisalpine Republic. But the Directors had other designs, and sent back the general to command the captured province of Venice.

In 1799, when the Austrians and Russians invaded Northern Italy, Serurier commanded a division of the army of occupation. During the operations which ended in the enemy forcing the Adda, his division got isolated from the main body. The old soldier, whose boast was that he never turned his back on an enemy, forgetful of strategy, and thinking only of honour, instead of attempting to escape and rejoin the rest of the army, took possession of an extremely strong position at Verderio, and soon found himself surrounded; after a gallant fight against an enemy three times his number, he was compelled to surrender with seven thousand men. The celebrated Suvaroff, the Russian commander, treated him with great kindness and invited him to dine. After his exchange on parole had been arranged, the Russian general asked him where he was going. 'To Paris.' 'So much the better,' replied Suvaroff; 'I shall count on seeing you there soon.' 'I have myself always hoped to see you there,' replied Serurier with considerable wit and dignity.

The general was still a prisoner on parole when Bonaparte returned from Egypt, and at once gladly placed himself at his disposal, and aided him during the coup d'ètat of Brumaire. It was because of this service, and of the strong affection which the old warrior bore him, that Bonaparte piled honours upon him, for Serurier had undoubtedly done less than anybody, save perhaps Bessières, to deserve his bâton. Still, Napoleon knew his devotion, his blind obedience to orders, and his absolute integrity. In December, 1799, he called him to the Senate. In April, 1804, he made him governor of the Invalides, and a month later presented him with his Marshal's baton, and created him Grand Eagle of the Legion of Honour and Grand Cross of the Iron Crown. But he never employed him in the field, though once for a short time during the Walcheren Expedition he placed him in command of the National Guard of Paris.

The old Marshal found a congenial occupation in looking after the veterans at the Invalides, while, as Vice-President of the Senate, he faithfully served the interests of his beloved Emperor. When in 1814 he heard that Paris was going to surrender, rather than that the trophies of his master's glory should fall into the hands of the enemy, on the night of March 30th he collected the eighteen hundred captured standards which adorned Nôtre Dame, and the military trophies from the chapel of the Invalides, and burned them, and he actually hurled into the fire the sword of the Great Frederick which had been seized in 1806 at Potsdam. Yet in spite of his devotion to the Emperor, a few days later he took part in the proceedings in the Senate, and voted for his deposition. Under the Restoration he was made a peer of France, but on Napoleon's return he hastened to greet him. But the Emperor could not forgive his desertion, and, thinking he would not benefit by his services, he refused them. When the Bourbons returned a second time the Marshal was stripped of his titles and, what caused him more grief, of his command of the Invalides. After parting from the veterans, whose welfare he had so long superintended, the old warrior withdrew into private life, and died at Paris on December 21, 1819, at the age of seventy-seven.

26

PRINCE JOSEPH PONIATOWSKI, MARSHAL

JOSEPH PONIATOWSKI, the nephew of King Stanislaus (the erstwhile lover of Catherine the Second of Russia), was born in 1762, before his uncle had been raised to the kingly rank. Like all Poles of noble birth, war and war alone could offer him a profession he was able or cared to pursue, and accordingly at an early age he served his apprenticeship in arms under the banner of Austria. Returning to his native country in 1789 with the experience of several campaigns against the Turks, he was entrusted by his uncle with the organisation of the Polish army. For the cast-off lover of the great Catherine was about to make one last effort to save his country from the greedy hands of Prussia, Russia and Austria. The great kingdom of Poland had fallen on evil days; she had no fortresses, no navy, no roads, no arsenals, no revenue, and no real standing army; while the King was elected by a Diet of nobles who thought more of foreign gold than of patriotism; the single vote of one member of this Diet could bring all business to a standstill. King Stanislaus's reforms were wise, but they came too late. The kingship was to become hereditary, the 'liberum veto', whereby business was paralysed was abolished, and a standing army was to be raised. But it suited none of her great neighbours to see Poland organising herself into a modern State, and before Prince Joseph had had time to raise and thoroughly drill his new model army, Prussia and Russia determined once and for all to wipe the kingdom off the map of Europe. In 1792 Prince Joseph found himself at the head of his new levies opposed by the trained troops of those countries. To add to his difficulties, the orders he received from his uncle were contradictory and irresolute, for King Stanislaus, though patriot at heart, had not the moral courage for so great an emergency. The new Polish troops gained some minor successes, but before the immense array of enemies the King's heart failed him, and he signed the Convention of Targowitz, which foreshadowed the dismemberment of his country. Prince Joseph, like many another of his brave comrades, unable to stomach such cowardice, threw up his commission and withdrew into exile. In 1794 Poland suddenly flew to arms at the command of the great-hearted Kosciuszko, and Prince Joseph, keen soldier and patriot, gladly placed himself under the orders of his former subordinate, and covered himself with glory at the siege of Warsaw. Again, however, the Polish resistance was broken down by force of numbers, and the Prince, turning a deaf ear to the blandishments of Emperor and Czarina alike, withdrew from public life and settled down to manage his estates near Warsaw. For eleven long years Poland lay dismembered, but the national spirit still smouldered, and broke into clear flame when, in 1806, the victorious French drove the battered remains of the Prussian armies across the Vistula. But Poland was a mere pawn in the game, to be used as a means of threatening or conciliating Russia, and in spite of the high hopes of the Poles the treaty of Tilsit, instead of reviving the ancient kingdom, merely established a Grand Duchy of Warsaw. The Emperor left Davout to watch over the weaning of the State, and appointed Prince Joseph to organise the national forces which were to supplement the French army of occupation. No better choice could have been made, for the Prince had the necessary tact to manage the imperious Davout, while his chivalrous nature, his well-known patriotism and his experience and ability, enabled him once more to accustom the Polish troops to the bit of discipline. When, in 1809, the great European conflagration forced Napoleon to leave the Grand Duchy to its fate, Prince Joseph was able to keep the Austrians in check, and actually to penetrate into Galicia before the battle of Wagram brought the war to an end. Poniatowski's campaign against Austria, glorious as it was for the Poles, was in reality the forerunner of disaster. During the campaign the Polish troops were supported by a Russian division. To Poniatowski, the Russians, the despoilers of his country, were more hateful than the enemy, and he so distrusted them that, at the risk of having to fight them, he refused to allow them to occupy any of the captured fortresses; this suspicion was increased by the capture of a secret despatch from the Russian commander to the Austrian

Archduke, congratulating him on the victory of Razyn, and expressing a wish that his standards might soon be joined to the Austrian eagles. The Prince at once sent the intercepted despatch to Napoleon, who summed up the situation with the words, 'I see that after all I must make war on Alexander.' So when the Grand Army assembled for the invasion of Russia, Prince Poniatowski with his Poles rejoiced at the call to arms, and brought thirty-six thousand well disciplined and well equipped troops to the rendezvous, while sixty-five thousand were left to garrison the fortresses: the years of peace had been spent by him in busy labour as Minister of War, providing for the necessities of the army, establishing engineering and artillery colleges, equipping hospitals and perfecting organisation and discipline. Smolensk, Moskowa, and many a skirmish proved that the labour of organisation had not sapped Prince Joseph's dash and courage, and the horrors of the retreat brought out to the full his chivalrous bravery and determination. Though wounded during the retreat, he was ready the following year to help the French in Central Europe. On the morning of the first day of the battle of Leipzig, Napoleon, to fire the Poles, sent their Prince his baton as Marshal. While esteeming the honour, Prince Joseph showed no undue elation, for, much as head admired the French, and grateful as he felt, he was at heart a Pole, and, as he said to a comrade, 'I am proud to be the leader of the Poles. When one has a unique title superior to that of Marshal, the title of Generalissimo of the Poles, nothing else matters. Besides, I am going to die, and I prefer to die as a Polish general and not as a Marshal of France.' But the Marshal did not allow his gloomy forebodings to interfere with his duty, and so fiercely did he face the enemy that after three days' fighting his corps had dwindled from seven thousand to a bare two thousand men. On the morning of the fatal 19th of October the Emperor sent for him and entrusted him with the defence of the southern suburb of Leipzig. 'Sire,' said the Prince, 'I have but few followers left.' 'What then?' rejoined the Emperor; 'you will defend it with what you have.' 'Ah, Sire,' replied the Prince Marshal, 'we are all ready to die for your Majesty.' Thus spoke the Pole, but many a Frenchman thought otherwise and hurried from the stricken field. With their hated enemies, the Austrians, Russians and Prussians surrounding them, the small band of devoted Poles fought to the last. When the bridge was blown up and ordered retreat was impossible, the Prince, drawing his sword, called out to those around him, 'Gentlemen, we must die with honour.' Severely wounded with a handful of followers, he fought his way through a column of the enemy and reached the bank of the Elster. Faint from loss of blood, he urged his horse into the stream, and by great exertions reached the other side; but the beast, worn out by the long days of battle, was unable to clamber up the steep, slippery bank, and the Prince Marshal was so faint that he could no longer guide his steed; so horse and rider dropped back into the stream and were seen no more alive. Two days later his body was recovered, and buried with all the honours due to his rank, in the presence of the allied sovereigns, his former enemies. Thus passed away Prince Joseph Poniatowski, whose chivalrous courage had won for him the title of the Polish Bayard, whose life had been spent for the welfare of his country, whose high military reputation was sullied by no inglorious act, and who at the last chose death rather than surrender.